THE WAY OF THE SPIRIT

A Bible Reading Guide and Commentary

THE WAY OF THE SPIRIT

A Bible Reading Guide and Commentary

Vol. 4

MY LORD AND MY GOD

**'The Writings' of the Old Testament
(Ruth, Chronicles – Song of Songs,
Lamentations and Daniel, plus Jonah)
John's Gospel
1–3 John
Paul's Captivity and Pastoral Letters
James, Peter and Jude**

JOHN McKAY

Kingdom Faith

First published in Great Britain in 1990
by Marshall Pickering

Reprinted, with corrections, in 1998
by Kingdom Faith Ministries,
Foundry Lane, Horsham, West Sussex RH13 5PX
Tel: 01403 211505, Fax: 01403 218463
E-mail: ws@kingdomfaith.org.uk

ISBN: 1 900409 21 6

Text Set in Times Roman by Kingdom Faith Ministries
Printed and bound by Creative Print and Design (Wales)

With gratitude to God for all who have
taught me the Lordship of Christ,
encouraged me in his wisdom,
and sustained me with their songs of worship.

Question: *What is the chief and highest end of man?*
Answer: *Man's chief and highest end is to glorify*
                  God, and fully to enjoy him for ever.

(The opening words of the Larger Catechism agreed
upon by the Assembly of Divines at Westminster in
1648.)

Thomas said to him, 'My Lord and my God!'

(John 20.28)

Contents

List of Maps

Charts and Diagrams

Acknowledgements

Since these Bible Reading Guides represent the deposit of a whole life of prayer and study, thanks are due to many more people than can be named here, to all who have contributed to the development of my understanding of the Christian gospel, even from earliest childhood: my parents, school and Sunday-school teachers, the ministers in the church of my teens, and countless others since.

Until my early thirties my Christian life was largely motivated by a desire Tennyson speaks of in his poem *Ulysses*, 'to follow knowledge, like a sinking star, beyond the utmost bounds of human thought'. That, coupled with the call of God, led me into the liberal theological departments of our universities and into ministry in the Anglican Church. Looking back on those years I acknowledge particularly John Gray, John Baker and Ernest Nicholson for the enthusiasm for Bible-study they imparted to me; Anthony Hanson and Norman Whybray for encouraging me as I learned to become a Bible teacher myself; Michael Hennell and Leslie Stanbridge for training me in ministry.

John says in his Gospel (16.13) that 'when he, the Spirit of truth, comes, he will guide you into all truth'. A total revolution took place in all my desiring and understanding when I allowed the Holy Spirit to have his way in me, and like St. Paul, it took me about ten years to come to terms with all he was showing me. I owe a deep debt of gratitude to many who stood by me at that time, particularly to Michael Hall for first introducing me to the Holy Spirit and his work; and to Ron Treasure, Donald Cameron, Mark Simons, Peter Vessey and John Daglish for helping me grow in the Spirit.

But it is in ministry that the value of faith and revelation

is discovered. Over that past eight years the truths the Spirit
has shown me have been well tested and the teachings of
earlier years thoroughly sifted. Much has been shaken out
and I trust it is mainly 'what cannot be shaken' that now
remains (Heb. 12.27). For these years I especially thank
Derek Rawcliffe, Bob Gordon and Colin Urquhart for all
their encouragement and support.

Thanks also to the staff of Marshall-Pickering for their
help and advice and for making the production of these
volumes possible. Also to Jim Penberthy and other fellowship members for all their support, and to James Verner and
others for encouraging me to develop the home study course
that goes with these books.

And finally, I thank Marguerite again for proof reading
and for her many helpful suggestions, both about the books
and the course. But most of all I thank her, and my sons,
James and Iain, for their great patience with me over the
past three years of writing, and indeed for their positive
enthusiasm for the work. They have all been a wonderful
source of support and inspiration to me.

John McKay
14th January 1990

Thank you to my son, James, for his patience in remaking
all the maps and charts for computerised printing, and to
David Stearns for redesigning the cover, with its illustration
representing the light of Christ dispelling the darkness and
illuminating the pages of God's Word.

26th May 1999

Preface

The theology of the way of the Spirit is really quite simple and easy to grasp. It can be summed up in the words 'continuity of vision and experience', or 'shared vision and experience'. That is, the vision of God's purposes in history granted to Biblical man was in its main theme and outline essentially the same in Abraham's, Moses' and Jesus' day and continues to be so in our own. And in the same way, the experience of God granted to Biblical man was also in essence the same throughout and remains so for us today.

It would, however, be far too naive to say without qualification that our understanding of God's purposes and our experience of him are identical with those of the ancients. We must allow for the effects of changed circumstances: historical, social, environmental, cultural, linguistic, political, etc. We must also allow for the unfolding of revelation down the centuries: Abraham surely did not understand all that was later revealed to Isaiah or Paul. Again we need to recognise that the means by which both the vision and the experience have been mediated to men are manifold: through angels and prophets, dreams and visions, words and awarenesses, and now, of course, most fully through Jesus' own life and teaching.

However, behind every act of revelation has stood the third person of the Trinity, sometimes hardly noticed, revealing the hidden things of God or calling them to remembrance. He showed Moses things he wished all God's people could see (Num. 11.24-29), Jesus promised he would lead us into all the truth (John 16.13), and in Paul's experience he lifted a veil from his mind, uncovering truths he had hitherto only dimly perceived (2 Cor. 3.14-18).

The heart of what the Spirit shows us must always be the

same, for he is the 'Spirit of Christ'. His main function is to
show us Jesus, that he is Lord and God, and to help us
understand the things that are his. 'Jesus Christ is the same
yesterday, today and forever' and is the focus of all revelation, whether granted to Old Testament men to prepare them
for his coming, or to us to help us understand it and prepare
for his return (cp. 1 Pet. 1.10-12). Hence, in the midst of
diversity, it is all one. Our experience and understanding of
God 'in the Spirit' are basically the same today as in Biblical times—and men without the Spirit are still as puzzled
about that as in Paul's day (1 Cor. 2.14).

What I have tried to do in these four volumes is outline
this simple way of the Spirit through Biblical history, but
these books can never be more than guides to you on the
way. Only the Spirit himself can fully show you the path.
Ask him to do so as you read.

The Overall Plan of Study.

This volume is the fourth in a series of four covering the
whole Bible. Each deals with a successive period of Old
Testament history, concentrates on the books of the Old
Testament associated with that period and examines particular aspects of faith related to it. Each volume then traces
the sequel to the story told in the Old Testament section
through books of the New Testament that seem to provide

	VOL. 1 THE CALL AND THE CROSS	VOL. 2 TIMES OF REFRESHING	VOL. 3 HEIRS OF THE PROPHETS	VOL. 4 MY LORD AND MY GOD
OLD TESTAMENT	2000-1230 BC	1230-500 BC	1050-400 BC	600-0 BC
	The Pentateuch	The Histories	The Prophets	The Writings
	Faith, obedience and sacrifice	The Kingdom, revival and Messianic hope	Prophecy, revival and charismatic faith	The Lordship of God in history, worship and belief
NEW TESTAMENT	Mark	Matthew	Luke	John
	Romans and Hebrews	Acts and Paul's mission letters	Selections from Acts & various epistles, Revelation	1-3 John, Paul's captivity & pastoral letters, James, Peter & Jude
	Jesus as Priest	Jesus as King	Jesus as Prophet	Jesus as Lord

an appropriate follow up, and in doing so separately examines one of the four well-known portraits of Jesus as Priest, King, Prophet and Lord.

The Purpose of the Series.

The purpose is to provide a commentary-guide to *the Way of the Spirit* through the Bible. Christians who have been influenced over the past 20–30 years by the Charismatic Movement have often spoken to me of a need for some such guide, one that would help them to understand their Bibles better in the light of their experience of the Spirit, and one that would help them to relate their Bible-reading to such matters as the Spirit's ways, the power of faith, the dynamic of the word, revival, healing, and so forth—in fact everything that relates to personal experience of God in the life of the believer. We shall therefore be endeavouring, as we trace the Bible stories, to lay bare the heart that pulsates within giving them life, to tap their dynamic source—which is, of course, the Spirit of God himself.

As we study the history of Israel, we shall see how, unlike secular history, it is very much a story about God's dealings with men. When we trace the accounts of individual lives, we shall find they too are stories about the working of God's Spirit in transforming men. And throughout we shall also discover just how much the Bible does delight in the very things many Christians love to hear about in the Church today: the miraculous, the prophetic, the visionary, the love and fellowship of Spirit-filled believers, and so forth.

Our aim is therefore to examine the foundations of Christian faith, vision and experience in Scripture. Hence, alongside the chronological and topical arrangement of each volume outlined above, there is another more embracing pattern relating to our overall purpose:

- Vol. 1 outlines the basic principles on which all Christian life and experience need to be founded: faith in God's promises, obedience to his call and acknowledgment of the saving power of Christ's sacrifice.

- Vol. 2 traces the main movements of revival in Biblical history, thus highlighting the principles by which God's kingdom operates and outlining the challenges and vision that inspire all men of the Spirit.

- Vol. 3 examines the experiences and teachings of prophets and other men of the Spirit in both Testaments more directly, demonstrating how their faith and vision are of the very essence of Biblical hope.

- Vol. 4 looks at the common approaches of Spirit-filled Christians and the Bible to worship, service, pastoral matters, the challenges of daily living, and the like.

How to approach the Way of the Spirit in the Bible.

These books are written as Bible-reading guides, hence for use in conjunction with the Bible.[1] As you read the Scriptures, besides looking to the notes for guidance, expect the Holy Spirit himself to interpret what you read—and more than that, to lead you to the very source of his truth in the life of God himself. Remember the words of our Lord Jesus: 'You diligently study the Scriptures because you think that by them you possess eternal life. These are the Scriptures that testify about me, yet you refuse to come to me to have life.' (John 5.39f)

The Bible can be read both for its information about the things of God and also for the enjoyment of its life. The first is theology, but on its own that can become the letter that kills, and so it needs to be coupled with the second, for 'the word of God is living and active ... it penetrates even to dividing soul and spirit ... it judges the thoughts and attitudes of the heart.' (Heb. 4.12) Our theology has to be living, and it is only the Spirit that gives life.

Paul speaks about the difference between reading Scripture with and without the illumination of the Holy Spirit in 2 Cor. 3.14-18, where he says that those who read without the Spirit do so with a veil over the eyes. 'But,' he continues, 'whenever anyone turns to the Lord, the veil is taken away.' Then he adds, 'Now the Lord is the Spirit ...' and this 'comes form the Lord, who is the Spirit'. This removal of a

---

[1] A simple reading guide is provided on pp. 241-7. Workbooks and teaching tapes are also available for those who wish to use this book as the manual for a full home-study teaching course—see p. 249.

veil is something Christians commonly experience after baptism with the Holy Spirit, and so my prayer is that you, the reader, will also know it being lifted as the Spirit enlightens God's Word for you.

Don't allow yourself to become too preoccupied with small details, the precise interpretation of individual passages, words or phrases, complex historical or theological issues, and the like, but rather see yourself walking on the stage of the ancient world, first with the men of Old Testament times, and then with Jesus and his disciples. Go with Jesus around Galilee, listen to him speaking, participate in the astonishment and excitement of the crowd, share in the puzzlement and the illumination of his disciples, get the feel of what you read. The information given in these pages is mainly intended to help you lay hold of that 'feel' for yourself, particularly as it relates to the vision, the power and the life of God these men of old knew.

Read your Bible in something like the way you would read a novel or watch a play. Take yourself into the life of its drama and let the feel of that life flow through your life as you walk and talk with the ancient men of God and with Jesus. Lay hold of their vision and let it become yours as well. Let their longings be your longings and their joys your joys, for therein lies the life God wants you to know in Christ.

All Biblical quotations are taken from the New International Version of the Bible. To avoid confusion, the conventions of the NIV translators have also been adhered to beyond the quotations, e.g., 'he' rather than 'He' for God, 'the Most Holy Place' rather than 'the Holy of Holies', 'Spirit' (of God) rather than 'spirit' in the Old Testament (contrast RSV).

PART ONE

INTRODUCTION

1

God's Waiting People

With this volume we come to the fourth and final part of our survey of the Way of the Spirit in the Bible.

In the first we saw how God called Israel's earliest ancestors, taught them to co-operate with him by faith and obedience in his plan for saving his world from the mess earliest man had made of it through sin, taught them about sacrifice as his remedy for sin, and then sent Jesus to live out that life of faith, obedience and sacrifice for our salvation.

In the second we traced the story of how God planted Israel in Canaan as a first colony of his kingdom on earth, how through times of faithfulness issuing in growth, of disobedience resulting in decline and of repentance leading to revival, he established it initially as the Davidic Kingdom in ancient Israel and then, after a time of severe discipline, established it as the Kingdom of God through the ministry of Jesus, now to spread out from its Israelite base into the rest of the world.

In the third volume we focused attention on the work and vision of those men through whom the power of God's Word and Spirit worked down the centuries enabling them to preach towards revival and to lead revivals, namely the prophets in Israel, then Jesus himself as *the* 'Prophet' or 'Man of the Spirit' par excellence, and finally the Spirit-filled Christians of the early Church.

In these three volumes we covered Israel's history down to the exile, spilling over only a little into post-exilic times; in this fourth we must therefore concentrate on the five-hundred or more years that remain before the birth of Christ. Similarly, we have studied the Pentateuch (Genesis – Deuteronomy), the Histories (Joshua – 2 Kings) and the

Prophets (Isaiah – Malachi); now we must review the rest of
the Old Testament, the books commonly known simply as
'The Writings'.

While the earlier phases of Israel's history can be char-
acterised as times of faith, kingdom-building, revival and
the like, the one word that best sums up the mood of the
post-exilic period is 'waiting'—waiting for God to come
and fulfil the promises he had made to and through patriarchs, kings and prophets in the generations gone by,
promises that were to find fulfilment in the life, ministry,
death and resurrection of our Lord Jesus Christ. These were
long years when men had to be reminded that God was still
sovereign, still faithful to his word, still absolutely powerful
and still very much in control.

The themes of God's sovereignty and his wisdom are also
focal elements in our New Testament study, where we shall
hear Paul speak of Jesus as 'the power of God and the wisdom of God' (1 Cor. 1.24).

The primary responses these attributes of God evoke from
us are worship and meditation, such as we find in Psalms or
Proverbs. In the New Testament these responses are best
exemplified in John's portrait of Jesus as the Lord of glory
in the fourth Gospel, or Paul's descriptions of the ascended
and glorified Christ in his letters from prison. So while we
looked in our earlier studies at Jesus as Priest, King and
Prophet, here we must think of him as Lord—and along with
that, of course, consider our own proper response to his
Lordship in meditation and worship.

But as a preliminary to that study, let us first remind
ourselves what the whole story is all about.

1. MARANATHA! OUR LORD, COME!

The Lord's people are a waiting people. So it has been since
earliest times, and so it remains today. The reason is that our
God is not one who sits in some remote place waiting for us
to find him, like the gods of most oriental religions, but One
who comes to his people. The initiative in salvation is always God's, not ours, and that is why we speak of 'good

news'—salvation does not depend on our capabilities, but
on the power of God, and the good news is that he has
wrought it through Jesus Christ. Our part is to receive with
gratitude what he has done and to wait expectantly for what
he has promised to do next. The pattern is the same
throughout the history of salvation.

IN THE BEGINNING (Gen. 1–11)

The story starts with God's initiative. He made the world
and 'saw that it was very good' (1.31). Man first received it
with gratitude, but then turned away to receive from another's hand and so lost everything. Sin, suffering and death
become his lot and God sees with sorrow 'how corrupt the
earth has become' (6.6,12). He demonstrates his power to
come in judgment through the Flood, but sin continues to
multiply. Man turns totally to do-it-yourself religion, building his Babel-tower to heaven, seeking to come to God
instead of waiting for God to come to him. The result is total
alienation—of God from man and man from man.

GOD COMES TO ABRAHAM (Gen. 12–50; c. 2000–1300 BC)

– with a promise that in a land of God's appointing he will
have descendants through whom God will restore blessing to
all mankind. Abraham's part is simply to go in faith and
expectancy, letting God do it through him. The Genesis
stories tell how he and his sons, after many disasters
resulting from trying to work things out for themselves,
learned to wait in faith for God to come and fulfil his word.
At the end we see them a waiting people in Egypt, with
Joseph on his death-bed looking forward in hope as he
reminds them of God's promises to Abraham.

GOD COMES TO MOSES (Exodus – 1 Samuel; c. 1300–1000)

– with a promise to bring his people out of Egypt and
establish them in Canaan. On the way, at Sinai, he reveals
his pattern of life that will ensure continued blessing in the
land (the Law). Their part is to live in faith in the revelation
and obedience to its requirements. When they do so God
blesses them with success, as in the exodus and the

6 Introduction

conquest, but on both counts they repeatedly fail and suffer the consequences. In the wilderness they rebel and so have to wander there for forty years. Then in Canaan they turn to pagan gods and so suffer repeated oppression, until finally they become slaves to the Philistines. They seek salvation through having a king like the nations, but he (Saul) fails to walk in obedience to God, and so ...

GOD COMES TO DAVID (1 Samuel – 2 Kings; c. 1000–540)
– with a promise to establish him and his descendants in a royal dynasty, living in peace and greatness (2 Sam. 7). His part is simply to live and rule in faithful obedience, waiting for God to fulfil his purposes through him. At first all goes well, for the glory of Solomon's reign recaptures something of Eden's splendour (1 Kings 4.20f). But Solomon and his successors repeatedly turn to other gods rather than wait for the LORD. The kingdom splits and slowly disintegrates until its northern part (Israel/Ephraim) falls to the Assyrians in 722 and the southern (Judah) to the Babylonians in 597. Jerusalem is finally destroyed in 587 and the people are taken into exile.

GOD COMES TO THE PROPHETS (c. 750–450)
– with a promise to bring all his earlier promises to fulfilment through a New Covenant, in which man's heart will be changed by the working of his Spirit. The new age is to be introduced by a descendant of David (Messiah) who will himself be full of God's Spirit, will be the embodiment of that righteous life called for in the Law of Moses, and will offer the perfect sacrifice to release us from the bondage of sin (cp. Hos. 2.14-23; Isa. 9.1-7; 11.1-9; 53; 61.1-3; Jer. 31.31-4; Ezek. 36.24-38).

THE PEOPLE OF GOD WAIT (c. 540 – BC/AD)
– for the coming of Messiah. When the Persians overthrew the Babylonian Empire in 539, Jews began to return home and rebuild a community around Jerusalem, encouraged by men like Haggai, Zechariah and Malachi to hold fast to the vision of the earlier prophets. As the years rolled by without evidence of the old promises coming to fulfilment, Jewish

religion became increasingly legalistic and ritualistic. Attitudes hardened into doctrines as parties, like the Pharisees and Sadducees, began to emerge.

In the middle of the fourth century BC the Persians were succeeded by the Greeks and then, after a brief spell of independence in the second, the Romans took over in the first. Though the cultural, political and religious changes during these centuries were immense, the heart of Judaism remained essentially the same: God's people became truly a waiting people, waiting for their Messiah and the new age of God's Spirit. Also, thanks to the exile, Jews were now strategically placed in all major centres of civilisation, thus preparing the whole of the ancient world for the coming of the Christ.

GOD COMES TO HIS PEOPLE (The Gospels; c. 5 BC – 30 AD)
– in Jesus Christ. 'When the time had fully come, God sent his son' (Gal. 4.4) and the long night of waiting came to an end—that is, for those who recognised and received him. To them he was the living fulfilment of the vision of kingship God gave to David, of the pattern of righteousness he gave to Moses, of the faith to which he had called Abraham—indeed of everything he had created Adam to be. He was thus a second Adam, come to restore all that the first Adam had lost. But more than that, he was the very embodiment of that wisdom of God that existed even before creation began and that found expression in the creative Word God uttered at the dawn of time. In him all God's promises find fulfilment, for he is himself the Wisdom of God, the Word of God and the creative Power of God—the Man for whom Israel had waited.

GOD COMES TO JESUS' DISCIPLES (Acts; c. 30 – 100 AD)
– in the power of his Holy Spirit. God sent Jesus to restore Eden's blessing to all mankind. The promise of the Spirit is thus for everyone, but is given only to those who receive it from the hand of Christ. By his touch, Jesus' followers found themselves living in Paradisal joy and sharing in his Messianic power. Through them the Kingdom spread and

very soon its fire was burning all over the Roman world.

(Jews, of course, do not accept Jesus as the Christ, and so are still waiting for their Messiah. Their hope is essentially the same as ours, only held at an earlier stage of development. They are a people locked in the faith of later Judaism, waiting for something we believe has already happened. That is why Jewish Christians often speak of themselves as 'fulfilled Jews'.)

GOD COMES TODAY

– in revival power. The message of the Bible is clear. Salvation is God's doing, not ours. We can wait for it, long for it and pray for it, but we cannot make it happen. Indeed, the harder we try, the more we hinder God's working. But the good news is that he has promised it and will grant it to all who seek him and wait for him. God continues to come to his people in the same way today. We call that 'revival'!

GOD WILL COME AGAIN

– in the end. That promise is as much his for us today as all the others. They have proved utterly reliable. This one will too. We are still a waiting people.

Maranatha! Our Lord, come!

2. THE POST-EXILIC AND INTERTESTAMENTAL PERIOD

Jewish political history in this period, between the fall of Babylon in 539 BC and the birth of Christ, is almost entirely governed by changes of empire—from Babylonian to Persian to Greek to Roman. There were also many religious and cultural changes, so many that we no longer speak about 'Israelites', but 'Jews'. The following are the most significant:

1. *The Dispersion* (or *Diaspora*): Israel was no longer a coherent Palestinian state, but a people dispersed through every country in the ancient world. They still looked on Jerusalem as their faith-centre and by New Testament times it had become a place of pilgrimage, but its centrality was

more religious than political. Israel had been a nation, Judaism became a world faith, though preserving a longing for restoration of national, political status as 'Israel'.

2. *The Temple and the Synagogue*: The temple was rebuilt in Jerusalem, but for scattered Jews it could not be a place of regular meeting. Synagogues began to appear locally as places of assembly, Scripture-reading, teaching and prayer, though not of sacrificial worship led by priests. For that a pilgrimage to Jerusalem was necessary.

3. *The Law* became more central to Jewish life, partly because it provided a basis for common cultural identity to the scattered people. Some laws became especially important since they provided, as it were, distinctive badges of Judaism: particularly circumcision, Sabbath-observance and the food-laws.

4. *A People of the Book*: This new emphasis on the law led to greater emphasis on the centrality of the written word, but gradually that made many Jews more legalistic and religiously dogmatic in the practice of their faith. Jesus found the Pharisees particularly so.

5. *The Priests* in Jerusalem found themselves with a new political status and authority now that there were no kings. The power they attained is clearly seen in the story of Jesus' trial.

6. *Fasting, Lamentation, Sin & Atonement*: On the more spiritual side, the exile had confirmed the truth of the prophets' message about sin bringing judgment. Hence we find a growing emphasis on penitence, fasting and the like. In fact, the Feast of Atonement became one of the most important of the annual festivals.

7. *Monotheism*: In pre-exilic times Israelites had repeatedly turned to the worship of other gods, thus stirring God's anger and rousing the voice of his prophets, but through the judgment of exile the battle for monotheism was finally won. By Jesus' time it was no longer a living issue.

8. *Messianic Hope* became much stronger in post-exilic times. Since there was no longer a king on the throne, the promise of eternal rule to David took on new significance as Jews set themselves to wait for a coming Son of David who would restore their kingdom. They came to speak of him as (the) Messiah. The title is simply Hebrew for '(the)

Anointed One'; the Greek equivalent is '(the) Christ'.

9. *Diversity of belief and practice*: Parties (a bit like our denominations, though not at all the same) began to appear and by New Testament times we find the Jews thoroughly divided, mainly among the Pharisees, Sadducees, Zealots, Essenes and Samaritans.

3. STUDYING 'THE WRITINGS'

What are 'The Writings' of the Old Testament?
Since the Jews do not recognise our New Testament as sacred Scripture, they do not refer to the Hebrew Bible as 'The Old Testament'. Their name for it is 'The Law, The Prophets and The Writings' (*Torah, Nebi'im uKethubim*).

'The Law' refers to the Pentateuch.
'The Prophets' refers to
  (i) the history books Joshua, Judges, Samuel and Kings ('the former prophets');
  (ii) the prophetic books Isaiah, Jeremiah, Ezekiel and the twelve Minor Prophets from Hosea to Malachi ('the latter prophets').
'The Writings' refers to everything else.

The books in the Hebrew Bible are arranged in that order, which is different from the English order.

What The Writings comprise.
(a) *History* (from Adam to Persian Times)—Chronicles, Ezra, Nehemiah.

1 Chron.1–9 covers the period from Adam to David in genealogies.

The rest of Chronicles is a history of the Davidic dynasty and the southern kingdom of Judah. It contains no account of the conquest, the settlement or Saul's reign, disregards the history of northern Israel entirely and omits all the prophet-stories found in Samuel and Kings, but it also adds information not found in them, particularly about the temple and its priesthood. Thus its accounts of David's and Solomon's reigns focus strongly on the building of the temple and the organisation of its worship, and the same interest in the affairs of the Levites continues through its account of the divided monarchy. We shall not be studying Chronicles here. It was reviewed in Volume Two.

The books of Ezra and Nehemiah continue the Chronicler's story of Jerusalem, its temple and its people into the post-exilic era. We shall turn to that presently.

(b) *Historical novels*—Ruth, Jonah, Esther.

Ruth is a tale about David's Edomite ancestors.

Jonah is the story of a prophet who was sent to prophesy in Nineveh, capital of the Assyrian empire.

Esther is a story about a Jewish girl who became Queen of Persia and rescued her people from persecution.

(c) *Wisdom literature*—Job, Proverbs, Ecclesiastes.

Job is a drama on the problem of suffering.

Proverbs is mainly a collection of wise sayings and advice.

Ecclesiastes is a meditation on the purpose of life.

(d) *Religious poetry*—Psalms, Lamentations, Song of Songs.

Psalms is a hymn-book.

Lamentations contains five hymns lamenting Jerusalem's desolation during the exile.

Song of Songs is a book of love-poems.

(e) *Apocalyptic prophecy*—Daniel.

Daniel is partly made up of stories about Jewish bravery at times of persecution by the Babylonians and the Persians (chs. 1–6), and partly of visions unfolding the future (chs. 7–12).

When were The Writings written?

The fact that we are studying these books in the context of post-exilic history indicates that some of them at least were written then, as is obviously the case with Chronicles-Ezra-Nehemiah, Esther, Lamentations and Daniel. There are also good reasons for believing, as we shall see later, that Ruth and Jonah may have been written in post-exilic times. On the other hand, Song of Songs, Proverbs and Ecclesiastes are said to date back to Solomon's time. Psalms also contains elements dating back to the early days of the Davidic monarchy, though some of the psalms are fairly late (e.g. Pss. 79 & 137, which tell about the destruction of Jerusalem and the sufferings of the exile). Job is virtually impossible to date and could have been written at almost any time before the third century.

It is important to recognise, however, that questions of date and authorship, interesting as they are in themselves, will not often affect our understanding of the way of God's Spirit in the books we shall be studying here.

Other post-exilic Jewish writings.

In the Old Testament itself Haggai, Zechariah, Joel and Malachi are post-exilic, but we have already looked at them in Volume Three.

There are also many other Jewish religious books from later pre-Christian and early Christian times that were never included in the Hebrew Bible. Many of these first appeared in Greek and are now contained in what we call *The Apocrypha*. (Roman Catholics include these in their Bibles, though Protestants generally do not.) Other Jewish books written in Greek that never found their way into anyone's Bible and are referred to as *Pseudepigrapha*.

These later Greek writings are useful for piecing together the history and theology of Judaism just before the time of Christ. Also most helpful are *The Antiquities of the Jews* and *The Jewish War* by Josephus, a first-century Jewish historian and theologian, giving an account of his people's history from creation to the fall of Jerusalem in 70 AD.

Jewish scriptures also began to appear in Greek translation, and in Aramaic as well. When Alexander the Great established his Hellenistic (= Greek) Empire in the fourth century, Greek became the international language of the ancient world. Before that Aramaic had served the purpose. After the exile Hebrew ceased to be a living language for the dispersed Jews, but most of them could speak Greek or Aramaic. The Aramaic translations are known as the *Targums*. They are often as much a paraphrase as a translation, and so help us to see how later Jews interpreted their sacred scriptures. The Greek translation is known as the *Septuagint*. It was produced in Alexandria, in Egypt, and adheres more closely to the Hebrew text, though it also includes the books of the Apocrypha.

(The Septuagint became the main version used by the early Church and continues to be so among the Greek Orthodox. A Latin translation of it, the *Vulgate*, replaced it in the West and became the Bible of Roman Catholicism. The Protestant reformers in the fifteenth and sixteenth centuries decided to return to the Hebrew text and make a fresh translation, and that is one of the reasons why few Protestant Bibles include the Apocryphal books.)

Other important, but later, Jewish books include the *Mishnah*, the authoritative collection of the Jewish oral law, supplementing the teaching of the Torah and covering most aspects of Jewish life (some Jews, particularly the Pharisees, believed it was revealed to Moses along with the written law at Sinai), and the *Talmud*, which incorporates the Mishnah and various records of Rabbinic debates about its interpretation.

Our purpose here is not to study Judaism, but to trace the way of God's Spirit in the Bible. We shall therefore be passing directly from our Old Testament studies into the New Testament without much reference to these later Jewish writings, except where they provide background information that will help us understand our Bible-story better.

THE BOOKS OF THE APOCRYPHA

1 Esdras: A parallel history with 2 Chron. 35 – Neh. 8, from Josiah's reforms to Ezra's reforms, but omitting the record of Nehemiah's work and a great deal else.

2 Esdras or **The Apocalypse of Ezra**: A series of seven apocalyptic visions granted to Ezra.

Tobit: A fictitious tale about how Tobit, an exile living in Nineveh, was blinded and healed, how his son, Tobias, recovered the family fortune and won his bride from a demon, all with the help of an angel.

Judith: A fictitious tale about a young Jewish widow befriending and beheading Holofernes, an Assyrian general who was besieging her town.

The Rest of Esther: Additional material to the book of Esther.

The Wisdom of Solomon: An extended meditation on the value of wisdom and the part it played in creation and history.

Ecclesiasticus or **The Wisdom of Jesus ben Sirah**: A wisdom collection in the style of Proverbs, arranged mainly in continuous passages, as in Prov. 1–9 or 30–31.

Baruch: Teachings of Baruch, Jeremiah's scribe, to encourage the exiles in Babylon.

The Epistle of Jeremy: An attack on idolatry in the style of a letter from Jeremiah to the exiles (cp. Jer. 29).

The Song of the Three Holy Children: A prayer uttered by Azariah and a song that he and his two companions sang in the fiery furnace (= *The Benedicite* in Christian worship).

Daniel and Susanna: A story about a virtuous woman falsely accused, but rescued from her death sentence by Daniel.

Bel and the Dragon: A couple of stories about how Daniel demonstrated the falseness of Babylonian religion.

The Prayer of Manasseh: The prayer King Manasseh is supposed to have prayed when he repented in 2 Chron. 33.

1 Maccabees: A history of the Jewish revolt and the early Maccabean kings, 175–134 BC.

2 Maccabees: A less reliable, more legendary history of the early Maccabean era.

2

The Exile

The exile was more than a mere set-back for Israel in her history. It was an event so cataclysmic that the LORD's people were never to be the same again. At the time most Israelites must have viewed it as a tragic disaster, though a few individuals with deeper spiritual sensitivity and perception did view it with positive faith as an act of God for the judgment and refining of those he had chosen to carry his light to the nations of the world.

To understand properly the effect of these things on the development of Jewish faith after the exile, it is important for us to review first of all some of the main events that led up to the judgment and to trace the hand of God in them.

1. WHY THE EXILE?

Though God spoke to his people 'at many times and in various ways', as Heb. 1.1 puts it, for the most part he did so to remind them about three or four basic things he had already revealed to their ancestors about his purposes for them and the redemption of the world through them.

God's original purpose.
At the very beginning, when God first spoke to man, he revealed that his purpose for him was to 'Be fruitful and increase in number; fill the earth and subdue it. Rule over the fish of the sea and the birds of the air and over every living creature that moves on the ground' (Gen. 1.28). God created a good earth, a beautiful garden-kingdom, and in his goodness entrusted it to man to care for, enjoy and rule over

as its king.

All that was spoiled by the fall, after which man lost the fullness of his kingly authority. Life became a battle with his environment, as he tilled the soil with the sweat of his brow, cultivated it in competition with thorns and thistles, bore children in pain (Gen. 3.16-19), and eventually had to live in a relationship with the animal world governed by fear (9.2) and with the rest of mankind governed by suspicion, hostility and confusion (ch. 4; 11.1-9).

God's purpose to redeem the world.
It was not God's will to leave the earth thus, but to make it his kingdom again. And so one day he spoke again—to Abraham, outlining his plan for redeeming the world, and inviting him to co-operate in bringing it to birth.

The plan was very simple (Gen. 12.1-3):
1. God would lead Abraham to a land of his choosing;
2. there his family would so increase that one day they would become a great nation;
3. God would look after him and bless him in his co-operation;
4. and the outcome would be that blessing would eventually be restored to all peoples on earth.

God made no great demands of Abraham, other than that he trust him and set out for his new home. He did not say Abraham would have to work or try hard at anything; redemption would be God's doing, not Abraham's. All he had to do was make himself available to father a family in Canaan so that it might in turn become the nucleus of a nation through which God could re-create his kingdom on earth. God was only asking for his co-operation and trust—his faith.

Genesis shows us some of the problems Abraham and his descendants had in sustaining that co-operation. It tells a story full of dramatic tension. They now receive and then lose sight of the call and promise of God; they now show faith and then fail to stand firm in it. Abraham, Isaac and Jacob were all either tempted to, or actually did flee from Canaan in time of stress, and the story ends with the infant nation well and truly out of the promised land. God had made no great demands, only promises. All he asked for was faith, but they clearly found that difficult.

In the end the answer lies with God, not man; it is his promise and his purpose. In the closing verses of Genesis we see Joseph remind his brothers of that truth and encourage them to look forward in faith to the day when God would bring them back home to Canaan again (50.24).

What God was doing in those early days was giving the people he had chosen basic revelation about his redemptive plan and showing them the kind of co-operation he wanted from them. That is, he was imparting vision and teaching the need for simple faith in him to fulfil it.

As the story progresses through the Old Testament and other dimensions are added to the vision, these basic ingredients remain foundational for all God does in Israel. We listen to leaders, kings and prophets, just like Joseph on his death-bed, reminding the descendants of Abraham about the promise God made to their forefather, about the high calling he has given them, and about their constant need to walk in faith in that calling, vision and promise.

God's purpose to create a holy nation.
God spoke again when he called Moses and brought the Israelites out of Egypt through the desert to Mount Sinai (Exod. 1–19). There he spoke of his plan for them to be his 'treasured possession, a kingdom of priests and a holy nation', a people set apart for his work, and outlined the basic principles by which they were to live in order to be so (the Ten Commandments, etc). Then Moses and the elders, on the people's behalf, entered into covenant with him to become that holy nation (Exod. 19–24).

Moses also received further instructions about worship, sacrifice, priesthood, religious purity, moral conduct, social behaviour and other aspects of the life of holiness that was to be lived in Canaan (Exod. 24 – Num. 10). Because of grumbling and disobedience it took the Israelites another forty years before they were ready to enter the land (Num. 11–36), but then, on the eve of their crossing over, Moses, in his last sermon (Deuteronomy), reminded them about the urgency for obedience to this pattern of life God had shown them.

Obedience would secure all the rich blessings he wanted them to have in the land. But the call was absolute: to be holy, to be God's people, totally dedicated to him and to his law. And so, alongside the promises stand very solemn warnings about the disastrous consequences of disobedience: 'I have set before you life and death, blessings and curses. Now choose life, so that you and your children may live ...' (30.15-20). God's will, as he had first promised to Abraham, was to bless, but two ways lay before Israel, and only one of them would lead to that blessing, namely the way of obedience and faith. The other would most surely lead to curse, suffering and destruction.

Israel's call was therefore more than just to become a nation, but to become God's holy nation, the expression of his kingdom on earth. God's plan was ultimately to restore his Eden-kingdom, and Israel was to be its first planting, a kind of colony of the kingdom of heaven on earth, a base from which the rest of the world was to be won back.

Thus, in his covenant with Abraham God gave promises to be received in faith; in his covenant with Moses he gave commands to be responded to in obedience. Throughout Israel's history up to the exile these standards are appealed to time and again to explain what has happened and to warn about what might happen.

God's purpose for the Davidic king.
Israel's early history in the land illustrates the outworking of these standards. At first, through their faithful obedience Joshua and his men conquered Canaan, but in the generations that followed faithlessness resulted in moral, social and political decline. Of course, whenever the people returned to the LORD in repentance, he granted times of restoration and revival, as he did repeatedly in the age of the judges, but a thorough restoration only took place after total humiliation when the people were forced to turn wholeheartedly to God again in Samuel's time. And then in David's day God spoke once more.

The establishment of David's kingdom introduced a new political structure in which the welfare of the nation, while still depending on the people's conduct, now depended more on the king himself. So when God spoke to David, he reminded him of his responsibility, but he also made him a promise that he would care for him, bless him and establish his throne for ever (2 Sam. 7).

The history of David's throne was not always happy. At first it was, under Solomon, but then the kingdom split in two and was never reunited. None the less, as the years rolled by, the sons of David continued to reign in Jerusalem, just as God had said they would, and increasingly the people of Judah found security in his promise. If Jerusalem was 'the City of David' and 'the house of the LORD' stood in it, how could any enemy ever take and destroy it? That sense of security is reflected in some of the Psalms, such as 2 and 46.

However, it was not only to David that God had spoken. To Abraham he had explained that his purpose was to restore blessing to all mankind, and to Moses he had revealed how the Israelites were to live in order to enter into that blessing themselves. Therefore when kings and people strayed into wrong ways, as they did increasingly with the passage of time, it became obvious to some that the outworking of the promise to David was not going to be straight-forward and without pain.

God's purpose in judgment.

Presently the warning voices of prophets were being heard in Jerusalem and throughout the land: unless men return to God in repentance, he must intervene and discipline. Unfortunately their warnings were not often heeded. On one or two occasions they were and the LORD granted times of revival, but for the most part they were not and so his hand fell in judgment.

First it was the Northern Kingdom that felt the brunt of his anger. When the Assyrians took Samaria in 722, they dealt with it brutally. They virtually depopulated the land, deporting Israelites to various parts of their empire and resettling the land with foreigners, so much so that the North well nigh became pagan territory (2 Kings 17).

In the South the Davidic kings still reigned in Jerusalem. When the Assyrians failed to take the city in 701 BC (2 Kings 18–20), popular faith in God's promise to David must have soared. However, the king on the throne at that time, Hezekiah, was a faithful man of God who had just led his

people into revival, but his successors were quite unlike
him. Paganism ran rampant in Jerusalem throughout most of
the seventh century and the warning voice of the prophets
was effectively silenced (2 Kings 21). In 622 BC King
Josiah initiated a movement of reform and revival, but it
was too late to save the nation (2 Kings 22–23). He died in
609 and his successor, Jehoiakim, allowed paganism to
flourish again. Finally Jerusalem was taken by the Babylonians in 597 and destroyed by them in 587. The verdict of
the Chronicler reads:

> *The LORD, the God of their fathers, sent word to them*
> *through his messengers again and again, because he had*
> *pity on his people and on his dwelling-place. But they*
> *mocked God's messengers, despised his words and*
> *scoffed at his prophets until the wrath of the LORD was*
> *roused against his people and there was no remedy.*
>
> (2 Chron. 36.15f)

To be sure, in the midst of all their warnings the prophets
did say that God would bring restoration after judgment.
They even foretold that he would speak again and inaugurate a new covenant age in which the old promises to
Abraham, Moses and David would find a greater measure of
fulfilment than known hitherto, the age of his Spirit which
would mark the final thrust of his kingdom into the rest of
the world.

Nevertheless, Jerusalem now lay in ruins, burnt to the
ground, together with her temple and palace that had so
livingly symbolised God's promise to David. After the first
deportations in 597 some refused to accept that what had
happened was anything more than a temporary set-back, a
mere hiccup in history that would soon pass (Jer. 28.3). The
disastrous finality of 587 dispelled such vain hopes.
Distress, incomprehension, bewilderment, even disillusion-
ment with God must now have overtaken many Israelites.
Such was the setting for the book of Lamentations.

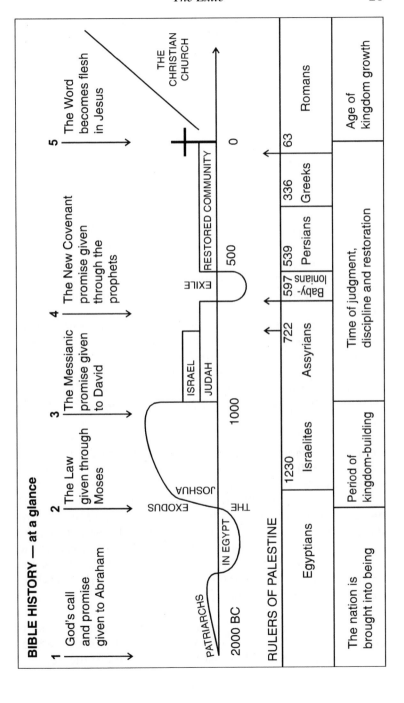

BIBLE HISTORY — at a glance

1 God's call and promise given to Abraham

2 The Law given through Moses

3 The Messianic promise given to David

4 The New Covenant promise given through the prophets

5 The Word becomes flesh in Jesus

THE CHRISTIAN CHURCH

PATRIARCHS

IN EGYPT

THE EXODUS

JOSHUA

ISRAEL

JUDAH

EXILE

RESTORED COMMUNITY

2000 BC   1000   500   0

RULERS OF PALESTINE

Egyptians	Israelites	Assyrians	Baby-lonians	Persians	Greeks	Romans
	1230	722	597	539	336	63

| The nation is brought into being | Period of kingdom-building | Time of judgment, discipline and restoration | | | Age of kingdom growth |

2. SONGS OF A CHASTENED PEOPLE (LAMENTATIONS)

Lamentations is a collection of five psalms. The first four are acrostics, i.e., their verses are arranged in (Hebrew) alphabetical order. The fifth is not an acrostic, but like the others it does have 22 verses, the same as the number of letters in the Hebrew alphabet. In the third chapter each of the three lines of the verses begins with the same letter— hence the number 66 (= 3 x 22). As we shall also see, the spiritual intensity is strongest in ch. 3.

There is a tradition that Jeremiah wrote Lamentations, but that is based on 2 Chron. 35.25 which actually refers to some other collection of laments commemorating King Josiah after his death in 609 BC. That collection must now be lost. It can hardly have been the same as our book of Lamentations, for what it laments is the fall and destruction of Jerusalem and the conditions prevailing in Judah thereafter.

Lamentations may be a song-book that was used during the exile by mourners who gathered at the ruined temple site on special days of fasting and lamentation, when they wept over the sins that had caused the disaster. Two passages in particular suggest something like that: Jer. 41.5 tells of a company of eighty pilgrims dressed as mourners bringing offerings to the temple area in the early days of the exile; and Zech. 7.1-5 makes reference to times of fasting and mourning in the fifth and seventh months that had been observed with unbroken regularity for seventy years from the destruction of Jerusalem in 587.

Pss. 74 & 79 vividly recall the actual plundering of the city and the sanctuary, and Ps. 137 shows something of how the Babylonian exiles lamented their fate. Lamentations, on the other hand, is concerned mainly with conditions of life for those left in Judah. From it we get an impression of the spiritual temperature of Palestinian Judaism during the years of the exile. It is a very emotional book!

The laments themselves are not just five separate poems conveniently collected in one book, but are closely interrelated compositions with a distinct progression of theme.

Ch. 1: Is any suffering like my suffering?
As it laments the tragic affliction that has befallen the city, the first poem views the disaster almost entirely from the perspective of personal grief. It is essentially a cry of self-pity, bewailing the humiliation of Zion (even if also acknowledging it is merited because of sin, vv. 5,18,20), how the proud city is now deserted, how her people suffer, her enemies gloat over her, and there is no-one to give comfort. The cry of this first lament is aptly summed up in the words of v. 20: 'See, O LORD, how distressed I am!'

Ch. 2: The LORD has abandoned his sanctuary.
The fall of Jerusalem is now viewed from God's perspective and we see that his mood is anger. 'Without pity the Lord has swallowed up ... In fierce anger he has cut off ...' (vv. 2f) The bitterness of the desolation is expressed just as strongly as in ch. 1 (v. 11), but now it is acknowledged that God has only acted as he said he would (v. 17), that is, that the prophets (not the false ones that had spoken only peace, v. 14) had got it right after all.

Ch. 3: Let us return to the LORD.
The mood shifts again. Acknowledging that the suffering is the LORD's doing and no mere accident of history (vv. 1-20), 'therefore I have hope' (v. 21). The theme of hope and waiting patiently for God to move again in compassion and in accordance with his faithfulness to his ancient promises (vv. 22-33) leads directly to an admission of his justice and a call for repentance (vv. 34-42) which in turn leads on to a plea for deliverance.

Ch. 4: It happened because of our sins.
The continuing lamentation over Jerusalem's desolation contains further acknowledgment that, sad though the disaster is, it is indeed punishment (v. 6), particularly for the sins of her religious leaders (v. 13). But equally the conviction is expressed that 'your punishment will end; he will not prolong your exile.' (v. 22)

Ch. 5: Restore us to yourself, O LORD.
Still lamenting the suffering, still confessing sin and

acknowledging the justice of the punishment (v. 7), the plea now climaxes with a call for restoration.

The progression in these laments is entirely spiritual and reflects a common chain of human reactions to divine chastening, moving from an initial outburst of self-pity through various stages of recognising God's anger, perceiving his hand at work, believing there must yet be hope, turning to him in repentance, acknowledging the justice of what has happened, and then finally to expecting restoration.

At the heart of the book, in the middle of ch. 3, we find ourselves occupied entirely with statements of faith—about 'the LORD's great love', that 'his compassions never fail. They are new every morning', that 'The LORD is good to those whose hope is in him.' Clearly what was learned through the chastening of exile was acceptance of the prophetic message about judgment, the wholesomeness of repentance and sorrow for sin, and the need for faithful waiting on God for restoration. Thus God's promise to David may seem to have failed (4.20), but he is faithful and somehow will yet fulfil it. The temptation is always to think he has gone back on his word, but faith says wait. At the heart of Lamentations is one of the strongest statements of belief in God's continuing faithfulness in the whole of the Old Testament.

A helpful book when your own world seems to be falling apart!

PART TWO

THE SOVEREIGNTY OF GOD

The exile, as we have already noted, radically changed the Lord's people. Among the many lessons they learned through it probably the most profound was about the need for obedience to God's revealed will. It taught them reverence for the laws of Moses and for the prophets' calls to repentance. In due course the law and obedience to its demands were to become of paramount importance in Judaism.

Equally profound was what they learned about faithfulness to their one God and about faith in his purposes. The fall of Jerusalem seemed like a death-blow to all their hope for fulfilment of his promises to Abraham and David, but already beforehand the prophets were saying it would not be so and that restoration would eventually come. During the exile the prophetic word continued to speak reassurance and hope, particularly through the utterances of Isa. 40–55. The message of the prophets was the subject of Volume Three and so need not be repeated here, but when it was seen to be vindicated in the return from exile, consciousness of God's sovereignty over the affairs of nations as well as over Israel itself began to grow more positively than ever before.

It is perhaps that sense, that God is in control, that he is the One who guides or restrains the hand of governors and emperors, that emerges most vividly in the story of the post-exilic community as we read it in the books we are about to study. The earlier prophets always taught God's universal sovereignty, in the exile Isa. 40–55 had proclaimed it more strongly than ever, and now the Jews could see it in the events of history. Their sense of national destiny in the wider context of international affairs was becoming supremely important: God is truly in control and his ancient promises will indeed be fulfilled; it may be difficult to see how, but they will; we must therefore wait in hope and faith.

3

Creating the Jewish Community

EZRA AND NEHEMIAH

The books of Ezra and Nehemiah cover a period of just over a hundred years, starting with the return from exile and taking us down towards the end of the fifth century BC. Nothing of the story of the last four centuries before Christ is told in the Old Testament, except prophetically in the visions of Daniel. That is because the story of the Jews was completed by 400 BC—not in the sense that nothing else happened in their history, but in that God had finished his preparatory work among them by then. What they had to do now was wait. Certainly the religious, social and political thinking of Jews continued to develop, and still does so, but they remain essentially a waiting people, waiting for the fulfilment of the revelation that was completed in Old Testament times. What we are about to read now is the story of their regathering and of the final touches being added.

Ezra and Nehemiah are the continuation of the work of the Chronicler. That is clearly shown by the fact that the first few verses of Ezra are the same as the last few of 2 Chron. 36. However, it is not at all clear when they were written or by whom. Whoever the author was, he seems to have made fairly full use of the personal diaries of Ezra and Nehemiah, sometimes unedited, judging by the fact that much of the book of Nehemiah is written as if by Nehemiah himself.

The period covered spans the reigns of five Persian emperors. Daniel, Haggai, Zechariah, Esther, Malachi and possibly Joel also belong to different parts of this era, but we shall see how they fit into the story as we go along.

THE PERIOD COVERED BY EZRA AND NEHEMIAH

Cyrus 559–30
> Cyrus takes Babylon in 539.
> Many exiles return to Jerusalem with Sheshbazzar in 537 (Ezra 1–2).
> Daniel's last years (Dan. 9–12).

Cambyses 530–22
> Not mentioned in the Old Testament.

Darius I 522–486
> Haggai and Zechariah start prophesying in 520.
> The temple is rebuilt, 520–15 (Ezra 3–6).

Xerxes I (= Ahasuerus) 486–65
> Objections lodged against the people of Jerusalem, 486 (Ezra 4.6).
> Esther becomes queen and prevents a massacre of Jews in Susa.
> Joel ?

Artaxerxes I 465–24
> Work of rebuilding the walls of Jerusalem stopped (Ezra 4.6-23).
> Malachi
> Ezra is sent to conduct religious reforms in 458. He brings more exiles home with him (Ezra 7–10).
> Nehemiah comes to Jerusalem as its governor in 445 and rebuilds the walls (Neh. 1–7).
> Scenes of revival as Ezra reads the Law and the walls are dedicated in the autumn of 445 (Neh. 8–12).
> Nehemiah goes back to report of Artaxerxes, 433 (Neh. 13.6).
> He returns 'some time later' and has to re-establish his reforms (Neh. 13. 7-31).

---

1. THE FIRST TWENTY-FIVE YEARS (EZRA 1–6)

Chs. 1–2: The first group of exiles returns home.
The opening date refers to the establishment of the Persian Empire. Cyrus became king of Persia about 559. Ten years later he began his conquests: first Media in 549, then Lydia (modern Turkey) and Assyria by 546, until finally he took

over the whole Babylonian Empire when his troops marched into Babylon in 539.

Almost immediately he issued an edict encouraging exiles of all nations to return to their homelands. That was a total reversal of the policies of the Assyrians and Babylonians before him. They had held conquered regions in subjection by removing the leading citizens, any they considered capable of rousing rebellion. By contrast the Persians encouraged local citizens to return and shoulder responsibility for their own regions. They divided the empire into twenty 'satrapies', each overseen by a governor known as a Satrap, and each further subdivided. Judah was a subdivision of the satrapy known as Trans-Euphrates (NIV), or Beyond the River (RSV), that is, the territories west of the Euphrates, including Syria in the north.

As part of their policy of rebuilding the regions they restored the local gods and temples, so that throughout the empire men could 'pray for the well-being of the king and his sons', so that local gods might be kept happy and not rise in 'wrath against the realm of the king and of his sons' (Ezra 6.10; 7.23). The Jews had no idols to take home, so they brought their temple treasures instead.

In 537 one called Sheshbazzar was appointed governor of Judah and he led the first returning party. As they came bearing their restored treasures and gifts from their neighbours in Babylon, they must have felt a bit like their Israelite forebears at the time of the exodus when they set out for Canaan carrying the treasures of Egypt (ch. 1). On arrival in Jerusalem, some of their leaders gave further contributions towards building a new temple, but in the meantime the priests and the people had to go and establish themselves in their homes.

In this sequence of events the Jews clearly saw the hand of their God at work. In 1.1 we read that these things happened because 'the LORD moved the heart of Cyrus' and because they had already been prophesied by Jeremiah. The reference must be to passages like Jer. 29.10-14 and 31.38-40, but even more striking are the prophecies in Isa. 44–45, such as 45.13: 'I will raise up Cyrus ... He will rebuild my city and set my exiles free', or 44.28: '... who says to Cyrus, "He is my shepherd and will accomplish all that I please; he

will say of Jerusalem, 'Let it be rebuilt,' and of the temple,
'Let its foundations be laid.'" Of course, Isaiah was well
aware that Cyrus was a pagan and not one who acknowledged God (45.5), but none the less, this was God's doing.
Rationalism sees only military and political policy; faith
detects the sovereign working of God.

Chs. 3–4: The foundation of the temple is laid.
In the autumn the returned Jews rebuilt the altar and re-
started sacrificial worship, under the supervision and
direction of Jeshua, the high priest (called Joshua by Haggai
and Zechariah), and Zerubbabel (grandson of Jehoiachin, the
Davidic king exiled in 597) who was presently to take over
from Sheshbazzar as governor (3.1-6).

Preparatory work on the temple was also begun and the
following spring the foundation was laid amid loud rejoicing
and a great deal of mixed emotion. However, the work soon
ran into opposition. People in the land were naturally
interested and eagerly offered to help, but the exiles did not
welcome their offer. The result was a backlash of opposition
that brought the work to a standstill for the next fifteen years
(3.7 – 4.5).

The exiles rejected this offer because they regarded the
people who made it as semi-pagans. To begin with, they
were not of Israelite blood, but descendants of the foreigners
the Assyrians had resettled in Samaria. Yes, they had
learned the ways of the LORD, but they also clung to the
worship of their old gods: 'Even while these people were
worshipping the LORD, they were serving their idols. To this
day their children and grandchildren continue to do as their
fathers did.' (2 Kings 17.41) How pagan they still were in
536 is not clear, and in later years their faith certainly
became purer, but the Jews and their descendants never
accepted each other. They are the ancestors of the Samaritans of New Testament times.

In 4.6 we are suddenly carried forward some fifty years to
486, to the beginning of the reign of Xerxes I, and then in v.
7 even later, to the reign of Artaxerxes I, to times when
similar opposition brought work on rebuilding the city walls
to a standstill. Presumably the reason for including these
verses here was simply to point out the similarity, that the

opposition to the building of the temple was just like the opposition that later brought work of rebuilding the city and its walls to a halt (vv. 6-23).

Chs. 5–6: The temple is rebuilt.

The date is now 520. Apparently work on the temple had continued after the foundation was laid in Sheshbazzar's time (5.16), but it had progressed very slowly. Meanwhile, judging by some of Haggai's comments, it seems that the mood in Jerusalem, after a series of bad harvests and other economic disasters, was rapidly degenerating into depression (Hag. 1.2-11). He and his fellow-prophet, Zechariah, therefore spoke up to encourage the new governor, Zerubbabel, and the priest, Jeshua, to restart the building-work, and thanks to their enthusiasm the mood quickly swung to one of revival.

Then a surprising thing happened. As might have been expected, there was renewed opposition, but that led to a search which uncovered a decree of Cyrus authorising the rebuilding and enjoining that costs be met from the royal treasury—which effectively meant out of the pockets of those senior officials who were trying to stop the work!

The work now moved rapidly to completion. The new temple was dedicated and Passover celebrated in it for the first time in the spring of 515 BC amid great rejoicing, particularly over the miraculous provision from the royal treasury!

'The king of Assyria' in 6.22 is simply the Persian Darius as ruler of the empire that was formerly Assyria. Some such fluidity of expression seems to have been common, for Artaxerxes is also called 'king of Babylon' in Neh. 13.6.

2. NEHEMIAH AND THE REBUILDING OF JERUSALEM (NEH. 1–7)

These chapters were clearly written by Nehemiah himself and taken by the historian from his diaries. We pass directly to them from Ezra 6 so that we can follow through the story of Jerusalem's rebuilding uninterrupted.

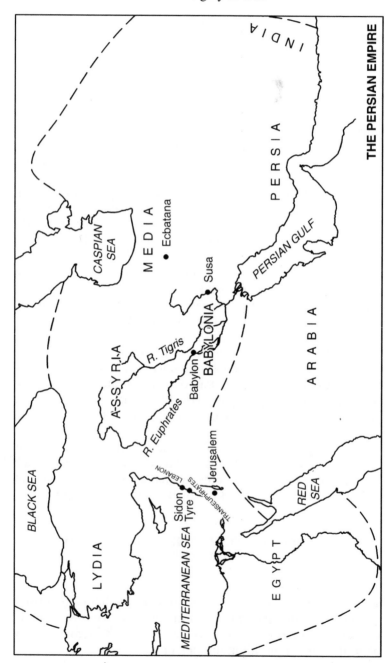

After the temple was completed the rebuilding of the city seems to have continued slowly over the next forty years until the Jews started to work on the walls. As we saw in Ezra 4.6-23, an objection was lodged in 486, at the beginning of the reign of Xerxes I, and then, sometime after 465, Artaxerxes I brought it all to a halt. Ezra came to Jerusalem and began his religious reforms in 458, but we shall return to that later. Here we take up the story again in Neh. 1, in the twentieth year of Artaxerxes, 445 BC.

1.1 – 2.10: Nehemiah comes to Jerusalem.
Nehemiah was a Jew with a trusted position at the court of Artaxerxes. His job, to serve the king's wine, ensuring it was not poisoned, gave him direct daily access to the royal presence. That, however, did not make what he had to do any easier.

When he heard from his brother, Hanani, about the sorry state of Jerusalem and took the burden of it to the LORD in prayer, he knew he had to take action on his people's behalf. But it was by decree of Artaxerxes himself that the work of rebuilding had been stopped, and so it was no mere formality that his prayer should end with a plea to be granted favour in his presence. With considerable trepidation he approached the king, but contrary to all expectation, the favour was granted and Nehemiah was appointed governor of Judah. Indeed, not only did he come with permission to resume the work of rebuilding Jerusalem and its walls, but he even came accompanied by a military escort and with a letter of recommendation to the satrap of Trans-Euphrates.

Not everyone in Judah was pleased. The local opposition that had already halted work on the temple and the walls was still there, headed now by two men in particular, Sanballat and Tobiah (2.10).

2.11 – 3.22: He starts work on the city-walls.
Nehemiah's approach to the LORD's work is consistently a mixture of the spiritual and the practical. He had prayed for Jerusalem, but also taken steps to come and rebuild. And that was how he continued. Though he knew 'what my God had put in my heart to do' (2.12), yet it was practical diplomacy to make his tour of inspection in secret, for the

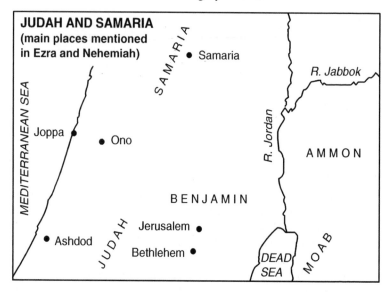

JUDAH AND SAMARIA
(main places mentioned
in Ezra and Nehemiah)

SAMARIA

• Samaria

R. Jabbok

MEDITERRANEAN SEA

R. Jordan

Joppa

• Ono

AMMON

BENJAMIN

JUDAH

• Ashdod

Jerusalem •

Bethlehem •

DEAD SEA

MOAB

moment he announced his purpose his opponents spoke up.
His answer to them again shows the mixture of spiritual and
practical: 'The God of heaven will give us success,' and
'We his servants will start rebuilding' (2.20).

So Nehemiah set the people to work on the walls. It
seems almost everyone took part, for the list in ch. 3 mentions priests, perfume-makers, district-rulers, goldsmiths,
merchants and women, though it also notes that some
noblemen would not put their shoulders to the work (v. 5).
Nehemiah's business sense is again seen in the fact that he
made people responsible for the sections nearest their own
homes for which they would inevitably have a special
interest (cp. v. 28).

Ch. 4: Handling the opposition.
Nehemiah's zeal immediately stirred Sanballat, the Samari-
tan governor, and his associates to anger. They did all they
could to discourage the builders and stop the work. At first
they sought to undermine Jewish enthusiasm with ridicule,
but when that failed and the wall reached half its height,
they turned to sabotage. Nehemiah again took both spiritual
and practical action: 'We prayed to our God and posted a
guard' (4.9). In the same way he encouraged his tiring work-

force: 'Don't be afraid of them. Remember the Lord ... and fight' (4.14).

Thorough and laudable as his defensive arrangements were, it must have seemed a tiresome and wasteful distraction from the work of rebuilding to have to make them at all. However, that is so often how it is in the LORD's work, for there will always be something that tries to interfere with it.

Ch. 5: Troubles within.

As if Sanballat and his men were not trouble enough for Nehemiah at that time, there were domestic problems as well! When trouble comes from outside, it usually shows itself inside the body at the same time, as still in our own churches today. The problem for Nehemiah was taxation—rich officials exploiting the poor. He was justifiably angry. Though in the past they had been used to governors who cared little for the people (v. 15), he had been buying back Hebrew slaves (v. 8), lending the poor money and grain (v. 10), and refusing to demand his own allowance as governor 'because the demands were heavy on these people' (v. 18). His priority was the work on the wall (v. 16), the work God had sent him to do.

Chs. 6–7: Completing the wall.

Sanballat now realised that the only way to stop the building was to get rid of Nehemiah himself. But Nehemiah did not fall for his attempts to lure him out of the city for talks (6.2-4), to blackmail him (6.5-9) and to intimidate him (6.10-14).

The wall was completed in fifty-two days (6.15), an amazing feat by any reckoning, and Nehemiah was now able to turn his attention to matters of city-government, housing and registering the population of Jerusalem. The only list he seems to have had to work with was 'the genealogical record of those who had been the first to return' (7.5; this list in ch. 7 is basically the same as that in Ezra 2).

Nehemiah's story in these chapters is one of success based on strong faith, unshakeable determination and careful strategy. In the end, even his enemies had to admit that God was with him (6.16).

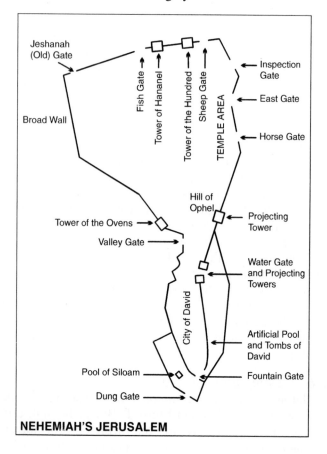

NEHEMIAH'S JERUSALEM

3. EZRA'S REFORMS AND REVIVAL (EZRA 7–10; NEH. 8–10)

We now go back to 458, the seventh year of Artaxerxes (Ezra 7.8). By that date some work had been done on rebuilding the city and its walls (4.12), but Artaxerxes had called a halt to that for the time being. Meanwhile, the spiritual temperature in Jerusalem had plummeted. From Malachi we learn that the fresh enthusiasm of the early days when the temple was being rebuilt had not lasted. Priest and people alike had grown careless about the service of God. Reform was badly needed.

Just as Neh. 1–7 is drawn from Nehemiah's personal record of events, so most of Ezra 7–10 is taken from Ezra's, as the first-person style clearly indicates.

Ezra 7–8: Ezra comes to Jerusalem.

Surprisingly, it was Artaxerxes who was the one most concerned about Jewish religious apathy. He apparently feared lest the God of the Jews should become angry and 'there be wrath against the realm of the king and of his sons' (7.23), so he sent Ezra, a priest and teacher of the Law of Moses, with orders to execute reform and encourage revival. He also provided Ezra with generous financial help to refurbish the temple and put new life into its sacrificial worship (7.13-24), and gave him full authority to teach the law and appoint magistrates to uphold it (7.25f).

Ezra was a man of profound faith. Not only was he 'a teacher well versed in the Law of Moses' (7.6), but also one who sought the LORD in fasting and prayer and trusted 'the good hand of God' to guide and protect him. Hence, when he set out for Judah with the party of exiles that returned with him, he began the journey by making the company fast and pray for safe conduct, rather than belie his faith by asking the king for a military escort to protect them and the royal treasures they were carrying from the bandits that endangered travel in those days.

His faith in God shows itself in many ways, but perhaps nowhere more clearly that in his heart-felt expression of gratitude at being granted permission to go to Jerusalem (7.27f), and then in his very different reaction to what he found when he arrived there.

Ezra 9–10: Ezra's Reforms.

The first challenge that confronted him was the appalling effect of mixed marriages in drawing the LORD's people away into unfaithfulness. This was by no means a minor issue, for it affected the leadership of the community as well and, according to Mal. 2.10-16, some had even divorced their Israelite wives in order to marry young pagan girls.

Ezra's way of handling the problem was to fall on his face before God and stay there praying, confessing and weeping until the LORD answered him. And as he prayed

others were moved in spirit and began to gather to him,
themselves now moved to repentance and tears. Soon the
support was sufficient for him to summon all the returned
exiles to assemble in Jerusalem. Meantime he continued in
prayer and fasting. It was mid-winter and raining when they
came together, but they fell under such conviction as he
spoke that they agreed to rectify the problem. Only four
opposed him!

It took three months for the committee he appointed to
deal with the individual cases, and we are not told how it
did so, but by the time Nehemiah came to Jerusalem the
issue seems to have been resolved.

Neh. 8: Ezra re-establishes the Law.

We have no idea what Ezra did in the thirteen years before
Nehemiah arrived, but here we meet him once more, in the
autumn after the walls were rebuilt.

Nehemiah built walls and faith, Ezra built 'church'. His
burning passion was for the Law of Moses, and so when the
people assembled in the autumn to celebrate the feast of
Tabernacles, he read it aloud to them 'from daybreak till
noon' (8.3) and got Levites either to interpret it or translate
it into Aramaic as he read, so that everyone could understand. It is significant that he did that at their own request
(8.1)! Nehemiah's faith-building had clearly had an additional impact beyond getting walls constructed.

The first effect of reading the Law was a strong conviction of sin, but then Ezra and Nehemiah encouraged the
people to make a proper start to keeping its requirements by
observing the feast in the manner it prescribed. Thereafter
Ezra read from the Law to them every day of the week-long
festival. It seems as though it was a book that was not very
familiar to the people of Jerusalem at that time, but they
apparently found much joy in re-discovering it.

Neh. 9–10: Renewing the covenant.

The impact of Ezra's law-reading was that the Israelites
gathered a fortnight later to observe a day of fasting and
penance. Again there was much law-reading, but also prayer
and confession of sins. The day ended with the leaders,
Levites and priests signing an agreement to keep the law

henceforth. This was now the second occasion in Israel's history that law-reading had led to revival (cp. 2 Kings 22–23).

The details of the covenant specify the need to observe three sets of laws:

1. those relating to mixed marriages (as agreed thirteen years earlier; 10.30, cp. Ezra 10),
2. those relating to the Sabbath (10.31),
3. those relating to taxes, tithes and offerings for the upkeep of the temple and its services and the maintenance of its staff, namely the priests and the Levites (10.32-9).

Ezra's lasting achievement was to establish the Jews as a people of the Law, thus eventually giving Judaism its peculiar flavour that has lasted down to today. It is doubtful that Ezra would have foreseen the legalism of Jesus' day, for his intention was simply to preserve the identity of a people in danger of becoming absorbed into its semi-pagan environment. In that he seems to have succeeded admirably.

4. THE CONCLUSION OF EZRA'S AND NEHEMIAH'S MINISTRIES (NEH. 11–13)

With the wall completed and the law re-established by the signing of the covenant, Nehemiah turned his attention to the residential needs of Jerusalem's citizens.

11.1 – 12.26: The population of Jerusalem.
Jerusalem was now a substantial city, but still thinly populated, so places were offered to volunteers from the nearby territories of Judah and Benjamin to come and live in it (11.1f). What follows after 11.3 is simply an account of the city's population at the time and a list of its priestly and Levitical families according to the register of those who originally returned from exile.

12.27-47: The dedication of the walls.
The story of Nehemiah's governorship is fittingly rounded off with a brief account of the dedication of his new walls. Two processions, each led by a choir, the one headed by

Ezra and the other by Nehemiah, marched round the top of
the wall in opposite directions until they met up together.
Then they assembled in the temple courts for a final service
of thanksgiving with sacrifices. It was a time of great joy—
'The sound of rejoicing in Jerusalem could be heard far
away' (12.43).

Ch. 13: Nehemiah's return visit.

Nehemiah continued in Jerusalem as its governor for twelve
years, and then went back to report to Artaxerxes (on the
title 'king of Babylon' in v. 6, see above, p. 33), presumably
satisfied with his achievements, for the city was now
strongly established both politically and religiously. However, during his absence things began to slip and on his
return 'some time later' (v. 6) he was confronted with many
of the old problems all over again:

- The Levites were neglecting their temple duties in order
  to work their fields for food because tithes and dues
  were not being paid for their upkeep (vv. 10-14).
- The laws governing Sabbath-trading were being flouted
  in every way imaginable (vv. 15-22).
- Mixed marriages were again on the increase and some
  of the offspring of these marriages were more foreign
  than Jewish (vv. 23-29).
- The greatest insult came from the high priest, Eliashib.
  He had given a room in the temple to Tobiah, one of
  those who originally opposed Nehemiah's building pro-
  gramme (vv.7-9), and had sanctioned the marriage of
  his grandson to the daughter of Sanballat, Nehemiah's
  other arch-enemy (v. 28; cp. Neh. 4.1-3 & 6.1-14).

In all these cases Nehemiah was not slow to take the most
decisive action! (See especially vv. 8f, 21, 25, 28.)

It must, however, have been sad for him to see much of
what he had spent his life and energy to build up being
eroded. It is so often the way that men of vision build for
God and are succeeded by others who either do not have
the same vision themselves, or lack the drive to sustain it.
Many Church leaders will readily sympathise with
Nehemiah.

The first returning Jews must have been full of hope that God would soon usher in the age of restoration and blessing of which their prophets had once spoken. But with the passage of the years enthusiasm waned and the LORD's people found they had to reconcile themselves to waiting, possibly a very long time. We detect hardly any sense of expectancy in the history we have studied. Yes, there were still a few prophets, and they did speak of the things to come, but much of their message was directed to encouraging the Jews to rebuild. The primary focus of the age was on establishing a political and religious system that would endure and would ensure continued national solidarity.

In these days the voice of prophecy finally fell silent, and the Judaism of the Book, with all its formal and legal ways, now began to take shape. Whilst Ezra's own ministry generated considerable revival enthusiasm, the law he came to establish gradually fossilised into the rather rigid legalism Jesus encountered among his contemporaries. That in itself, however, was not entirely negative in its effects, for it provided a strong, even if arid and unbending, focus and foundation for the faith of the Jewish people and in the long run ensured that they remained identifiably the LORD's people down the long centuries until Jesus' birth, learned in their sacred traditions, and so the better prepared for his coming. Judaism, religion for a waiting people, was slowly crystallising.

4

Jews and Gentiles

The closing of Jewish ranks around the Law had positive benefits, but it also led to an exclusivist attitude in relation to the rest of the world. The last resolution the people of Jerusalem made on the basis of Ezra's law-preaching was that they 'excluded from Israel all who were of foreign descent' (Neh. 13.3). While it had been absolutely essential to do something radical about the paganising effects of mixed marriages, the emerging attitude somehow seems to contradict God's call on Israel to be 'a light to the Gentiles' (Isa. 42.6; 49.6). Doubtless some in Jerusalem at the time must have thought so. Of the three little books we shall now look at, two read almost as if they could have been published as a caution against such hardening anti-Gentile attitudes. The third glories in Jewish superiority.

1. THE BRIDE FROM MOAB (RUTH)

Ruth is the first of the two books that read like a plea against hardening, exclusivist attitudes in relation to non-Jews. It is written in the style of a historical novel about times long ago (1.1), when men had social customs long since forgotten in Israel (4.7), and tells a beautiful, moving story about how a foreign girl became great-grandmother to King David.

Chs. 1–3: Ruth and Boaz.
The story starts and ends in Bethlehem, David's ancestral

44

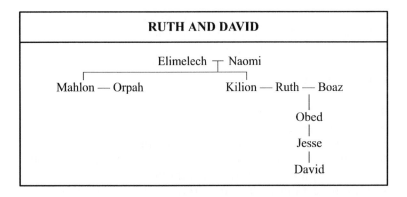

RUTH AND DAVID

Elimelech — Naomi

Mahlon — Orpah   Kilion — Ruth — Boaz

Obed

Jesse

David

home, but its central figure is the Moabite girl, Ruth, who married the son of a Bethlehemite widow, but was herself widowed while still childless. Israel had a law for protecting a dead husband's name and property in such circumstances (Deut. 25.5-20). It prescribed that the nearest kinsman should act as 'redeemer' and marry the widow to have children who would then become heirs to the dead man's property. It was because of this law that Ruth, 'a foreigner' (2.10), became ancestor to David.

The legal details are interwoven through an enchanting love-story in which Ruth is presented as a beautiful, faithful, loving and virtuous girl, and Boaz, her Israelite lover, as a wealthy, upright, respected citizen. There are many touching moments in the narrative.

Ch. 4: Ruth and David.

Ruth's story was not told just as a fragment of ancient history or simply to entertain. Repeatedly it emphasises Ruth's foreignness; she is pointedly called 'Ruth the Moabitess' over and over again. The fear of marrying her shown by her nearest kinsman (4.6) manifestly reflects an age when there was strong antipathy to mixed marriages— probably in Ezra's time, when the book would have been written as a plea not to regard all foreign marriages as necessarily dangerous.

Ruth is compared to Rachel and Leah (4.11) who were also foreign girls. Israel's history was built on mixed marriages, some of them very crucial ones, and some of them very lovely! They did not all cause the husbands to be led astray—after all, did not Ruth change her nationality and religion (1.16)? It was not always the pagans that won the converts! The plea of Ruth is clearly to beware of throwing out the baby with the bath-water.

Together with Jonah, this little book probably did much to prevent post-exilic Judaism from becoming totally exclusive in its attitudes to the Gentile world. But it is important not to regard it simply as a piece of anti-Ezra political propaganda. Its plea in no way contradicts the law that Ezra sought to establish, for it certainly does not approve of intermarriage with pagans. Ruth is of a totally different spirit from the pagan wives of Ezra's day. Though she actually lived at a time when pagan influences were strong in Israel, towards the end of the period of the judges, she herself stood quite apart from them. She accepted her mother-in-law's faith, supporting her with outstanding sacrificial love (1.16), and Boaz recognised that she had done so with complete sincerity (2.11f).

The law of Moses is God's law and when rightly applied it does leave room for the Spirit to perform beautiful works of grace. The danger, however, is that our narrow, legalistic interpretations of it frequently obscure that truth.

But above all that, the book is a wonderful testimony to how the grace of God works for good in the lives of those who give themselves unreservedly to him. Ruth's decision to unite with the Lord's people had eternal consequences far beyond her own imagining. The immediate result was a new and good husband, but more than that, it led to her becoming great-grandmother to David, and so ultimately one of the ancestors of Christ, thus gaining for herself a place in the annals of the New Testament (Matt. 1.5).

2. THE RELUCTANT PROPHET TO THE GENTILES (JONAH)

Jonah lived in the eighth century BC, about the same time as Amos (2 Kings 14.25), but the book about him was written much later, when Nineveh was no longer a thriving city

(Jonah 3.3). It is unique among the prophetic books in that it tells us hardly anything about the prophet's teaching. Like Ruth it is a story-book, a historical novel. And also like Ruth, its theme is Jewish attitudes to the Gentiles.

To a Jew Nineveh epitomised the Gentile world at its worst. The Assyrians wiped out half of Israel, ravaged the land and flooded it with paganism. They were the last people a righteous Jew would want to preach to, so Jonah ran away when called (ch. 1). Eventually he obeyed and saw an amazing response to his preaching (chs. 2-3), but he was also displeased that God should show such compassion on pagans. He withdrew in a sulk to wait and see whether God would come round to his point of view, and so God had to show him just how flimsy was the selfish structure of the faith under which he sheltered (ch. 4).

The book of Jonah also has a powerful lesson in obedience to teach. It is impossible to run away from God's call for ever (cp. Ps. 139), for that only leads to severe distress (ch. 1), but on repentance, God is prepared to grant restoration (ch. 2), to renew his call and lead us into fruitful ministry (ch. 3). Even if our first fears and discernments of the consequences of obedience are absolutely true (4.2), God still wants the job he calls us to do done and so needs that obedience (ch. 4). His vision, after all, is far wider than ours!

Jonah is an amazingly powerful little book. Like Ruth it was probably published in the post-exilic age when Jewish attitudes to the Gentiles were hardening. It was the exclusivist attitude that eventually became predominant, and was even passed on to the early Church. Paul had to fight hard to combat it among the Christians in Jerusalem (cp. Acts 15 and Galatians), but already, several hundred years before him, another prophet had been taught the vision that was to become his. Jonah's story must have done much to encourage those engaged in the wider outreach of the gospel in New Testament times, as it still does today.

3. FOR SUCH A TIME AS THIS (ESTHER)

Esther was a Jewish girl who, because of her beauty, was taken for wife by Xerxes I, King of Persia. The marriage was miraculously timely, because her new status enabled her to avert a persecution planned against Jews throughout the empire. The story reads so easily that it hardly needs any comment here. The key passage is 4.13f.

The last chapters tell how the tables were turned against the persecutors in a veritable blood-bath and how the Jews established their annual Feast of Purim to celebrate the remembrance of this deliverance.

The attitude to Gentiles here is very different from that in Ruth and Jonah, reflecting more the superiority and exclusivism that became characteristic of the thinking of many later Jews. Most Christians will find themselves more naturally in tune with the mood of Ruth and Jonah, for while we rejoice at the miracle of deliverance in Esther, many find it difficult to share in the glorification of its all too human sequel.

There is, however, a Christian application of Esther that enables us to cherish its message still today, and that is found in translating what it teaches of the ways of warfare against the enemies of God into the language of Christian spiritual warfare. Paul says, 'For our struggle is not against flesh and blood, but against the rulers, against the authorities, against the powers of this dark world and against the spiritual forces of evil in the heavenly realms' (Ephes. 6.12). Although God is never actually named in Esther, he is still very active behind the scenes, for he never leaves his people defenceless. But as he prepared Esther 'for such a time as this', so also when the time comes it is important that the defender God has prepared should not remain silent in the face of evil (4.14). Then once he has put the (spiritual) enemy to flight, it is important to see that he is thoroughly routed (ch. 9).

Though the context is different, the lesson is still the same as in Esther's time. Jesus is our Esther and he won a resounding victory over the devil who would have destroyed God's people. We can therefore still celebrate our version of

Purim and proclaim that 'we are more than conquerors through him who loved us' (Rom. 8.37).

As we have reviewed the Persian era, we have stumbled repeatedly on amazing traces of God's sovereign intervention on behalf of Israel through the apparently ordinary events of secular history. For example, we saw how the rebuilding of the temple came to be funded out of the pockets of those who tried to stop the work. We saw how Artaxerxes' fear of political unrest led to Ezra's reforms and how the LORD opened this same king's heart to send Nehemiah to rebuild the walls of Jerusalem. Similarly, the timing of Esther's marriage was hardly coincidental. The Persian period may have produced no revival movements as spectacular as in some other ages, but 'the good hand of God' was very much on his people throughout it, rescuing, guiding, restoring and building them into a unit established and strong enough to survive the long age of waiting that lay ahead. The Lordship of God was very evident in these times, though only to the eyes of faith. But even before there ever was a Persian Empire it was foreseen that God would be working that way, for Isa. 45.1-7 had foretold that the rise of Cyrus the Persian, unbeknown to him of course, would be 'for the sake of Jacob my servant, of Israel my chosen'. That was how the Persian era started, and so it continued— controlled by the hidden but sovereign hand of God 'for the sake of Jacob my servant'. What the Jews made of the various opportunities God gave them is, however, a different matter, as we have also seen.

PART THREE

WISDOM AND WORSHIP

ౙ

Wisdom and worship may at first sight seem strange part-
ners, but in the context of our experience of God they are
certainly not so, as is attested by the oft repeated statement,
'The fear (reverence) of the LORD is the beginning of
wisdom' (e.g. Prov. 1.7; 9.10). Wisdom in the Bible is
God's wisdom, and his wisdom is one of the reasons why
men worship him. Today this wisdom has become incarnate
in Christ, and is now revealed to us by God's Spirit (1 Cor.
1.30–2.10). Wisdom and worship are therefore both integral
to our life in the Spirit.

The books covered in this section are all part of the
Writings of the Old Testament, but not all post-exilic in
origin. Rather the contrary, for Proverbs, Ecclesiastes and
Song of Songs are traditionally associated with Solomon and
the Psalms with David. That does not mean that David or
Solomon wrote everything in them. In Proverbs, for example, the last two chapters are headed 'The sayings of Agur'
and 'The sayings of King Lemuel' respectively, while most
of chs. 22-24 is described simply as 'the sayings of the wise'
(22.17; 24.23). Presumably the compilation of Proverbs
started in Solomon's day, but continued down the centuries
after him. Indeed 25.1 tells us the book was still being
edited in Hezekiah's time, some 250 years later. Perhaps
such editing also continued on into post-exilic times.

Similarly many of the Psalms are ascribed to persons
other than David, such as Solomon, Asaph, the sons of
Korah, or Moses (cp. Pss. 72–90), and some psalms are
clearly exilic or post-exilic, such as Ps. 137. Again we may
imagine a Davidic core being supplemented over the years.
Ecclesiastes and Song of Songs, on the other hand, do not
show such evidence of continuous editing and are both said

to be Solomonic. The book of Job is quite impossible to date, though Ezek. 14.14,20 suggests links between Job himself and very ancient times.

The literature contained in these books is almost entirely poetic. Hebrew poetry functions on different principles from English. It does have rhythm, but not rhyme; instead it uses what we call parallelism, which takes the sense of one line and either repeats it or elaborates on it is the next. For example:

What is man / that you are mindful of him,
  the son of man / that you care for him?

(8.4)

For the LORD / watches over / the way of the righteous,
  but the way of the wicked / will perish.

(1.6)

With various modifications and elaborations, this is the basic literary structure used in all Biblical poetry. It is perhaps most clearly seen in Prov. 10.1–22.16 where virtually every proverb or verse is a self-contained parallel couplet.

5

The Wisdom of the Wise

PROVERBS AND ECCLESIASTES

Wisdom is God's wisdom, but it is not just concerned with theological or religious matters, though these are naturally included in it. When Solomon asked God for wisdom, he asked for ability to distinguish between good and evil and for endowment with political skill. He was also granted judicial skill, power to write poetry, and knowledge of the sort one finds in an encyclopaedia (1 Kings 3.9,16-28; 4.32f). But wisdom is also more than intellectual achievement, or technical training; it is a totally embracing, life-related moral and intellectual education. It is partly the sort of thing one gains from home upbringing and parental teaching (Prov. 4.1-5), partly from listening to older and more experienced men (Job 29.7-25), and partly through training, education and experience in cultured social circles (1 Kings 10.6-8). Wisdom teaches men how to handle the challenges of life in society.

The Old Testament contains three wisdom books, all very different from each other: Proverbs, Ecclesiastes and Job. Though only three, they actually represent a major element in Israelite faith. Hence fragments of wisdom appear from time to time in the Psalms and other parts of the Old Testament (e.g. Ps. 34; Isa. 28.23-29), but there was even more to wisdom than that, far more than collected proverbs and the like, for it was a veritable third stream in society alongside the law and prophecy. Thus in Jer. 18.18 we read of the priest, the wise and the prophet as three influential leadership groupings.

In that respect Israel was not unique, for other ancient

cultures had similar wisdom traditions, and schools of wise men that fostered them. The Egyptians, for example, had an extensive wisdom literature which was studied in educational establishments, some of it not unlike the kind of thing we find in the wisdom books of the Old Testament, though predictably its faith-level was quite different. So the books we are about to study are not simply additional to the main stream of Israelite and ancient Near Eastern life and culture, but a vital and integral part of it. Likewise they also belong to the main stream of Israel's faith and so, in God's economy, to the way of the Spirit.

1. PROVERBS FOR ATTAINING WISDOM (PROVERBS)

Before studying Proverbs it is worth observing how the Old Testament speaks about Solomon's part in its compilation. Besides noting in 1 Kings 3–4 that his wisdom was a gift from God, rather than one of his natural endowments, and that he applied it extensively to composing proverbs and poems about a wide variety of topics, it also gives us a fascinating insight into how he did so in Eccles. 12.9-12:

> *He pondered and searched out and set in order many proverbs. The Teacher searched to find just the right words, and what he wrote was upright and true.*
> *The words of the wise are like goads, their collected sayings like firmly embedded nails—given by one Shepherd.*

These words themselves are worth pondering because they give us a clue to understanding how to read Proverbs and tap its spiritual dynamic. It is clearly not a book to be read at one sitting, but an anthology of life-related sayings to be mulled over and slowly digested, like a collection of nails, each of which needs to be hammered home separately.

Again, unlike other wisdom books, it does not debate deeper issues about the purpose of life. The proverbs themselves are pithy, declaratory statements, not written to resolve philosophical questions, but to build faith and instruct men how best to live their lives in society. They teach about attitudes and conduct at home, at work and at places where people meet, about decision-making and justice, indeed about everything we do, say or think. But always the view-point is that 'the fear of the LORD' is foundational.

That view-point is clearly stated right at the beginning, in chs. 1–9, which contain longer, sermon-like passages teaching the nature and preaching the value of wisdom. There it is firmly taught that wisdom is inseparable from God himself. It is his wisdom, and men find it in him.

Chs. 1–4: Get wisdom, get understanding.

The young (and the not so young), as they learn to make their way in life, constantly have a choice to make: whether to go God's way or the world's. God's way is the way of wisdom, understanding, knowledge, discretion, prudence, discipline, righteousness, goodness, peace, and the like— everything that is wholesome and has its foundation in the fear of the LORD; the world's way is the way of folly, sin, evil, greed, adultery, violence—in fact, everything that is un- wholesome and has no foundation in the fear of the LORD.

Ch. 1 draws the contrast vividly: Beware of heeding secret enticements to follow sinners into evil, and equally beware of rejecting the open warnings of wisdom about the consequences of such ways.

Instead, call out to God for wisdom, for it is in him that wisdom is found (2.1-8). It will protect you from the ways of wicked men and seductive women and will keep you on the right path (2.9-22).

With wisdom come many blessings money cannot buy, such as faithfulness, security, prosperity and peace (3.1-18). Wisdom is as old as creation itself, but is still the principle by which God wants his world to work (3.19-35).

So get wisdom. At whatever cost get wisdom. Avoid the way of the wicked. And guard your heart. (ch. 4)

Chs. 5–7: Beware of folly.

In ch. 6 we find warnings against some foolish ways, such as putting up security, idleness and various forms of deceit, but the main burden in all three chapters is to warn

against the dangers of adultery. Paul also considered
sexual immorality more serious than other sins, because it
defiles our body, which is the temple of the Holy Spirit (1
Cor. 6.12-20).

Chs. 8–9: Wisdom's invitation.
Unlike the crafty approach of the adulteress in ch. 7, Wisdom calls out openly to all men (8.1-5). What she offers is
beyond price, but it bestows honour and prosperity (vv. 6-
21). That is because she is the very wisdom of God himself
and knows the ways of the world better than any, for she
was begotten of him before creation and was the craftsman
at his side when he planned and made it all (vv. 22-31). To
find her, therefore, and heed her call is to find life (8.32–
9.12); whereas to heed the call of Folly is to head for the
grave (9.13-18). This portrayal of Wisdom and Folly as two
women both inviting men, simple men, to be their guests,
the one serving a feast of life, the other a feast of death,
aptly summarises the whole sermon of Prov. 1–9.

When we come to look at what the New Testament says
about Christ and the wisdom of God, we shall have to recall
Proverbs' teaching about wisdom existing with God before
creation and being his architect in it and we shall see that
there is an intimate and inseparable link between God's
wisdom and his Spirit (see pp. 185f).

10.1–22.17: The Proverbs of Solomon.
These chapters are mostly made up of short, single-sentence
sayings giving instruction about social, moral and religious
affairs, covering almost every conceivable aspect of daily
living. The advice may often seem very secular, about not
much more than good manners and sensible behaviour, but
in fact the religious foundation is totally clear—it is still that
'The fear of the LORD teaches a man wisdom' (15.33; cp.
10.27; 14.26f; 15.16; etc.). We are not called to super-
spirituality, but to total integratedness in every aspect of life,
and that flows first out of a right reverence for God.

Clearly space does not permit us to discuss these and the
following chapters in any detail here, but at least we can
make some general observations about the main categories
of sayings and themes in them. To that end we can divide

the proverbs into three broad categories:

1. *Religious teaching.*

The themes covered are mainly the same as those in chs. 1–9, including reminders about wisdom being God's standard for life that leads to all that is good, about folly being the converse way of human frailty and sin, and about the fear of the LORD being the undergirding motive for all faithful living.

2. *Moral teaching about personal virtues.*

We find certain virtues strongly praised, such as self-control, restraint in speech, truthfulness in bearing witness, humility in conduct, honesty in commerce, compassion for the poor, and diligence at work. Conversely, certain wrong attitudes are condemned, such as pride, anger, gossiping, laziness and sexual waywardness.

3. *Social teaching relating to the community.*

Much is said about the family, the basic unit in society, and particularly about the woman's responsibility in maintaining a good home. In the same context the need for repeated teaching of the young and for firm discipline is emphasised. There is also quite a lot said about right relationships between those in authority and those under them, mainly with reference to masters and servants or to kings and their subjects. And in a similar vein we find a lot about relationships between rich and poor. Neither wealth nor authority are condemned. In fact both can be blessings bestowed by wisdom. But care for the poor is strongly urged.

22.17–31.31: Various collections of proverbs.

In these chapters we have six different sections. One of the main differences between them and 10.1–22.16 is that their sayings are often more extended than the simple two-line couplet and sometimes they show a greater degree of connectedness between each other. They are not, however, as extended or connected as in chs. 1–9.

The three main categories of sayings and the themes in them are the same as in the Proverbs of Solomon, but again space does not permit us discuss these in detail. It will also be evident in reading that these chapters contain reflections and exhortations that sometimes remind us of the sermons in chs. 1–9.

The Sayings of the Wise (22.17–24.22)

In the composition of this first section it seems that use was made of Egyptian wisdom sources, for almost every verse in it has a parallel in *The Teaching of Amenemopet*. Nevertheless, its sayings have been so rewritten that they are thoroughly Israelite and its teaching is entirely in line with everything we find earlier in Proverbs.

Further Sayings of the Wise (24.23-34)

These continue in the same vein as 22.17–24.22.

More Proverbs of Solomon (chs. 25–29)

Here the proverbs are again expressed in the same form of short couplets as in 10.1–22.16. It is interesting to note that they were edited by Hezekiah's men, for his reign was marked by revival in Jerusalem (2 Kings 18; 2 Chron. 29–32), and that reminds us once more that wisdom was not just secular advice on how to get on in life, but very much part of the full counsel of God.

The Sayings of Agur son of Jakeh (ch. 30)

Agur's sayings differ from Solomon's in that they are mainly in the nature of reflections on the unfathomable ways of life, and as such are more akin to some of the sayings we find in Job.

The Sayings of King Lemuel (31.1-9)

This little collection is mainly advice to rulers not to seek their own pleasure, but to alleviate the lot of the poor.

The sayings of Agur and Lemuel are certainly of foreign origin, though, just like the sayings of the wise in 22.17–24.22, they are entirely in keeping with the flavour of Israelite wisdom. The Hebrew is difficult to interpret, but one translation suggests both men belonged to Massa, an Arab tribe (30.1; 31.1–NIV footnote; cp. Gen. 25.14).

A Portrait of a Wife of Noble Character (31.10-31)

This beautiful portrait makes a wonderful ending to a book that has had so much to say about adulterous women and quarrelsome wives. In it we see that wisdom's true view of womanhood and family life is one of high appreciation.

Some of that appreciation is revealed in the fact that it is written as a beautiful acrostic poem, its twenty-two verses beginning with the twenty-two letters of the Hebrew alphabet. It makes a delightful ending to a most encouraging and instructive book.

2. THE MEANING OF LIFE (ECCLESIASTES)

'Ecclesiastes' is a Greek word that means 'Speaker', 'Preacher', or 'Teacher'. His book is very different from Proverbs. It is basically a discussion about the meaning of life and as such it can make depressing reading. The Teacher tells how he has explored every aspect of life. He has devoted himself to study, given himself to pleasure, amassed wealth, attained the pinnacle of success, witnessed oppression and friendlessness, pursued religion, and so forth, but after all that comes to the conclusion that everything is meaningless, utterly meaningless.

However, his book is not simply negative. There is a dimension to life that eludes the Teacher: the eternity God has set in man's heart (3.11). He knows it is there, but cannot fathom it, so he returns to it again and again, sometimes with puzzlement, sometimes with resignation, sometimes with positive hope. It is as though he is saying: I have tried everything and find satisfaction nowhere, but always there is God, himself an unfathomable mystery, and after exploring all else I find myself back with him in the end.

1.1–4.8: Everything in life is meaningless.

This opening section gives an introductory summary of the Teacher's theme: that everything is repetitive and pointless (1.2-11). That, he says, he knows from his own experience of life. He has applied himself to wisdom, but found it a wearisome business (1.12-18). Equally he has sought pleasure in drink (2.3), has known the satisfaction of success in business (2.4-7), has tasted the glory of wealth and fame (2.8f), but surveying it all it seemed utterly empty (2.10f). To be sure he found the way of wisdom better than the way of folly, but the end of both is the same, namely death (2.12-16). Furthermore, you can put as much as you will into life, or get as much out of it, but ultimately you leave everything to another who may care nothing for all you have achieved (2.17-26).

He acknowledges that there is a time for everything (3.1-8), that God's will for man is good, for him to enjoy life (3.9-14), and that in his time he will bring judgment (3.15-17), but for the present everything seems pretty meaningless. Man hardly has any advantage over the animals; the best he can do is enjoy himself as fully as possible (3.18-22).

Most aspects of life are meaningless. Many people are so oppressed they would be better off dead (4.1-3), while others are vainly trying to outdo their neighbours (4.4-6), or aimlessly labouring for wealth (4.7f)—all, he says, 'a miserable business'.

4.9–11.6: Some advice on making the best of this meaningless life.
This central section contains, alongside continuing reflections on the emptiness of life, proverbial teaching similar to what we find in the book of Proverbs, and some of it is quite positive.

For example, he speaks of the value of companionship (4.9-12), of the importance of careful forethought about promises made to God (5.1-7), of the blessing of wealth when it is God's gift (5.16-20), of proper conduct before the king (8.2-6), of enjoying yourself while you can (9.7-12), of the value of quiet, unacclaimed wisdom (9.13-18), indeed of the generally superior quality of a life guided by wisdom (ch. 10).

But equally we find plenty negative reflections. Thus he speaks of the emptiness of gaining popularity just to lose it again (4.13-16), of the deception of hard-won wealth that vanishes so easily (5.8-15), of the vanity of not being able to live and enjoy the LORD's blessing when he gives it (6.1-6), and of the vanity of wisdom that sometimes seems just so many words (6.7-12). Good men and evil have a common fate in death, and that he finds hard to make sense of (8.7-17). Then finally he speaks of the desolation of life's end (9.2-6). Without the hope of an afterlife, of which he has no personal assurance (3.18-21), everything looks meaningless.

Read in one way, all that could seem utterly negative and depressing, but in the middle of it all his more positive philosophy of life does show through from time to time, especially at the end of this section, in chs. 9–11.

There he reflects that all men, good and bad alike, have a common fate, namely death (9.1-6) and so his advice is to make the best of what you have now (9.7-12). But in saying that he is not recommending a licentious free-for-all. To him the way to make that best is the way of wisdom, not folly (9.13-18). The wise and the fool may both come to the same end, but who wants to live like the fool? See what his ways are like (ch. 10). Live rather as wisdom's precepts decree, making the most of the time you have (ch. 11).

But even that could seem shallow if we did not also see him groping after something deeper, as we do in ch. 7, for example. There we find a mixture of proverbial advice and reflections on the nature of wisdom, much of it of the same positive nature as in Proverbs, but in the middle of it all we hear him cry:

> *I am determined to be wise—*
>   *but this was beyond me.*
> *Whatever wisdom may be,*
>   *it is far off and most profound—*
>   *who can discover it?*
> *So I turned my mind to understand,*
>   *to investigate and search out wisdom and the scheme*
>   *of things.*
>
> (7.23-25)

Here is the cry of a man who knows there is a reality beyond the apparent meaninglessness of life, and he longs to tap it, but for the moment somehow cannot.

11.7–12.14: The conclusion of the matter.

Again the advice is to make the most of life while you can, in your youth before old age overtakes you and it is too late (11.7–12.5), for the end of all things is death and in the light of that 'Everything is meaningless!' (12.6-8)

This is the philosophy of a man who sees nothing beyond

death. Old Testament man had no fixed conception of what
happens after death. Depending on how we interpret them, a
handful of passages do suggest some positive belief in a life
hereafter, such as Job 19.25-27; Ps. 16.9; Isa. 26.19; Dan.
12.1-3, though others, such as Ps. 6.5; 88.10-12, imply there
was nothing much to look forward to beyond the grave.
Even in Jesus' time the Jews had come to no agreement on
the matter, for 'The Sadducees say that there is no resurrection, and that there are neither angels nor spirits, but the
Pharisees acknowledge them all.' (Acts 23.8)

Paul describes the situation another way: that 'death
reigned from the time of Adam', but now what Christ has
done 'brings life for all men' (Rom. 5.14,18). Had the
Teacher (Ecclesiastes) lived in our times he might not have
written all he did about death making life meaningless.

Even so, Christians today with all the gospel of life in
Christ, if they are honest, will admit they do sometimes feel
just as the Teacher did. It is one of the glories of the Old
Testament that it does not camouflage the hard realities of
life. The truth is that people do get depressed, gospel or no,
and when they do, they find in Ecclesiastes a sympathetic
voice.

However, that is not the note on which his book ends.
There is more after 12.8. Despite everything, he still comes
back to the point at which all wisdom starts, namely the fear
of the LORD, and that for him, as it is the beginning of
wisdom, is also the conclusion of the matter. It is that that
keeps him from abandoning everything and lapsing into the
foolish ways of the world. It is that that still sustains hope.
Wisdom may be elusive and beyond understanding and
everything else may seem meaningless, but there is still
God. He is always there—the ultimate and unchanging
fountainhead of all things. The meaning of life ultimately
rests, not in a philosophy, but in God.

> *Now all has been heard;*
> *here is the conclusion of the matter:*
> *Fear God and keep his commandments,*
> *for this is the whole duty of man.*
>   (12.13)

6

Wisdom and the Spirit

JOB

It is sometimes said that the Holy Spirit enthusiasm of charismatic Christianity has little in common with the rational approach to life found in Israel's wisdom literature. Our study of Proverbs and Ecclesiastes should already have shown how shallow such an estimate of both wisdom and the Spirit is, for wisdom is clearly not the same as intellectual assessment, but something much more profound, partaking of the very personal nature of God himself. It is his wisdom, not ours, and as St Paul says in 1 Cor. 2.10-12: 'God has revealed it to us by his Spirit ... no-one knows the thoughts of God except the Spirit of God (and) We have received ... the Spirit who is from God, that we may understand ...' That same link with the Spirit is also the foundation of the Old Testament's teaching about wisdom, and nowhere more clearly than in the book of Job.

1. IT IS THE BREATH OF THE ALMIGHTY THAT GIVES UNDERSTANDING (JOB)

The theme of Job is the age old problem of suffering: If God is good and just, why does he let innocent people suffer? The question is still as much a living one today as it was Job's time.

For Job the issue was more than philosophical, for though he was a righteous man, he was himself suffering bitterly, having lost everything, even his health. Three friends try to

reassure him at great length by trotting out standard theological answers: basically that it is God's will that the
righteous should be blessed and that consequently his
suffering must be punishment for sins he has committed. Job
refuses to accept that it is so simple and his speeches
fluctuate between anger and anguish, interspersed with cries
to God to hear and answer him.

A young man called Elihu then speaks up, declaring that
the answer lies with God's Spirit, not in doctrine. He does
run over the standard arguments again, but leads Job beyond
them into contemplation of God's majesty and finally into
the presence of God himself, whose voice then takes over
from Elihu's. God gives no explanations, only a reminder
that he is the majestic Creator of the universe, but by the end
Job is crying out in repentance, whereupon his restoration
begins.

The message is clear: Salvation lies, not in acceptance of
doctrines, however true and correct they may be, but in
personal encounter with the living God. There we find not
rational answers so much as a new perspective, which itself
gives healing, new faith, vision and joy.

There is only one way to appreciate the full significance
of this book and that is to read it as you would a play.
Though there is much debating in it, it is not first and
foremost a philosophical treatise, but a life-related drama.
The words of Job and his friends are not spoken by disem-
bodied voices, but by real flesh-and-blood men with
recognisable human personalities. Certainly they have points
of view, but to consider only these is to miss the whole point
of the book. We need also to weigh the personalities of the
actors, enter into the flow of the drama and, as it were, take
ourselves on stage just as we would if we were at the theatre
watching it all. As a series of debates, Job is a dull book, but
as a living drama it is one of the most exciting books in the
Bible, and one in which Spirit-filled Christians should find
themselves very much at home.

We shall read it as if it were a four-act play with prologue
and epilogue. The division is somewhat artificial, but it
helps to catch the flavour and progression of the drama.

PROLOGUE (Chs. 1–2)

Imagine a narrator come on stage and tell the story in these chapters as introductory background to the play you are about to watch. The setting is Uz, somewhere east of Palestine, and the event is quite undated. But these things are unimportant, as is the question of the date of the book itself, which could be almost any time before the end of the Old Testament period. The subject matter is itself timeless.

Job is introduced to us as 'blameless and upright, a man who fears God and shuns evil' (1.8). That is God's own verdict on him and even after the many tragedies that befell him it remains so (2.3). Job's faith is summed up in his own words: 'The LORD gave and the LORD has taken away; may the name of the LORD be praised.' (1.21) As he sits on his ash-heap scratching himself with a piece of broken pottery and his wife nags him to give up his high faith, he is a man totally alone, with no idea why he should be suffering so much. And that is how his friends find him.

ACT 1 (Chs. 3–14)

In this and the next act all three friends speak with Job in turn. They are elders in society, wise men steeped in the thinking of their age, who have studied the ways of life, have learned much from their own experience and also from the wisdom of others before them. Their theological viewpoint is consistent throughout: that God blesses the righteous and punishes the wicked. Though Job questions that view, he does not so much deny its truth, as complain that it offers him no help or comfort in his own suffering.

It is Job who breaks the silence with a heart-rending cry of desolation.

Ch. 3: Job speaks.
Curse the day I was born (vv. 1-10). Why did I not die at birth? At least there is peace in the grave (vv. 11-19). Why are people allowed to live in misery anyhow? (vv. 20-26)

Chs. 4–5: Eliphaz.
Eliphaz's response is not to sympathise or offer comfort, but

to reason with Job, giving him a lecture like some school-teacher might. His approach is thoroughly pedantic. Note his style: 'Think how you have' expressed yourself on such matters to others and heed your own reasonings now (4.1-6). 'Consider now' the logic of suffering (4.7). 'As I have observed', it is the wicked who suffer (4.8-11). I even had a weird dream that showed me that (4.12-21). 'I myself have seen' it work out in life (5.1-7). 'But if it were I, I would appeal to God ... do not despise the discipline of the Almighty'; he'll look after you, if you submit to him (5.8-26). 'We have examined this, and it is true. So hear it and apply it to yourself.' (5.27)

This is indeed the style and approach of school-teachers: a mixture of doctrinal lecture and pep-talk, though doubtless offered with a good heart.

Chs. 6–7: Job.
Listen! My crying is not for nothing (6.1-7). Oh that God would end it all! What's the point anyhow? (6.8-12) What you have said is no help to me. Would someone tell me what I've done wrong! (6.13-30) Do I have to end my life like this? (7.1-10) Why is your hand so heavy against me, O God (7.11-21).

Ch. 8: Bildad.
But God is just. If you look to him, he'll restore you (vv. 1-7). 'Ask the former generations and find out what their fathers learned' (v. 8). Bildad speaks on like a wisdom teacher, drawing parallels with nature to illustrate his point (vv. 9-22). Like Eliphaz, his heart towards Job seems good, but again his approach is thoroughly academic.

Chs. 9–10: Job.
I know what you say is true, but something doesn't tally (9.2). God is so powerful and I don't know how to dispute his wisdom (9.3-20), but it does not fit my case. It seems 'He destroys both the blameless and the wicked' (9.21-24). I try to think differently, but I still must suffer and I have no-one to mediate for me (9.25-35). Why do you get at me like this, O God? (10.1-17) Why was I ever born? (10.18-22)

Ch. 11: Zophar.

How can you speak like that? I wish God would show you the truth himself (vv. 1-6). He knows much more than you do and he sees your deceit (vv. 7-12). Reach out to him in repentance and he'll restore you (vv. 13-20). The patience of the friends is beginning to get stretched, but the mood is still encouraging at the end of this chapter.

Chs. 12–14: Job.

I know all you are saying (12.2f). I know God has the power to make and unmake people (12.4-25). I know all that, but I want to speak with God (13.1-3). You charge me with lying and speak to me proverbs of ashes (13.4-12), but I want to plead my innocence before God (13.13-19). O God, stop tormenting me like an enemy (13.20-28). Man's life is so short and troubled. A tree has more hope for renewed life than a man (14.1-12). I wait for renewal, but you wear my life away to nothing (14.13-22).

ACT 2 (Chs. 15–21)

In this second cycle of speeches the friends become increasingly irritable and impatient with Job, and Job equally becomes more agitated and distressed in return.

Ch. 15: Eliphaz.

Eliphaz's first speech was good-hearted, if academic, but now he becomes hot-tempered and personal. Job's speech, he says, is rash and sinful (vv. 1-6). It stands opposed to all the wise men teach about God's ways (vv. 7-16). They have taught us just how very badly the wicked suffer for their sins (vv. 17-35).

Chs. 16–17: Job.

Some comfort you offer me! I know all these arguments well (16.1-5), but the fact is that God is tearing me to pieces (16.6-14) and I can't see that I deserve it (16.15-17). Even now my plea goes to heaven, but my life is cut short (16.18–17.2). O God, please help me, because they cannot (17.3-9). They have it all back to front, saying there is hope for me, when my only hope is the grave (17.10-16).

Ch. 18: Bildad.

Bildad speaks in indignation at Job's low opinion of their good advice (vv. 1-4) and, like Eliphaz, launches into a horrifying account of what happens to the wicked (vv. 5-21), which is certainly no answer to give to a man in distress.

Ch. 19: Job.

How long will you torment me. Can't you see God has wronged me (vv. 1-7). He has made me suffer terribly (vv. 8-20). I ask for pity from you, not further persecution (vv. 21f). But I know I will see God in the end and be vindicated, so you yourselves should fear his judgment (vv. 22-29).

Several times Job has called out to God and longed to speak with him. Here for the first time he catches some certainty that he will.

Ch. 20: Zophar.

Zophar speaks out of hurt pride (vv. 1-3), but like both Eliphaz and Bildad, the only justification he can give is that ancient wisdom tells how terribly the wicked must suffer (vv. 4-29).

Ch. 21: Job.

Listen. If what you say is right, why do the wicked generally do so well in life while God does nothing about it (vv. 1-21). Your arguments are nonsense and of no consolation to me (vv. 22-34).

ACT 3 (Chs. 22–31)

In this third cycle the friends' arguments tail off and fritter out to nothing. They exhausted their store of theological wisdom in the first cycle, their portraits of horror in the second simply showed the bankruptcy of their views, and now they have little left to say.

Ch. 22 Eliphaz.

Eliphaz started off as a gracious enough theologian-counsellor, but Job would not accept his wise counsel. So now, perhaps smarting at the rejection of his good advice, he accuses Job of being a hypocrite and sinner (vv. 1-11, the total opposite of what chs. 1–2 say), warns him of the dire consequences of his stance (vv. 12-20) and advises him to submit to God in repentance (vv. 21-30).

Chs. 23–24: Job.
Job's reply pays scant regard to Eliphaz's challenge: If only I could find God, I would state my case to him (23.1-9), but even so, he already knows, and anyhow, who dares do such a thing, for he is the Almighty (23.10-17)? Why does he not intervene to put an end to the injustice and evil in the world? (24.1-17) Yet it is true that the wicked are only like surface foam (scum!) that soon vanishes (24.18-25).

Ch. 25: Bildad.
Bildad's reply is utterly pompous. Judging by its opening words it could have become one of the most majestic speeches in the play, but he has run out of fire and his, and so also his friends' final words of comfort to Job are that man is but a maggot, only a worm! So much for the theological wisdom of the wise!

Chs. 26–31: Job.
Job's complaint is not that wisdom is futile, but that his friends' understanding of it is, and that the spirit that instructs them in it is wrong (26.1-4). There is a much deeper power and wisdom in God, of which we see 'but the outer fringe' (26.5-14).

Job therefore refuses to deny his innocence which is still the truth as he sees it (27.1-6), even though he does recognise, just as his friends have repeatedly asserted, that suffering is the normal fate of the wicked (27.7-33).

But God's wisdom is more profound than that, indeed so profound that no man can find it, not in the depth of the earth, nor of the sea, nor even at the very gate of death. Only God knows where it is to be found, and so he has told us that to fear him is wisdom (ch. 28).

Job recalls the days of his well-being, when he was a respected man in society, when he was able to care for the poor and when men eagerly listened to his advice (ch. 29). But now all that has changed and men mock him instead

(30.1-19). I cry out to God, he says, but he does not answer (30.20-23), and instead of blessing, I am plunged in suffering (30.24-31).

All that has befallen me even though I have avoided lustful thoughts and ways (31.1-4,9-12), have dealt justly in business and with my employees (31.5-8,13-15), have been generous to the needy and turned no-one away (31.16-23,31f), have not made a god of money or anything else (31.24-28), have not gloated over another's misfortune (31.29f) and have not harboured any secret sin (31.33f).

Job therefore challenges God to answer him. If his suffering is merited, he wants to know why (31.35-40).

ACT 4 (32.1–42.6)

Quite unnoticed to this point there is a bystander on stage, a young man called Elihu. Out of customary respect he has kept silent in the presence of his elders, but when Job lays his challenge before God, he bursts forth, as it were in answer, into a stream of uninterrupted speech that is best likened to a sermon—and a most powerful sermon it proves to be, for it leads directly to the revelation Job needs.

Elihu is a much misunderstood young man who has suffered a great deal at the hands of antipathetic commentators. He has been dismissed as pompous, abrasive, uninspiring, irrelevant, and some would even drop his speech from the book as an intrusion. However, the very opposite is the case. Yes, he is young and enthusiastic, but he knows that himself and apologises for it with some embarrassment. Yes, he repeats many of the same arguments as Job's friends, but his approach as he does so is quite different from theirs.

Job had questioned the spirit with which his friends spoke (26.4). Elihu's spirit is very different. He does not quote, as they did, what former generations of wise men taught, or what has been observed to be the case from life's experience. He is, in fact, not very academic at all in his approach, but more excited and enthusiastic. He is also a much warmer person. Job's counsellors may be called his friends, but they never once addressed him by name; Elihu does (33.1; 37.14). Their personalities are almost hidden behind their arguments; Elihu's is obvious from the outset.

Moreover, he tells us the spirit by which he speaks is 'the breath of the Almighty' (32.8). If he were alive today, we would not hesitate to call him a charismatic. And like his modern-day counterparts, his speech is full of God-talk. Indeed it is that that enables him to make his breakthrough with Job, because what in effect happens is that in his enthusiasm he lifts Job out of his self-pity and questioning into the very presence of God.

Chs. 32–37: Elihu.

He begins, amid profuse apologies for interrupting, by declaring that wisdom does not come through years of learning, but from the Spirit of God—and that is his licence to enter the debate (32.4-14), for he feels so full of the Spirit that he just has to speak (32.15-22). However, he reassures Job, perhaps because he saw him shrink back before this exuberant outburst, that while the Spirit is the motivating force in him, he is no different from Job himself in God's sight (33.1-7).

We were told that he spoke up because he was angry that God's reputation was being worsted in the earlier debates. Elihu's heart, like that of his near name-sake, Elijah, is to defend his God, and so he challenges Job on some of the things he has said (33.8-13). God does speak, perhaps in a dream that frightens us (not the spooky sort Eliphaz reported in 4.12-21) to save us from pride and destruction (33.14-18), or perhaps through suffering to discipline us (33.19-22), so that when we are restored to health we will be humble before him, acknowledging his salvation and glorifying him before men (33.23-28). God may lead us through such things again and again to save us from hell and lead us to 'the light of life' (33.29f).

He then turns to the friends: You may be 'wise men' and 'men of learning', but you have miserably failed to refute Job's insinuations about God's injustice (34.1-9). And so he launches into a long defence of God, not by highlighting the horrors he makes the wicked suffer, which was their main tactic, but by reasoning about God's own goodness and his utter abhorrence of evil (34.10-37). Here, in fact, we have one of the most God-centred speeches in the whole book so far. Elihu's theology may be no more scholarly than Job's friends', but we cannot but be impressed by his zeal for defending his God.

We begin now to see the drift of Elihu's sermon. The debates with his friends left Job full of doubts about God's justice and so with no basis of faith for healing. Elihu has set himself to counteract all that and by firmly portraying God's life-giving graciousness and utter goodness is constructing a platform of faith, a kind of launching-pad for the healing work of God.

Hence, in ch. 35, he considers how we may draw close to this wonderful God. Firstly, we cannot persuade God to intervene by our actions; they may affect other men, but not God, for he is too highly exalted (35.2-8). Secondly, we cannot persuade him to intervene by our words, particularly by self-centred prayers, or expostulations about him not answering (35.9-14).

On the other hand, mighty as he is, he does not despise men, but is keenly interested in both the righteous and the wicked (36.1-7). He uses suffering to teach them and restores those who heed his discipline, though those who do not must perish in their ignorance (36.8-16). It is therefore important to persevere in righteousness and heed God's discipline (36.17-21).

If Elihu had said no more, his theology would offer no more hope than the friends': God is unutterably good; we cannot persuade him to help us; but we should try to live a good life and heed his reproofs. That, however, was only preparation for what follows. His speech has already been more God-centred than anyone else's, but now it becomes fully so. The debate about suffering has been slowly receding before his growing concentration on the majesty of God, and at 36.22 the transition becomes absolute. Thereafter Elihu gives himself totally to extolling God and encouraging Job to praise him (36.22-25), thus drawing him into contemplation of his power in creation (36.26-33).

As he describes God's power in the thunderstorm, he becomes very excited: 'Listen! Listen to the roar of his voice …' (37.1). Indeed, his speech becomes so vivid we almost sense the very life of everything he is describing: the snow, the rain, the wind, the ice (37.2-13). Then he lifts Job personally into the vision with a series of questions: Do you know how God does all these things, Job? (37.14-20) And then he lifts our thoughts back to God again (37.21-24).

And out of the thunderstorm God speaks! (38.1)

Chs. 38–41: God.
Elihu has done his work. His voice recedes into the distance as the voice of God takes over. Job is drawn up out of his misery into the very life with which Elihu's dramatic speech pulsates. He is now no longer listening to the preacher, but to God himself. The arguments, questions and pictures are the same as Elihu's, but their vista widens as Job is conducted on a spiritual review of creation's wonders, but now we listen to them being framed with the divine 'I': 'Where were you when I laid the earth's foundation?' (chs. 38–39)

Job's sufferings are already forgotten—or almost so. At the beginning of ch. 40 there is a momentary break, suggesting he had a sudden surge of misgiving and was tempted to return to his questionings. But the moment passes as God's voice continues to speak out of the storm, drawing Job into even more profound mysteries, the strange contemplation of earth's more monstrous creatures. (Behemoth in 40.15 may be the hippopotamus and leviathan in 41.1 the crocodile, though that is by no means certain.)

42.1-6: Job.
Job's questions about injustice now lie far behind him; he is a man 'lost in wonder, love and praise' (42.1-3). So it ever must be in God's presence. God's speeches offer no explanations about the problem of suffering, but Job is better satisfied than any such answers could possibly make him. His faith has entered a totally new dimension. Whereas before 'my ears had heard of you', that is through the teachings of elders, wise men and theologians, 'now my eyes have seen you' (42.5). And like so many others who have had similar experiences, he finds the only possible response to God is repentance (42.6).

Ironically that is exactly what his friends had advised, but

on the ground of their advice it would have been a purely
mental or wilful exercise. As a result of Elihu's sermon it is
an act performed in response to God himself, not to any
man's promptings, and that is the truest form of repentance
there can be (cp. Isa. 6.1-5).

EPILOGUE (42.7-17)

Job's restoration is not just a naive, fairy-tale ending tagged
on as an after-thought. It is very much the direct conse-
quence of his repentance resulting from his encounter with
God. It is rather like the healing Christians find released in
their lives when a Spirit-filled pastor or evangelist leads
them through his preaching and ministry, as Elihu did Job,
into the faith-creating presence of God.

The play is still about wisdom, but its message is that,
whilst theological wisdom may be true enough in its statements, it does not readily bring either understanding or
healing. That is found in the wisdom of the Spirit that Elihu
preaches, in 'the breath of the Almighty', which lifts us
beyond rational argument into the living, powerful presence
of God himself, where alone true wisdom and healing and
peace and all good things are found.

Two other writings in the Old Testament bear witness to the
same truth. The book of Habakkuk handles the same theme
at national level. The prophet looks for answers to questions
about his people's suffering (ch. 1), but instead of answers is
given a statement about faith (2.4) and a powerful, Job-like
vision of God by virtue of which he finds he can rejoice,
whatever the circumstances (ch. 3). Ps. 73 tackles the
similar problem of the apparently unjust prosperity of the
wicked (vv. 1-14), finds it cannot be resolved by human
understanding (vv. 15f), but that in 'the sanctuary of God'
(v. 16) a new perspective on it may be found, which again
leads to rejoicing (vv. 17-28).

2. THE SEARCH FOR WISDOM

Whatever wisdom may be,
it is far off and most profound—
who can discover it?

(Eccles. 7.24)

So wrote the nigh-despairing Teacher, and Job felt the same way at one point. In ch. 28, when he described how men dig into the earth's darkest recesses to uncover wonderful treasures, he then had to cry, 'where can wisdom be found?' The only answer he had to give was that no-one knows except God—and his word to man is 'The fear of the Lord— that is wisdom.'

In Proverbs the approach was very different. Job and the Teacher were both searching for answers; Proverbs asked no questions because it started from a position of faith that the fear of the Lord is truly the beginning of wisdom. Its teaching was therefore entirely positive, extolling wisdom's virtues and instructing men about receiving it to themselves.

Furthermore, since the source of wisdom is in God, Proverbs speaks of it as a person, one more precious than silver, gold or rubies, whose gift is life and peace (3.13-18). Her ways are righteous and just (8.13,20), she rewards with riches and honour (3.16; 4.9) and she has been the power behind governments and kings (8.15f). But there is something yet more profound and mysterious about wisdom: she existed with the LORD before the dawn of time itself and witnessed it all come into being, for she was God's architect in creation (8.22-31). Finding her is thus more than just finding new knowledge; it is tapping the very life of God himself: 'For whoever finds me finds life and receives favour from the LORD' (8.35).

Though wisdom is so profound, she is also freely available, for she offers herself freely to any who will receive her (8.1-11): 'I love those who love me, and those who seek me find me.' (8.17) Indeed she openly invites men to come and share at her table (9.1-6). But then:

The fear of the LORD is the beginning of wisdom,
and knowledge of the Holy One is understanding.
(9.10)

When we come to look at Paul's teaching about Christ
and wisdom in the New Testament we shall have to recall
this portrait. For the moment simply note how much, despite
the male/female difference, it is like a portrait of Christ.
Paul's teaching, as we shall see, is that Christ is God's
wisdom and that we find that wisdom for ourselves by
revelation through his Spirit (see pp. 185–8). For us today
the answer to Job's and the Teacher's questions is therefore
simply 'in Christ, by his Spirit'. But from what we have
seen, that is an answer the wisdom writers of the Old
Testament would themselves have been happy to receive
(see also Isa. 11.2). The author of Job spells out the connection of wisdom with the Spirit explicitly, but the others, by
their acknowledgment that its basis is in the fear of the Lord
rather than human learning, virtually say the same thing.
That is doubtless why, for example, in Prov. 4, where we are
exhorted to heed parental teaching, we are also admonished
to 'Get wisdom' herself, to 'love her ... esteem her ...
embrace her' (vv. 5-8). Wisdom is not simply a system of
teaching or thought, but something thoroughly personal,
sharing in the very nature of God. And as the personal
nature of God's word was revealed to us when it became
flesh in Christ, so also, Paul would say, was the personal
nature of his wisdom.

7

The Praise and Worship of God

PSALMS

Just as wisdom is grounded in the fear of the LORD, so too is worship. An encounter with God leaves us, like Job and Habakkuk, not only with much to think about, but overwhelmed with a sense of awe and love that we can only express in praise and adoration. It evokes from us the cry of Thomas that has been taken as the title for this volume: 'My Lord and my God!' The psalms either express such heartfelt worship, or voice a longing for conditions that will permit such worship.

The Book of Psalms was Israel's hymnbook. Its Greek title, *psalmoi*, means 'songs'; its Hebrew title, *tehillim*, means 'praises'. It contains all the variety of any modern hymn-book: songs for different seasons and festivals, penitential poems, prayers of petition and supplication, songs of thanksgiving, hymns of praise and adoration, etc. (A full descriptive list is given below on pp. 85–9.)

Psalms are also found in other parts of the Old Testament. Some of them have been incorporated into the Psalter, others have not. For example, the psalms in Exod. 15 and Hab. 3 have not been included, whereas 2 Sam. 22 has become Ps. 18. In the same way today, not every hymn that is written is incorporated in our standard hymnbooks.

1. READING AND PRAYING THE PSALMS

Whilst the psalms are beautiful literary creations, it is important to remember that they are first and foremost expressions of the heart, not the head. Some of them are deeply agonising cries of distress, others songs of profound trust, others outpourings of love and adoration. They were written to be prayed, not analysed. Learn to pray them. Feel the joy or the agony of the psalmist for yourself. Let your heart unite with his heart as you cry out to God using his beautiful words. They were written for you to use to address your God.

Psalms as poetry.
Bear in mind that what you are handling is poetry. We have already noted that Hebrew poetry functions on different principles from English: that, though it does have metre, it has no rhyme, but uses parallelism instead (see above, p. 53). Nevertheless, it is still poetry, not prose, and may therefore employ the same kind of poetic licence as we find in the songs and poems of any other language.

For instance, the mood in some psalms may appear to be communal, in others very personal: hence, some celebrate God's dealings with Israel in history, others his work in the private life of an individual worshipper. While it is often possible to distinguish the private from the corporate psalms by their use of 'I' or 'we', perhaps it is not always correct to make that distinction as though we were handling the more fixed literary expressions of prose-writers. Even today in corporate worship a whole congregation will happily sing a hymn like 'When *I* survey the wondrous cross', or an individual pray in private '*Our* Father in heaven', without any sense of contradiction. The same sort of fluidity was doubtless part of Israel's worshipping tradition.

Again, fluidity must often be assumed in the use of any particular psalm's poetic imagery. For example, Ps. 22 paints vivid word-pictures of one who is suffering severe bodily pain, seems to have a high fever, is near to death, and is lost in a jungle where he is surrounded by head-hunters and ravenous wild beasts. Yet the psalm is normally applied by Christians without any sense of awkwardness to the story of the crucifixion, which has little to do with any of these images. That is, of course, possible because poetry allows the free use of metaphorical language.

The psalms and revival.

Down the centuries of Christian history hymn-writing has regularly gone hand in hand with revival. At times when men have discovered God afresh, there has usually been a fresh burst of praise that has issued in a flood of new songs. So it was in the Wesleyan revival of the eighteenth century, so also in the last century during the campaigns of Sankey and Moody, then again at the beginning of this in connection with the Pentecostal revival, and now today with the spreading of charismatic Christianity.

It seems that something similar happened in ancient Israel. One of the reasons why the psalms are so firmly associated with David, apart from the fact that he is said to have written some of them, is that it was during his reign that public worship in Israel was first expressed in music and song, that is, as well as in the sacrifices prescribed by Moses (see 1 Chron. 15.16; 16.4-7,39-42; 25.1,6f).

Certainly the introduction of music in worship reflects David's own interest in song, but that in turn seems to reflect the effects of Samuel's revival on him in his youth. David's biographer includes one or two of his songs in his life story (2 Sam. 1,22,23), but apart from that only mentions his musical skills at the beginning, soon after he introduces him to us (1 Sam. 16). At that stage David was closely associated with Samuel and his prophets, who themselves enjoyed worshipping with music (1 Sam. 10.5). Before their time there is no record of any public or corporate worship accompanied by music in the Old Testament. Yes, there were poems and songs written and sung by individuals, such as Moses or Deborah (Exod. 15; Judg. 5). Moses even composed one the Israelites had to learn by heart to help them remember how God had cared for them, but we do not know if it was ever intended to be sung corporately in public worship (Deut. 31.19; 31.30–32.43). The law says nothing about music in worship and so the impression we get is that it was an innovation of David's day, with its origins lying further back in the outburst of prophetic praise that accompanied Samuel's revival. If some of the psalms do originate in a flood of new praise songs associated with that early revival, others, of course, were written later and in different circumstances.

David and the psalmists.
Many of the psalms have titles or headings that associate them with various people. A large number are ascribed to David (most of Pss. 3–41 and many others), two to Solomon (Ps. 72, 127), one to Moses (Ps. 90), several to Asaph, the sons of Korah and other Levites who served as singers and musicians in the temple (mostly in Pss. 42–89). There are also plenty, particularly in the last third of the Psalter, that have no personal ascription; these are sometimes referred to as 'orphan' psalms.

It may be that these ascriptions are meant to tell us who the authors were, though that is not at all clear. One theory is that the collection of psalms as we now have it in the Psalter was compiled from a number of earlier hymn-books and that the ascriptions indicate which collection they were originally contained in, such as a Davidic Psalter (the hymn-book of the royal chapel?), an Asaphite choir-book, a Korahite one, and so forth. One thing is clear: though David is traditionally associated with the Psalms, he could hardly have written all of them, for some are as late as the time of the exile, for example, Pss. 74 and 137.

Musical, historical and other notes.
Since the psalms were written to be sung, some of them have headings that give instructions about what musical instruments should be used to accompany them or what tunes are appropriate for them (cp. the titles to Pss. 4–9).

Some of the psalm-headings contain allusions to episodes in David's life, suggesting they were originally composed as a result of the experience alluded to. Perhaps the best known example is Ps. 51, which the title associates with David's penitence after his affair with Bathsheba. For us today such titles are useful as guides to the sort of situations in which we might find the psalms that have them appropriate. Ps. 51

has certainly proved invaluable as a penitential psalm to countless Christians down the ages.

There are also notes indicating that the Psalter is divided into five parts or books:

> Book 1: Pss. 1–41
> Book 2: Pss. 42–72
> Book 3: Pss. 73–89
> Book 4: Pss. 90–106
> Book 5: Pss. 107–150

Most of the psalms ascribed to David are in Books 1 and 2; most of the psalms ascribed to the Levites are in Books 2 and 3; and most of the psalms in Books 4 and 5 are orphan psalms. It is only possible to make very general observations about differences between these books, for they all contain a mixture of basically the same kinds of psalms. It may, however, be noted that proportionately more in the first two books are cries for help than in the last two, and that there is a greater concentration of pure praise in the second half of the Psalter than in the first, coming to a tremendous climax right at the end.

The praise of God in the psalms.

Whoever the original psalm-writers may have been, their songs are a continuing witness to a vibrancy of faith that we would do well to recapture today. Although they do not use the New Testament vocabulary of faith, their approach to God is essentially no different from Paul's or any other early Christian writer's.

A number of psalms are entirely hymns of praise, extolling God for his goodness, his creation, his salvation through history, his bounteous provision, and the like. Others are thanksgivings for victory, deliverance, protection, and various personal blessings. Some are statements of profound confidence in God's sustaining power and love (for examples, see the following pages). In most of these the praise flows from a heart filled with joy, thanksgiving and love.

However, praise can also be an expression of longing, anticipation and faith, such as we find in other psalms that are essentially heart-rending cries for help in time of dire national or personal distress. Almost every one of these (Ps.

88 is the exception) either concludes with or incorporates some statement of trust or some element of praise. Ps. 13 is an excellent brief example.

Many people have been puzzled by the seeming contradiction of praising God in the middle of a cry of distress, especially since the praise is not an expression of hope that help will come, but of faith that the answer is already given. But then it seems that the ancient psalmists knew the power that faith-filled praise could have in helping us to combat and overcome the circumstances of life. We saw something of that principle in operation in Job and Habakkuk, but it was also a principle that New Testament Christians understood very well (cp. Phil. 4.4-7; 1 Thes. 5.16-18) and it is one that many are rediscovering in our own day.

Psalm 22 is probably the best known example of this principle in operation. It opens with the words Jesus uttered in his cry of dereliction from the cross ('My God, my God, why have you forsaken me?'), but ends with such an outburst of praise that many have thought Jesus, far from crying out in distress, was starting to sing a song of victory. Both interpretations are partly correct, but the full truth must be much more profound than either. Jesus' sense of dereliction was totally real and his faith was equally real, but the fact of the matter is that faith's metal is only discovered and proved in the experience of life's depths. Both truths are expressed in Ps. 22, and we must not minimise either in the experience of Jesus. He was, however, heir to a long and rich heritage of faith and praise in suffering, and as the One sent by God to effect man's salvation he had to live its experience to the uttermost to prove its utter validity.

2. DIFFERENT KINDS OF PSALM

In a book this size there is space only for the briefest note on each individual psalm, but some general comments on their different kinds should help you find your way around the whole collection more easily.

In the lists that follow the groupings partly indicate how psalms might originally have been used and partly how they may still be used today, but sometimes they also indicate what the psalm is about, what its theme is, or quite simply what it says. Because some psalms are adaptable for different uses, they appear under more than one heading.

The psalms may be divided into five broad categories: hymns of praise, national prayers, private prayers, thanksgivings and teaching psalms. These five encompass all the psalms in the Psalter. The two additional categories listed below overlap with them and are not distinct from them: the first simply indicates which psalms Christians have interpreted as prophetic of Christ's life and the second lists some special smaller groupings.

1. Hymns of praise.

These are mainly songs of praise, focusing either on who God is, or on what he has done for his people, or on what he will do.

Pure praise has always been close to the heart of men and women who have experienced personal rebirth, Holy Spirit baptism, church renewal, communal revival and the like. Many of the new songs of today's renewal and revival movements are of this nature, and doubtless many of those listed here came out of hearts filled with the same kind of love for God.

In praise of God for what he is, good, loving, faithful, etc.:
100, 103, 111, 113, 134, 145, 146, 150.

To God the Creator: 8, 19, 24, 29, 104.
To God the bounteous Provider: 65, 84, 144, 147.
To God the Lord of Israel's history: 68, 78, 105, 111, 114, 117.
To God the Creator and Lord of history: 33, 89, 95, 135, 136, 144, 148.
To God the mighty, the victorious: 68, 76, 149.

Celebrating the coming, final victory of God and his people: 46–48, 68, 93, 96–99.
Celebrating the fact that 'The LORD is King': 47, 93, 96–99.
Celebrating God's protection of Zion ('Songs of Zion', cp. 137.3): 46, 48, 76, 84, 87, 122.

2. *National Psalms.*

In this category we find two sub-groups. Firstly, there are prayers for the nation itself, whether specifically for deliverance from enemies, famine, plague and such like, or more generally for restoration, blessing and prosperity. Secondly, there are psalms relating to the king, some of them prayers for his blessing, others expressions of confidence in God's promise to uphold him (cp. 2 Sam. 7.5-16). Some of the psalms in this second group came to be recognised as prophecies of the coming of Messiah.

Prayers for deliverance or victory: 44, 60, 74, 79, 80, 83, 85, 89, 108, 126, 129, 137, 144.
Prayers for blessing and continued protection: 67, 115, 125.
Prayers for revival: 80, 85, 126.
General prayers for mercy or restoration: 90, 106, 123.
Psalms that call the people to obedience: 81, 95.

Psalms of confidence in God's promise to uphold the king ('Royal Psalms'): 2, 18, 20, 21, 45, 72, 89, 110, 132.
Other psalms that include prayers for the king: 61, 63, 80, 84.
Other psalms that make reference to the king: 78, 122, 144.

3. *Prayers for use by individuals in time of need.*

This is the largest of our five categories. Its prayers are found scattered throughout the whole Psalter, but by far the greatest concentration of them is in the first half, where most of the psalms ascribed to David are also found. Part of the reason for that must be that many of them come, as some of the headings indicate, from times in David's life when he had to do a lot of crying out to God for help.

These psalms speak about suffering in a variety of ways: in terms of illness, injustice, harassment by enemies, attack from wild beasts and using other nightmarish images— sometimes a mixture of them all. Indeed it is not always clear what the precise trouble is, but that is not always clear when we are in the throes of suffering anyhow. What is frequently stated, however, is that in the midst of his distress the psalmist feels very far from God and longs for his nearness. Christians have often found these psalms helpful in times of spiritual warfare, when they have been aware spiritual warfare, when they have been aware that their suffering has a spiritual as well as a physical cause.

At some point in most of them the mood changes to one of trust or praise. Only in a handful of psalms (mainly the 'Penitential Psalms') do we find repentance expressed as the ground for restoration. Mostly the psalmist is like Job, not knowing why he should be suffering, sometimes even denying that he deserves to be (cp. Ps. 17). The passage from cry for help to song of praise must therefore, as we have already noted in discussing Ps. 22, rest on the ground of faith in God's mercy and justice. Some of the psalms in this group, in fact, have no cry for help, only the expression of trust, and some of these have proved exceedingly helpful to folk in times of distress down the centuries, by far the most popular of them being Ps. 23, of course.

Prayers for protection, deliverance or vindication in the face of persecution: 3, 5, 7, 12, 17, 25, 35, 40, 41, 54–57, 59, 64, 70, 86, 120, 123, 140–143.

For use in time of suffering and dereliction: 6, 13, 22, 28, 31, 38, 39, 42–43, 69, 71, 77, 88, 102, 143.

Prayers for justice or personal vindication: 7, 17, 26, 35, 69, 94, 109.

Prayers for forgiveness: 6, 25, 38, 51, 130.

Expressions of deep longing for the nearness of God: 22, 25, 27, 38, 42, 51, 61, 63, 73, 77, 84, 130, 143.

Expressions of confidence or trust: 4, 11, 16, 23, 27, 52, 62, 91, 121, 131.

The 'Penitential Psalms' in Christian tradition: 6, 32, 38, 51, 102, 130, 143.

Some psalms are well suited for use at night, when a sufferer might be looking for deliverance to come with the new day: 5, 17, 22, 27, 30, 46, 57, 59, 63, 108, 143.

4. Thanksgiving Psalms.

Strangely this is the smallest group, but then most of the hymns of praise could equally well fulfil the function of a song of thanksgiving.

For national deliverance: 118 (?), 124.

For personal deliverance: 18, 30, 34, 66, 116, 118, 138.

For forgiveness: 32.
For the knowledge of God's continuing love and care: 92, 107.

5. Psalms giving instruction or containing meditations on various themes.

The psalms listed in this section, or many of them, are sometimes referred to as 'Wisdom Psalms', because they deal with the same topics as the wisdom literature, use the same vocabulary, and may even read just like a piece of wisdom teaching. They speak about the fear of the LORD, about the attributes of a good citizen, about the ways of wisdom and folly, and so forth. For the most part they are addressed to men, rather than to God. They are essentially teaching psalms.

On the Law: 1, 19, 119.
On the qualities required in citizens of God's kingdom: 15, 24, 101, 112.
On corruption in society: 11, 12, 14, 53, 55, 58, 82, 94.
On the lot of mankind, the problem of evil and suffering, the ways of the godly and the wicked: 1, 9–10, 14, 36, 37, 39, 49, 52, 53, 58, 62, 73, 90, 92, 94, 112.
On God's judgment: 50, 75, 82.
On God's blessings: 127, 128, 133.
On God's omniscience: 139.

6. Psalms generally accounted Messianic in Christian interpretation.

The psalms listed here will all be found already in the five groups above. They are simply the ones that Christians have believed prophesy various aspects of Christ's ministry.

The royal Messiah: 2, 18, 20, 21, 45, 61, 72, 89, 110, 118, 132.
The suffering Messiah: 22, 35, 41, 55, 69, 109.
Christ as second Adam, fulfiller of man's destiny: 8, 16, 40.
Psalms describing God as King, Creator, etc., applied to Jesus in the New Testament: 68, 97, 102.

7. Special Categories.

There is no special theme that holds this group together.

Acrostics, or alphabetic poems (see p. 22): 9–10, 25, 34, 37, 111, 112, 119, 145.

Songs of ascent; the title in the psalm-headings perhaps indicates that they were written for pilgrims to sing on their way up to the temple: 120–134.

The Hallel Psalms, used by Jews at Passover, and so perhaps also by Jesus at the Last Supper (Mark 14.26): 113–118.

The Hallelujah Psalms, so called because they each begin and end with 'Praise the LORD', which is 'hallelujah' in Hebrew—a fitting group with which to end the Psalter: 146–150.

(The categorisation of the psalms is as in J.W. Rogerson & J.W. McKay, *Psalms*, The Cambridge Bible Commentary on the New English Bible.)

3. THE THEMES OF THE PSALMS

The numbers in brackets refer to the categories above.

BOOK 1

Ps. 1: The way of the righteous and the way of the wicked. The one is blessed by God and flourishes; the other comes to nothing. Compare Jer. 17.5-8. (5)

Ps. 2: The LORD delivers and establishes his anointed king. Zion and its king are protected by God according to his promise to David in 2 Sam. 7.8-16. Prophetically this psalm speaks of our security under Christ's kingship. (2,6)

Ps. 3: The LORD is my shield, I may rest secure. The man of faith can feel secure in the most frightening circumstances. (3)

Ps. 4: The LORD puts great joy and peace in my heart. A lovely psalm of assurance to read at bedtime! (3)

Ps. 5: I believe the LORD will hear me in the morning. Note the sense of certainty that God is righteous and that it is worth waiting for his help (3)

Ps. 6: Be merciful to me, O LORD; do not be angry with me. This is the first of the seven Penitential Psalms. The cry for mercy is real enough, but so also is the faith that it will be answered. (3)

Ps. 7: God is a righteous judge; he will save me. Sometimes our suffering is because of our sins, but not always. Sometimes we need to cry out for justice. (3)

Ps. 8: The majestic Creator has crowned man with glory and honour. Just enjoy this meditation, then read Heb. 2.5-9. (1,6)

Pss. 9–10: A prayer to God the protector of the poor. One continuous psalm in the Septuagint and Vulgate. An acrostic. (3,5,7)

Ps. 11: Society may be lawless, but God is watching over his people. Read this one when you feel like running away from everything. (3,5)

Ps. 12: Society may be corrupt, but God will keep us safe. For when you feel alone in a hostile environment. Read 1 Kings 19.1-18. (3,5)

Ps. 13: How long, O LORD? For use when you seem to be getting no answer from God. (3)

Ps. 14: Society may be godless, but God looks down on us. Virtually identical with Ps. 53. Read 2 Chron. 16.9. (3,5)

Ps. 15: Who may dwell in God's presence? For preparing to draw near to God. See also Ps. 24. (5)

Ps. 16: In God's presence is full security and joy. A rich psalm of confidence. Note vv. 8-11, then read Acts 2.22-36. (3,6)

Ps. 17: My plea is just; I shall see God's face. Note the ultimate blessing of the faithful, namely to see God's face. (3)

Ps. 18: God keeps faith with his Anointed One. David's thanksgiving for deliverance during his life (2 Sam. 22); prophetic of Christ's victory over evil and death. (2,4,6)

Ps. 19: The glory of God and the perfection of his law. Contemplating creation and God's law (Scripture) leads to a prayer for grace to be faithful. (1,5)

Ps. 20: The LORD gives victory to his Anointed. V. 7 gives the key to the faith behind this prayer. (2,6)

Ps. 21: The king rejoices and trusts in God's strength. A

psalm that celebrates Christ's ascension and his final triumphant return. (2,6)

Ps. 22: My God, my God, why have you forsaken me? On the crucifixion see v. 16 and compare vv. 1,7,8,18 with Matt. 27.46,39f,43,35. Note also the resurrection faith of vv. 22-31. (3,6)

Ps. 23: The LORD is my shepherd. And Jesus said (John 10.11), 'I am the good shepherd'. (3)

Ps. 24: Who may stand in the presence of the King of glory? See also Ps. 15. God comes to his temple in his glory (1 Kings 8.11). Today our body is God's only temple (1 Cor. 6.19), but if we open the gate of our hearts to his Spirit, he will still establish his glory in us (2 Cor. 3.18). (1,5)

Ps. 25: The LORD will guide me in his love. Note v. 14. God reveals his secret to us by his Spirit (1 Cor. 2.7-10). (3,7)

Ps. 26: Vindicate me, LORD; I love the place where your glory dwells. Similar in theme to Pss. 5, 7, 17. (3)

Ps. 27: I need fear no man, for the LORD will keep me safe. A beautiful expression of longing for God, to see his face, and of confidence that it is worth waiting for him. (3)

Ps. 28: I cry for mercy, but the LORD has heard. Note the strong expressions of trust. (3)

Ps. 29: On the power of God's voice and his glory. A prophetic picture of God coming in wind and fire to his worshipping people at Pentecost. (1)

Ps. 30: I cried to the LORD and he clothed me with joy. A rich testimony to the joy that results from returning to God. (3,4)

Ps. 31: Into your hands I commit my spirit; redeem me, O LORD. Note the intermixture of pleas for help and statements of trust and praise. Cp. Phil. 4.4-7. (3)

Ps. 32: Blessed is he whose transgressions are forgiven. A well loved psalm on the great joy of knowing forgiveness. (3,4)

Ps. 33: The LORD's word is trustworthy and he saves us. Note vv. 16-20. It pays to wait for God rather than look to men for their help. (1)

Ps. 34: Taste and see that the LORD is good. A testimony to God's goodness. An acrostic, twin of Ps. 25. Beautifully paraphrased in the hymn, 'Through all the changing scenes of life'. (4,7)

Ps. 35: Rescue me from my enemies. A plea for justice, like Ps. 7. Prophetic of the enmity shown to Christ. (3,6)

Ps. 36: On the sinfulness of the wicked and the love of God. A strong expression of trust in God's goodness amid godless wickedness. (5)

Ps. 37: On the blessedness of a life committed to God. A wisdom psalm, the reflections of an old man on trusting God amid the seeming injustices of life, in twenty-two proverbs arranged alphabetically. (5,7)

Ps. 38: Do not rebuke me in your anger; come quickly to my help. One of the Penitential Psalms; a plea for forgiveness. (3)

Ps. 39: Life offers little to hope for; my hope is in God. The prayer seeks an answer in this life, not in escape into the hereafter. (3,5)

Ps. 40: LORD, you have helped me before, please save me now. An excellent example of a request made to God with thanksgiving (Phil. 4.6) (3,6)

Ps. 41: The LORD protects the merciful; so LORD have mercy on me. A prayer for use in time of illness and loneliness. (3,6)

BOOK 2

Pss. 42–43: I long for God's presence again. Two psalms, but they read as one, in three parts, each with a refrain. (3)

Ps. 44: You helped our nation before; do not reject us for ever now. A national plea for justice, like the personal plea in Ps. 7. (2)

Ps. 45: A royal wedding song. Applied to Messiah in post-exilic times and to Jesus in Heb. 1.8f. (2,6)

Ps. 46: We will not fear, for the LORD Almighty is with us. A strong expression of confidence in God's eternal protecting presence among his people. (1,3)

Ps. 47: God reigns! A joyous celebration of God's sovereignty. (1)

Ps. 48: Our God makes his city secure for ever. Today we would think of the city as the Church or the heavenly Jerusalem. (1)

Ps. 49: No man can buy off death, but God will ransom

my life. The mood is like Ecclesiastes, but with a strong hope in salvation from death. (5)

Ps. 50: I want, not sacrifice or law-reading, but to be honoured. Our faith is not about rituals and dogmas, but about God, who lives, loves, judges and saves. (5)

Ps. 51: Cleanse me from my sin, and create in me a pure heart, O God. The best known of the Penitential Psalms. (3)

Ps. 52: You boast of evil, but I trust in God. The theme is the downfall of the wicked and the stability of the faithful, as in Ps. 1. (3,5)

Ps. 53: Society may be godless, but God looks down on us. See Ps.14. (3,5)

Ps. 54: Save me, O God; surely God is my help. Another prayer for help with a strong assertion of trust in God. (3)

Ps. 55: O that I could fly away and be at rest. Tempted to flee a hostile environment, our only sure refuge is to trust in God; cp. Ps. 11. (3,5,6)

Ps. 56: In God I trust. What can man do to me? A prayer for help in time of persecution. (3)

Ps. 57: Let your glory be over all the earth. The night of suffering is almost over and dawn is at hand. Used regularly on Easter morning. Vv. 7-11 = Ps. 108.1-5. (3)

Ps. 58: Surely there is a God who judges the earth. The vehemence of this psalm is a reminder of the reality of the law's curse on unrighteousness; cp. Deut. 28. (5)

Ps. 59: Deliver me. O God, my Strength, you are my fortress. A plea for deliverance from nightmarish enemies. (3)

Ps. 60: God has shaken our land, but with him we shall gain the victory. God's word from the sanctuary is a prophecy of victory. Vv. 5-12 = Ps. 108.6-13. (2)

Ps. 61: I long to dwell in your tent for ever. A prayer to be near to God, and for the king to be too. (2,3,6)

Ps. 62: My soul finds rest in God alone; he is my fortress. A strong statement of the value of trusting God. (3,5)

Ps. 63: O God, my soul thirsts for you; your love is better than life. A prayer of longing trust, very like Ps. 27. (3)

Ps. 64: Hide me from the conspiracy of the wicked. In the face of malice and slander our best protection is to seek refuge in God. (3)

Ps. 65: You have blessed our land, O God, with great abundance. A favourite psalm for use at harvest time. (1)

Ps. 66: Come and see what God has done—for us and for me. An invitation to the congregation to join in praise for deliverance, like Ps. 22.22-31. (4)

Ps. 67: May God be gracious to us and bless us. Another favourite harvest psalm (cp. Ps. 65), though the prayer is about much more than good crops. (2)

Ps. 68: Our God is a God who saves; so it has been, so it will be. A review of past victories (vv. 7-18) and a preview of God's final victory (vv. 19-31). (1,6)

Ps. 69: Scorn has broken my heart, but I will praise God's name. A cry of dereliction and praise, like Ps. 22. A favourite for Good Friday. Quoted frequently in the New Testament. (3)

Ps. 70: Hasten, O God, to save me; you are my deliverer. An urgent plea for help. Identical with Ps. 40.13-17. (3)

Ps. 71: God has been, is and will be my hope from youth to old age. An excellent expression of faith in the midst of suffering. (3)

Ps. 72: Endow the king with your justice, O God. A prayer for God's rule to be expressed on earth through the king, now Christ. (2,6)

BOOK 3

Ps. 73: I entered the sanctuary of God, and then I understood. See comments on p. 76. (3,5)

Ps. 74: They burned your sanctuary; do not forget us for ever. A prayer from the time of the exile (cp. Ps. 79), suitable for use when any work of God has been vandalised. (2)

Ps. 75: God is judge; he brings down and he exalts. An assurance of faith and a warning of judgment. (5)

Ps. 76: God's power is mightier than that of earth's armies. God is a mighty warrior, upholding justice for the afflicted. (1)

Ps. 77: When in distress I remembered God's past miracles. Recalling past mercies stimulates faith in present trouble. (3)

Ps. 78: How often our forefathers rebelled, and yet he was merciful. Even as recipients of God's mercies, we still turn our backs on him, as witness Israel's history from the exodus to David. (1,2)

Ps. 79: The nations have destroyed Jerusalem. Help us, O God. See on Ps. 74. (2)

Ps. 80: Restore us, O God. A prayer for communal revival. Note the refrain in vv. 3, 7 and 19. (2)

Ps. 81: If my people would but listen to me! This is like a sermon on the need for obedience to God's law in order to receive his blessing. Cp. Ps. 95. (2)

Ps. 82: God gives judgment among the 'gods'. The 'gods' are either unjust rulers, or else the heavenly beings to whom God committed the care of the nations; cp. Deut. 32.8–NIV footnote; Dan. 10.13. (5)

Ps. 83: LORD, let your enemies know that you are the Most High. A prayer to God to defend his people and his own honour. (2)

Ps. 84: How lovely is your dwelling-place, O LORD Almighty! So blessed are those who draw near to God that they even transform life's valley of tears (Baca). (1,2,3)

Ps. 85: Will you not revive us again? A prayer for revival, like Ps. 80, trusting it is God's will to give it. (2)

Ps. 86: Hear and answer me, O LORD. You are kind and forgiving. One of the greatest encouragements in time of need is a sign or token of God's continuing favour (v. 17), that he still cares. (3)

Ps. 87: The LORD loves Zion. This psalm looks forward to the day when all mankind will be united in the joy of Zion, which for us today means the Church, and in the end the heavenly Jerusalem. (1)

Ps. 88: Why, O LORD, do you hide your face from me? A cry of unrelieved anguish, a reminder of the terrible reality of dereliction, such as Jesus must have experienced in his suffering. (3)

Ps. 89: LORD, you made a covenant with David—help him now. Like other Messianic psalms, a prayer for God's rule to be established among men through Israel's kings, and then through Christ. (1,2,3,6)

BOOK 4

Ps. 90: Life is short; help us to make the best of our days. And the way to do that is by wisdom originating in the fear of the LORD. (2,5)

Ps. 91: If you make the Most High your dwelling, no harm will befall you. A welcome expression of assurance to counterbalance Ps. 88. (3)

Ps. 92: God is just: evildoers will perish, the righteous flourish. See on Pss. 1 and 52. (4,5)

Ps. 93: The LORD reigns and he is mightier than the thundering sea. Because he is creator, he is the one in charge, not earth's violent forces. It is not just any god we trust. (1)

Ps. 94: The LORD knows, and he avenges his people. Note the reasons for confidence: God knows, the upright recognise his hand, and I have known his care. (3,5)

Ps. 95: Let us bow before God and heed his voice today. An invitation to worship God, creator of the world and yet shepherd of his people. On vv. 8-11 see Heb. 3.7–4.11. (1,2)

Ps. 96: Say among the nations, 'The LORD reigns.' Another psalm proclaiming God's universal rule, like Ps. 93, but also looking forward to his coming to establish it fully on earth. (1)

Ps. 97: The LORD reigns, let the earth be glad. As Ps. 96, but concentrating more on his coming to establish justice. (1,6)

Ps. 98: Shout for joy; the LORD comes to judge the earth. As Ps. 97. (1)

Ps. 99: The LORD reigns, let the earth tremble. This psalm celebrates God's rule and his justice, but, in contrast with Pss. 96–98, says nothing about his coming. (1)

Ps. 100: Know that the LORD is good. Enter his courts with praise. An ideal psalm for preparing our hearts and minds for worship. (1)

Ps. 101: I will be careful to lead a blameless life. Righteousness relates as much to the company I keep and what I allow in my home as to what I actually do. (5)

Ps. 102: I am afflicted, my life is short, but God remains the same. This looks like an exile's psalm, praying for personal restoration and the rebuilding of Zion. (3,6)

Ps. 103: The LORD is compassionate and gracious; he forgives my sins. This reads like a thanksgiving for the prayer of Ps. 102 being answered. A beautiful statement about God's compassion. (1)

Ps. 104: On the bounteousness of God in creation. Note how everything is dependant on God, both for its original creation and for its continued sustenance. (1)

Ps. 105: On God's bounteous fulfilment of his promise to Abraham. Meditating on the history of God's faithfulness to his part in the covenant should lead us to rededicate ourselves to our part (v. 45). (1)

Ps. 106: We have sinned like our fathers. You forgave them; save us. Meditating on the history of man's faithlessness to his part in the covenant should lead us to appreciate God's part in it (v. 48). (2)

BOOK 5

Ps. 107: They cried to the LORD in their trouble, and he saved them. Whether trouble comes because of our sin or not, God is a bountiful saviour to those who call on him. (4)

Ps. 108: With God we shall gain the victory. This is Ps. 60 with its opening verses replaced by those in Ps. 57.7-11, giving it a stronger note of confidence. (2,3)

Ps. 109: Silence my accusers and save me. Like Ps. 58, a reminder of God's curse on evil, though we might find it hard to use today. (3,6)

Ps. 110: My Lord sits at God's right hand and is priest for ever. A Messianic psalm, cited several times in the New Testament; e.g., Heb. 1.13 & Heb. 7. (2,6)

Ps. 111: The LORD has shown his people the power of his works. An acrostic series of statements about God's faithfulness, etc. (1,7)

Ps. 112: On the blessings of the man who fears the LORD. An acrostic series of statements about the God-fearer's blessings. (5,7)

Ps. 113: The LORD is exalted, but he stoops down to help the poor. The same theme is found in Hannah's and Mary's songs in 1 Sam. 2.1-10 and Luke 1.46-55. (1,7)

Ps. 114: When Israel came out of Egypt. Its celebration of the exodus-wilderness story makes this an ideal psalm for Passover. (1,7)

Ps. 115: The nations' idols are powerless; the LORD will bless us. A rich statement of God's unique divinity and care for his people. (2,7)

Ps. 116: The LORD heard my cry and delivered me. A thankful testimony to God's help. (4,7)

Ps. 117: Praise the LORD for his love and faithfulness. The shortest psalm, but with a wide perspective, inviting 'all nations' to praise the LORD. (1,7)

Ps. 118: Give thanks to the LORD, he is my helper. The picture of a joyous procession entering the house of the LORD and proclaiming the words of v. 26 reminds us vividly of Jesus' entry to Jerusalem on Palm Sunday. (4,6,7)

Ps. 119: On the goodness of the law and the blessings of keeping it. Note the warmth of appreciation and deep love for God's law. Here is no arid legalism. (5,7)

Ps. 120: Too long have I lived among those who hate peace. The first of fifteen 'Songs of Ascents', perhaps for use by pilgrims. (3,7)

Ps. 121: The LORD watches over you. Here is faith's antidote to the problem of Ps. 120. (3,7)

Ps. 122: Pray for the peace of Jerusalem. Clearly a pilgrim psalm, on the joy of going to God's house. (1,2,7)

Ps. 123: Our eyes look to God till he shows us mercy. Note the expression of pure trust in v. 2. (2,3,7)

Ps. 124: If the LORD had not been on our side. Thanksgiving for deliverance and for God's vigilant care. (4,7)

Ps. 125: Peace be upon Israel. God's purpose is to protect his city and his people. (2,7)

Ps. 126: Restore our fortunes as before. A prayer for revival, incorporating a rich memory of what revival experience is like. (2,7)

Ps. 127: Unless the LORD builds the house. One of the blessings in a godly home is a populous household. (5,7)

Ps. 128: On the family blessings of all who fear the LORD. Another blessing in a godly home is a happy family life. (5,7)

Ps. 129: Let all who hate Zion be turned back in shame. The theme and style are similar to Ps. 125. (2,7)

Ps. 130: With the LORD there is forgiveness. A beautiful statement of God's willingness to forgive and redeem us. (3,7)

Ps. 131: I do not concern myself with things too wonderful for me. An excellent psalm to read when confronted with circumstances too complex to handle. (3,7)

Ps. 132: LORD, remember David. You swore an oath to him. The Davidic kings ruling in Zion represented God's favour and protection for his people. Similarly Christ's rule for the Church. (2,6,7)

Ps. 133: When brothers live together in unity there is rich blessing. That truth is soon recognised when Christians fail to do so. (5,7)

Ps. 134: Lift up your hands in the sanctuary and praise the LORD. A suitable song of blessing to round off the 'Songs of Ascents'. (1,7)

Ps. 135: Praise the LORD; he is greater than all men and gods. So we quickly learn from a glance at Israel's early history. (1)

Ps. 136: Give thanks to the LORD. His love endures for ever. God's goodness and love are seen in creation and in the way he has cared for his people. (1)

Ps. 137: The song of an exile remembering Jerusalem. A beautiful psalm apparently spoiled at the end. But justice also operates in our world. Jerusalem itself felt the weight of that too—hence the exile. (2)

Ps. 138: The LORD's glory is great; he will fulfil his purpose for me. In praise of God for his faithfulness, goodness, care and power. (4)

Ps. 139: Where can I flee from your presence? The flavour of this psalm is caught beautifully in the opening prayer of the Anglican Communion service: 'Almighty God, to whom all hearts are open, all desires known and from whom no secrets are hidden, cleanse the thoughts of our hearts by the inspiration of your Holy Spirit, that we may perfectly love you and worthily magnify your holy name.' (5)

Ps. 140: Protect me from men of violence. Note how this prayer is accompanied by faith that God will do so. (3)

Ps. 141: Let not my heart be drawn to what is evil. It is not enough to pray for protection from evil men. Evil itself can draw us. (3)

Ps. 142: Set me free from my prison that I may praise your name. The desperate cry of a lonely man, but not without faith. (3)

Ps. 143: May your good Spirit lead me. An urgent prayer for forgiveness, deliverance and a closer walk with God. (3)

Ps. 144: Blessed are the people whose God is the LORD. A little anthology of prayers, meditations and praises. (1,2)

Ps. 145: Great is the LORD, compassionate, faithful and loving. A lovely song in praise of God's graciousness. (1,7)

Ps. 146: Trust not men, but the LORD, who remains faithful for ever. Pss. 146–150 all begin and end with 'Praise the LORD'. (1,7)

Ps. 147: How the LORD delights in those who fear him. He is Creator, but he cares for us, and that is why we serve him. (1,7)

Ps. 148: Let everything in heaven and on earth praise the LORD. Note how his own people have a special place, close to his heart. (1,7)

Ps. 149: Let God's saints praise his name, because praise enables victory. We would normally relate vv. 6-9 to spiritual warfare today. (1,7)

Ps. 150: Let everything that has breath praise the LORD. A happy cry of praise with which to round off the Psalter. (1,7)

8

His Banner over me is Love

The title, 'Song of Songs', simply means 'the best of songs'. Unfortunately, other problems relating to this little book are not so easily resolved. There have been so many different interpretations of the Song that it would be quite impossible to review them all here. Some have argued that it is just a collection of love-poems, others that it is a drama with two (or three) actors and with (or without) bystanders participating in the dialogue. Jews have interpreted it allegorically of God's love for Israel, Christians of Christ's love for the Church or believers, though many have insisted that it should only be read as literally about love between man and woman. Further suggestions include relating it to wedding ceremonies, to temple rituals, or to particular events in Solomon's lifetime.

For simplicity's sake, without discussing the merits and short-comings of all these theories, the interpretation here will follow the annotation of the NIV, which assumes that we are reading a dramatic dialogue between a lover and his beloved interspersed with comments from bystanders. According to the text itself Solomon appears to have been the original lover (1.5; 3.7-11; 8.11), though the poetry of the Song equally permits that it be used of any couple in love and also in the traditional way as an expression of the love-relationship between Christ and the Christian.

When read as a drama in this way, we can trace a definite progression in the love-relationship, with recognisable longings and emotions of a beautiful love-affair. Some of the ancient oriental expressions may seem quaint and ungainly, but their sentiments are clear, and when reapplied to the developing relationship between Christ (the Lover) and the believer (the Beloved), we can see in them the whole gamut of emotions normally associated with attraction to Christ, conversion, baptism in the Spirit and growth in discipleship. The Lover's love is constant and consistent, the Beloved's vacillates between longing and self-consciousness, but repeatedly we see his love overcome her self-consciousness and satisfy her longing.

Perhaps the message of the Song is best summarised in the words of the anonymous fourteenth-century writer who taught how to get through the 'cloud of unknowing' that separates us from God:

> *Lift up thy heart to God with a meek stirring of love ... By love may He be gotten and holden; but by thought never ... Therefore, if thou wilt stand and not fall, cease never in thine intent, but beat evermore on this cloud of unknowing that is betwixt thee and thy God with a sharp dart of longing love.*
>
> (*The Cloud of Unknowing* 3, 6)

In some ways that teaching encapsulates at its best the heart of a people waiting for their God, as the Jews in post-exilic times were—indeed as God's people still are. But it is the heart of a people who wait because they have already met with God and know how wonderful his love truly is. Thus their longing originates in the love of the Lover himself, not just in their own desires, and so it reaches out for his love again. It is the love-longing that lies at the heart of all meditation and worship, and so of Israel's wisdom and of her psalms. It is the cry that rises from a heart that has known the touch of God's Spirit and longs for that touch again. The Song of Songs has always been particularly precious to Christian mystics and charismatics who have known the overwhelming power of the knowledge that 'God has poured out his love into our hearts by the Holy Spirit, whom he has given us' (Rom. 5.5).

1.1-7: First attraction and longing.
Imagine the Beloved with her friends and the Lover coming

among them. She is instantly drawn to him and longs to be alone with him (vv. 2-4). Her friends start to flatter him (v. 4), but she stands there self-conscious, bothered by her own weather-beaten appearance. None the less, the attraction is too strong, and so she asks where she may join him alone (vv. 4-7).

The parallels with man's first encounter with Christ are manifest.

1.8–2.7: Their first conversation immediately leads to the development of a warm, loving relationship.

Here the dialogue switches rapidly between Lover and Beloved as they express their love for one another with all the freshness of a new-found relationship (1.8–2.2), concluding with a statement of deep satisfaction on the part of the Beloved (2.3-7).

In Christian reapplication these verses speak of the great delight that attends conversion and of the joy in knowing that Christ loves us every bit as much as we love him.

2.8-17: The Lover's invitation to come with him.

Imagine a new scene. Sufficient time has passed for the Beloved to find herself longing to meet the Lover again. Suddenly she sees him coming and all the thrill of their first encounter rises inside her again (vv. 8f). Then she hears him call, inviting her to come away with him and enjoy the spring-time freshness of their new relationship (vv. 10-13). After some words that tell of playful pleasure of youthful courting (vv. 14f), the Beloved again expresses her deep satisfaction (vv. 16f).

The image speaks magnificently of the first flowering of the young Christian's relationship with Christ.

Ch. 3: After the thrill of first courting, their relationship takes on a more serious tone.

Here we have two new scenes. First we see the Beloved love-sick and restless at night, rising and searching for the Lover till she finds him and is comforted by the security of his embrace (vv. 1-5). Then we see her watching him come majestically in full regalia attended by his royal escort (vv. 6-11).

This chapter reminds us that our relationship with Jesus cannot be a passing fantasy, for though there be all the joy of a young love-affair in it, he is nevertheless the King of Heaven.

4.1–5.1: An invitation to a deeper relationship.

The Lover expresses his delight in his Beloved (4.1-7), but it seems she has withdrawn into herself, standing as it were on a remote, inaccessible mountain crest. The Lover pleads with her to come down (v. 8), reassuring her of his deep love (vv. 9-11), but complaining that she is like a beautiful garden inaccessibly locked up to him (vv. 12-15). His loving pleas touch her heart and she calls out to the wind to blow her open to her lover (v. 16), whereupon he comes instantly (5.1).

The parallel for the Christian is found in the action of the Holy Spirit (Hebrew *ruach* means both spirit and wind), usually some time after conversion, in filling us and opening us up in a new and fuller way to the unflagging love of Christ that has never let us go.

5.1–8.14: The testing and the triumph of love.

These last four chapters are perhaps best read as one continuous act in the drama, in which the love of the Beloved is tested in the presence of her friends.

The Christian parallels should be self-evident as you read. Hear for yourself the voices of your own worldly friends encouraging you to forget about Christ and seek their pleasures; feel for yourself the sense of dereliction when things go wrong and Christ seems far away; share the determination of the Beloved not to let go of love, that is, of the love you know in Christ; sense the approval that comes from the Lover when you do remain faithful; and above all find reassurance in the knowledge that his love for you remains constant and unchanging.

The curtain rises to a table scene. The Friends are having a party (5.1) and the Beloved enters in great distress, telling how her lover came to visit, but while she fussed over her appearance, that she was not ready to greet him, he became weary of waiting outside her door and left. She went searching for him, but could not find him (5.2-6).

In her distress she soon discovers who her true friends are not. She was roughly treated by the watchmen in the streets and now her 'friends' unsympathetically challenge her: 'What's so special about your boyfriend anyhow? There are plenty of other men.' (5.7-9)

Her answer is to affirm that her lover is 'outstanding among ten thousand', beyond compare as far as she is concerned (5.10-16).

Again her friends taunt her: 'Since you are so persistent, where is your lover now?' (6.1)

Her reply visualises him waiting in his garden and asserts that she knows they belong to each other (6.2f).

Thereupon, in response to such faithful, loving devotion, the Lover appears with words of love professing his devotion to her (6.4-12).

When the friends see that she has found him again, they call on her to come back to them, her old friends (6.12), but she is not listening for her lover's voice continues to woo and hold her (6.13–7.9).

Then comes her final declaration of total commitment to her lover, that she truly belongs to him and is willing to go with him (7.9-13).

In the final chapter a more constant and peaceful mood prevails. The Beloved reaffirms her desire to be with him (8.1-4). The Friends express some puzzlement (8.5), but she proclaims that her 'love is as strong as death', that 'many waters cannot quench love' and that it is worth far more than 'all the wealth of his house' (8.5-7).

The Friends make one last attempt to spoil the relationship by deflecting attention away to a young sister (8.8f), but the Beloved is now secure in her relationship with the Lover and says so (8.10-12).

The drama ends with the Lover calling to his Beloved and her responding, calling him to herself, away off stage to 'be like a gazelle on the spice-laden mountains' (8.13f).

It needs little imagination to read in these chapters a poetic account of the ups and downs of our own love-relationship with Christ. The dramatic tensions of lost, tested and refound love are all familiar to Christians who seek to walk in faithfulness with their Lord in the Spirit.

If these things are unfamiliar in your own experience, but do form part of your heart-longing, then heed the initial advice the Lover gave to his beloved when she asked where to find him: 'If you do not know, follow the tracks of the sheep.' (1.8) Others have gone this way before you and entered into a beautiful relationship of love with Christ. If you have not found that love for yourself, follow their tracks and see where he grazes them.

PART FOUR

THE COMING OF THE SON OF MAN IN GLORY

God's timing is always perfect, but when we try to probe the future we quickly discover that it is equally always a mystery. Perhaps the only right way to look to the future is the way we have seen repeatedly in this book: trusting in his sovereignty over all history and especially over the affairs of his people, meditating on and worshipping him for his government and his love in life as we presently know it, and waiting expectantly for his coming with the longing love of a beloved.

Four centuries passed between the ending of Old Testament revelation in the days of Ezra and Nehemiah and the coming of Christ, long years of waiting for the LORD's people. These years are undocumented in the historical writings of the Old Testament. Some of them are covered in the Apocrypha, particularly in 1 and 2 Maccabees, which tell mainly of events in the second century BC. Other information can be gleaned from Jewish, Greek and Roman sources, enough for us to be able to piece together a sufficient history to carry us down to New Testament times. The details of that history need not concern us here, though its skeleton is important, because there is one book in the Old Testament that covers it, not in historical record, but in visions of what was yet to come, namely Daniel.

As God's people waited, he showed them what must take place: the coming and going of empires, the ebb and flow of blessings and persecutions, the judgment of God, the coming of 'one like a son of man', the establishment of God's kingdom, and the final judgment of men. While he asks us to wait for him, he does not leave us comfortless, but assures us of his continuing faithfulness—such is his love to us his children.

9

The Most High is Sovereign over the Kingdoms of Men

The book of Daniel is in two parts: chs. 1–6 tell of six episodes in the lives of Daniel and his friends; chs. 7–12 recount four visions unfolding the future. The theme of the first part is the opening of imperial eyes to the power of Israel's God; the theme of the second is the ultimate victory of Israel to be wrought by his power.

Daniel is included among the prophets in our English Bible, but among the Writings in the Hebrew. Though he is granted visions, Daniel is never called a prophet. Nor does he speak like one. We never hear him speak a prophetic message denouncing wrong and calling for repentance, like Isaiah and the others, but only tell of his visions concerning the future and his interpretations of them. The word that more appropriately describes such revelations is 'apocalyptic'.

'Apocalyptic' (or Revelation: Greek *apokaluptein* means to uncover or reveal) refers to a style of writing that became increasingly popular among the prophets during and after the exile. They continued to utter their warnings about sin and judgment, but also began to unfold the future beyond in visions which they describe for us in highly picturesque and symbolic language. We encounter rudimentary foreshadowings of such apocalyptic visions in Isa. 24–27, but they become more developed in Ezekiel and Zechariah.

Certainly the borders between prophecy and apocalyptic are blurred. The Apocalypse most familiar to Christians, the New Testament book of Revelation, actually calls itself prophecy (Rev. 1.3; 22.10,18f). But the distinction is worth bearing in mind while reading Daniel, for his calling was not like that of the other prophets. He lived his life as a 'wise man' or adviser at the imperial court (2.12-24) and never had any public preaching or prophesying ministry. He only advised the king and interpreted revelations for him. Besides that he wrote down his own visions, not so that they could be read to his contemporaries, but so that they could be sealed up and hidden away until the time they were needed (12.4).

1. THE HISTORICAL BACKGROUND TO DANIEL'S LIFE AND VISIONS

Daniel was a teenager when he was taken to Babylon (1.3f). There he served at the royal court throughout the Babylonian period and on into the Persian. In his later years he was shown in vision what would come after that. The total period covered by his life and visions together takes us down to Roman times—and beyond.

Daniel was taken to Babylon 'in the third year of the reign of Jehoiakim', several years before the fall of Jerusalem in 597 (1.1). As Jehoiakim became king in 609 BC, that must be 606, or perhaps 606-5, since the Jewish year and ours overlap. The Egyptians had put Jehoiakim on the throne to rule as their vassal, but in 605 the Babylonians defeated them and took control of Judah. That is probably the occasion referred to in 2 Chron. 36.6f, when Jehoiakim was seized and some articles from the temple were removed to Babylon. Some of Jerusalem's leading citizens may also have been taken to Babylon at that time as hostages to ensure Jehoiakim's good behaviour. Daniel would have been among them.

Life under the Babylonians.

Just as Lamentations affords us a glimpse of conditions under which the Jews lived in Judah during the exile, so Daniel gives us some idea of conditions in Babylon. Putting that together with what we are told elsewhere, we gather

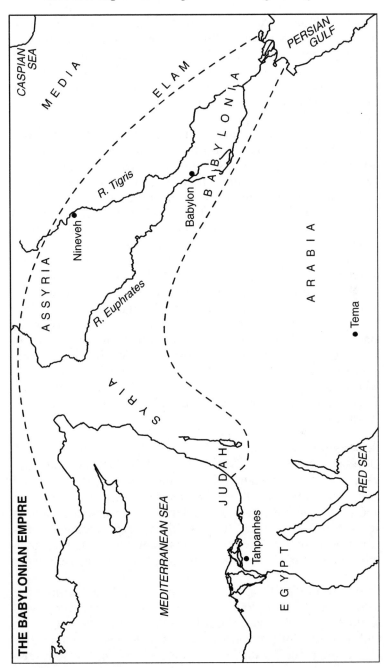

THE BABYLONIAN EMPIRE

that the exiles were resettled in Jewish ghetto-like communities, where they were allowed to build their own homes, develop their own industries and live as normal a life as possible in their new environment (Jer. 29.4-7). Some even rose to positions of political status and influence (Dan. 1), though they also suffered scorn and persecution from time to time (Ps. 137; Dan. 3,5).

Removed from the customary rituals of the temple they developed new forms of spirituality. Hence we find Ezekiel holding teaching meetings in his home (8.1; 33.31), and we see Daniel and his friends putting emphasis on the observance of food laws and on regular prayer and fasting (Dan. 1.8-16; 6.10f; 9.3; 10.2f). But these were essentially survival tactics, for the exiles' vision was never to establish Jewish religion in Babylon. Encouraged by their prophets, their vision was of a return to their homeland, and that in the not too distant future (see especially Isa. 40–55).

Nebuchadnezzar died in 562 and was succeeded by a number of weak, short-lived rulers. Then came the last king, Nabonidus, 556-39, who took little interest in the affairs of state. The Babylonian chroniclers inform us that early in his reign he 'entrusted the army and the kingship' to his son, Belshazzar, and retired to Tema in the Arabian desert, where apparently he remained till the fall of Babylon. Belshazzar was therefore effectively Babylon's last ruler (Dan. 5).

In Persian times.
Our studies of Ezra, Nehemiah and Esther have already shown that in Persian times, though many Jews returned home, conditions for those who chose to stay abroad continued to be much the same as under the Babylonians. Though Jews still had to face the possibility of persecution occasionally (Esther 3), they were encouraged to retain their own religion and many were able to rise in society, as Nehemiah did.

According to Dan. 5.31 it was one called Darius who took over the Babylonian kingdom when Belshazzar was slain. He was a Mede, not a Persian (5.31; 6.28; 9.1; 11.1) and he ruled until the accession of Cyrus the Persian (6.28). However, since Media was conquered by the Persians ten years earlier, his kingdom cannot have been separate from theirs. In fact, the Medes and Persians were allied like two horns on a ram (8.20), and so Darius had to uphold 'the laws of the Medes and the Persians' as one united administrative system (6.8,15). Though a Mede, he must represent the Persian regime.

Unfortunately no other record of his rule exists outside the book of Daniel. Though attempts have been made to identify him with a variety of people, none fits his description satisfactorily. One interesting candidate is Gubaru or Gobryas, the general who entered Babylon ahead of Cyrus and was entrusted by him with its government and with appointing its subordinate officials. It was he who killed Belshazzar (in a night assault, as Dan. 5.30 says) and although he was clearly not ruler of the whole empire, he may have been known locally in Babylon as 'King' during his brief administration there (6.6,9,25). If he was Daniel's Darius, the close relationship between his reign and Cyrus's implied in 6.28 is understandable (see NIV footnote).

Daniel himself lived on into the reign of Cyrus. We do not know when he died, but at the time of his last vision, in Cyrus' third year (10.1), 536 BC, he must have been about eighty years old, assuming he was a teenager when taken to Babylon in 605.

Apart from ch. 6, there is only one verse in Daniel that refers to historical events in Persian times, 11.2, but that really forms part of the history of the Greek era, to which we shall therefore now turn.

The influence of Greece.

Daniel's coverage of Greek history in 11.2-35 is amazingly comprehensive and accurate in its detail.

In the fifth century the Persian Xerxes I made war against Greece (11.2), but withdrew after being disastrously defeated at Salamis in 480. It was during these wars that, overwhelmingly outnumbered by the Persian invaders, the Athenians made their heroic stand at Marathon and the Spartans at Thermopyle. More than a century later the tables were turned when the Greek armies marched against Persia under the dynamic leadership of Alexander the Great. His conquering campaigns only lasted eleven years, but by the

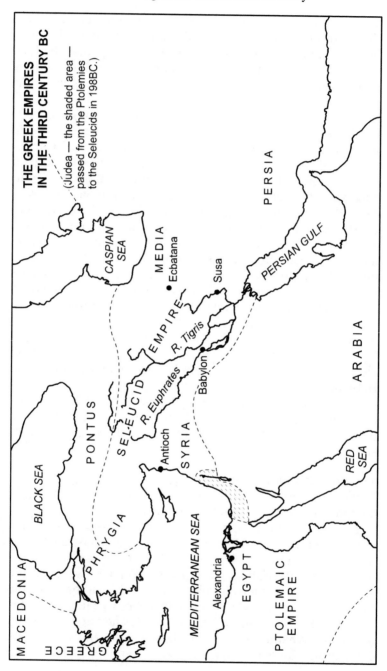

THE GREEK EMPIRES
IN THE THIRD CENTURY BC

(Judea — the shaded area —
passed from the Ptolemies
to the Seleucids in 198BC.)

end of them his control stretched south into Egypt and east into India. When he died in 323, his empire was divided among four of his generals (11.3f).

After initial squabbling between them, three relatively stable Hellenistic (= Greek) kingdoms emerged. The European part in Greece and Macedonia fell to one called Antigonus, the Asiatic part bordered by the Euphrates and the Mediterranean to Seleucus, and the African part in Egypt to Ptolemy. Because of their geographical location in relation to Israel, the last two rulers are called King of the North and King of the South respectively in Daniel (11.5).

Judea initially came under the control of the Ptolemies but disputes between them and the Seleucids, who ruled their territories from Antioch in north Syria, continued throughout the third century. An attempt to make peace through a marriage-alliance about 250 failed and the fighting continued (11.6-13).

Finally, in 198, the Seleucid Antiochus III defeated the Egyptians and Judea passed into his hands (11.14-17).

At first the Seleucids adopted a tolerant attitude to the Jews, but that did not last very long. In 196 Antiochus invaded Asia Minor and Greece, but he was driven back and thoroughly defeated by the Romans in 190, whereupon he lost all his Asian territories. Deprived of the wealth of Asia, his successor had to raise money elsewhere (11.18-20).

In 175 the murderous Antiochus IV Epiphanes came to power, and he raised his monies by brutality and plunder (11.21-24). In his time the fortunes of the Jews changed radically.

There are several reasons why he began to deal harshly with them, but he made his Hellenisation policy the main pretext for his persecution. One of Alexander the Great's aims had been to establish Hellenistic language and culture uniformly throughout his conquered territories. His successors continued to foster that vision, and so Greek ways became established everywhere, including Judea. While there were benefits associated with a common international language and culture, it meant that the LORD's people had sometimes to struggle to retain their Jewish identity. However, it was only in 168 BC that that became a serious problem, when Antiochus, angered by military and financial losses elsewhere, began to vent his wrath against the Jews.

In 170 BC he attacked and defeated Egypt, and on his way home plundered Jerusalem and slaughtered 80,000 people (11.25-28). Then in 168 he attacked Egypt again, but when his invasion was thwarted by a Roman fleet, he turned on Jerusalem again, plundering and desecrating the temple, determined to abolish the Jewish religion, and impose the worship of the Greek gods. To that end he instituted pagan sacrifices and set up an idol of Zeus in the temple ('the abomination that causes desolation'). Some Jews supported his Hellenisation policy, but the faithful would not (11.29-32).

Jewish resistance was passive to begin with, but it became militant when a priest called Mattathias refused to offer pagan sacrifice and slew an officer trying to enforce it. He and his five sons fled to the hills where others gathered around them and took their stand against the oppressor while they waited faithfully for God's appointed time of salvation (11.33-5).

At that point we pass beyond the details of history in Dan. 11. The rest of the story is, however, supplied in full detail in the books of the Maccabees in the Apocrypha.

Under the leadership of Judas Maccabeus ('The Hammer'), one of Mattathias' sons, the Jewish resistance began a guerrilla war that proved amazingly successful, the result of which was that the temple was rededicated in December, 164 (still celebrated by Jews in the feast of Hanukkah), and Judas established himself as ruler of what became virtually an independent kingdom.

The Maccabean state (or Hasmonean, as it came to be called) reached its zenith shortly before 100 BC, when Galilee and other neighbouring territories were annexed, restoring the kingdom to something like its old Davidic boundaries, and it lasted until the Roman general, Pompey, took Jerusalem in 63 BC. However, the details of Hasmonean history lie outside the scope of Daniel's visions and need not concern us here.

JUDEA UNDER THE GREEKS AND THE ROMANS		
336–23	Alexander the Great conquers his empire.	**P**
323–11	Ptolemy I and Seleucus establish their Egyptian and Syrian empires (see map on p. 115).	**T** **O** **L**
311–223	Judea is ruled by the Ptolemies who allow religious toleration to the Jews. Disputes between the Seleucids and Ptolemies continue.	**E** **M** **I** **E** **S**
223–187	Antiochus III Seleucid emperor.	
198	He defeats Egypt and gains control of Palestine.	
175–64	Antiochus IV Epiphanes Seleucid emperor.	**S**
168	He outlaws the Jewish religion and enforces Hellenism in Judea.	**E** **L** **E** **U**
167	The Maccabean revolt begins.	**C**
166–61	Judas Maccabeus leads the Jews in the fight for independence.	**I** **D** **S**
164	He takes Jerusalem and rededicates the temple.	
160–43	Jonathan, Judas' youngest brother, becomes leader and the fighting with Syria continues.	
143–35	Simon, Judas' last remaining brother, finally gains full independence and establishes the Hasmonean dynasty	
135–04	John Hyrcanus conquers Samaria and destroys the Samaritan temple.	**H** **A** **S**
104–3	Aristobulus conquers Galilee and enforces Judaism in the region which was mainly pagan since the Assyrians took it in 722 BC.	**M** **O** **N** **E** **A**
103–76	Alexander Janneus Slide into worldliness,	**N** **S**
75–67	Alexandra Salome and Hyrcanus II tyranny, murder,	
66–63	Aristobulus II family jealousies and intrigue.	
63	Pompey takes Jerusalem and Roman rule begins.	
63–40	Hyrcanus II rules subject to Rome.	
37–4	Herod the Great rules subject to Rome.	
19	Work on the building of his temple begins.	
5 BC	BIRTH OF JESUS CHRIST.	
4 BC	Herod dies and his kingdom is divided between his sons: Archelaus (– 6 AD) gets Judea and Samaria. Herod Antipas (– 39 AD) gets Galilee and Perea. Philip (– 34 AD) gets Iturea and Traconitis.	**R** **O** **M** **A** **N** **S**
6 AD	Judea ruled by Roman Procurators.	
26–36	Pontius Pilate Procurator of Judea.	
27–30	MINISTRY OF JESUS CHRIST.	
41–44	Herod Agrippa I King of Judea.	
52–60	Felix Roman Procurator of Judea.	
60–62	Festus Procurator of Judea.	
66	The Jewish Revolt begins.	
70	Fall of Jerusalem.	

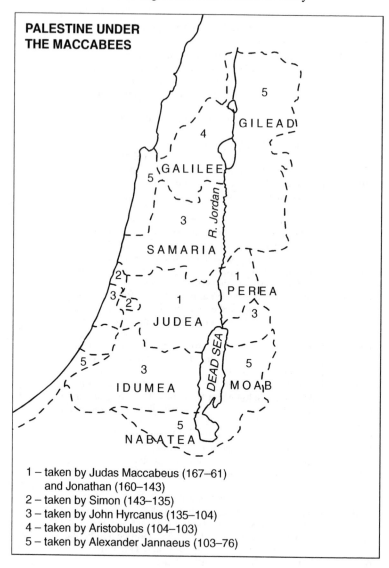

PALESTINE UNDER THE MACCABEES

GILEAD 5

GALILEE 4

5 GALILEE

R. Jordan

3

SAMARIA

2

3 2

1 JUDEA

PEREA 1

3

DEAD SEA

5

3 IDUMEA

5 MOAB

5 NABATEA

1 – taken by Judas Maccabeus (167–61)
   and Jonathan (160–143)
2 – taken by Simon (143–135)
3 – taken by John Hyrcanus (135–104)
4 – taken by Aristobulus (104–103)
5 – taken by Alexander Jannaeus (103–76)

The coming of the Romans.
By contrast with Greek, Daniel gives no details of Roman history, though the Roman era is embraced in his visions, and so a little needs to be said about it here, particularly as it

relates to the Jews.

The Romans allowed a measure of self-government to continue. Thus Herod the Great (39–4 BC), was able to build new cities, palaces and fortresses, and to begin rebuilding the temple in Jerusalem to more splendid proportions than ever before. On his death his kingdom was divided between three sons: Archelaus got Judea and Samaria, Herod Antipas (Luke 23.6-12) got Galilee and Perea, Philip got Iturea and Traconitis. Then in 6 AD Archelaus was exiled and his lands came under the direct governorship of Roman procurators, the fifth of whom was Pontius Pilate (Matt. 27). For a brief three years Philip's son, Herod Agrippa, ruled over all his grandfather's territories, but he died suddenly in 44 (Acts 12), and authority passed back into the hands of the procurators, two of whom were Felix and Festus (Acts 24–26).

The Jews never liked Herod the Great much, but they liked the Roman procurators even less. In their time there were repeated revolts against the Romans in Judea, mainly instigated by a new militant party known as the Zealots that came into being when a certain Judas the Galilean led a revolt in 6 AD, the very year the first procurator was appointed.

The procurators became less and less sympathetic with the Jews and their peculiar ways. Oppression and corruption increased until Jewish resentment finally erupted in a general revolt in 66 AD. That was thoroughly crushed in 70 AD when Jerusalem was sacked and its temple destroyed by the Roman general Titus. The Zealots held out for a few more years in their stronghold at Masada, but that fell in May, 73.

The kingdom of God.

There is one further imperial era in Daniel's reckoning: the age of Christ's kingdom. Again Daniel gives few details, except that unlike earth's empires it will be an everlasting kingdom (2.44; 7.14) and that it will be different in quality, for it will 'put an end to sin' and 'bring in everlasting righteousness' (9.24).

More than that, however, it will also inaugurate the time of the end. Daniel's visions carry us beyond history, through a last battle, resurrection of the dead, final judgment and on into the reaches of God's eternity.

When we look at Daniel's visions, we shall see that sometimes they omit intermediate stages and jump forward suddenly to the end itself. Sometimes we get the impression that the coming of Christ and the end are virtually the same, sometimes that the end is scheduled to follow the Greek period, sometimes the Roman, sometimes even later. (See charts on pp. 124, 126.) The fact is that the mark of the end is encounter with God in judgment, and so whatever period we live in, we can view it with the same faith that its end will be God's end, that all history is in the hands of God who can end it when he wills. The theme of Daniel is very much that 'the Most High is sovereign over the kingdoms of men'.

2. THE KINGDOMS OF EARTH AND THE KINGDOM OF GOD
(CHS. 1–6)

As we turn our attention to the spiritual message of Daniel, we need to remind ourselves that we are not abandoning history. C.H. Spurgeon once commented that the historical matters of Scripture constitute as it were the bones of its system; the spiritual matters its muscles, blood vessels and nerves. The one without the other falls apart. What we are looking at here are not detached spiritual ideas, but lessons the Jews learned from their history about the workings of God.

The primary lesson is not hard to discover: it is about God's sovereignty, or more specifically about how successive imperial rulers came to recognise his sovereignty. Chs. 1–4 tell how Nebuchadnezzar was brought to acknowledge it, ch. 5 how Belshazzar mocked it to his cost, and ch. 6 how Darius came to affirm it. The message is that Israel's God is not to be underestimated and his people are not to be despised, 'for he is the living God and ... his kingdom will not be destroyed' (6.26).

Ch. 1: Nebuchadnezzar recognises Daniel's superior wisdom.

Daniel and his friends, all young noblemen's sons, are trained by the Babylonians to become what we today would think of as high-level civil servants. They are determined not to compromise their faith by running the risk of defiling themselves through eating food forbidden by their law, but God's hand is wondrously on them. He sustains them physically, and in addition gives them knowledge and understanding beyond the measure of the education they receive. The king is most impressed. In Daniel and his friends we see living illustrations of the truth of the teaching of Proverbs, that wisdom originates in the fear of the LORD.

Their training puts them among the wise men of the east, most of whom, according to the customs of their age, are experts in magic, astrology, sorcery and the like. Daniel, however, never has anything to do with their pagan methods. The source of his wisdom is always God himself, as the following chapters clearly show. Though the story of his rise at court is different, he is constantly portrayed as one like Joseph, who through his supernatural wisdom once became vizier of Egypt.

Ch. 2: Nebuchadnezzar recognises the superiority of Daniel's God.

The story of the opening of the king's eyes takes a massive leap forward here. When his dream is interpreted, not only does he acknowledge Daniel's superior wisdom and suitably reward him with promotion, but now he perceives that the source of that wisdom lies in his God. Whereas the Babylonian magicians plead that their gods cannot help him (v. 11), Daniel assures the king that his God can (v. 28), and so the chapter ends with him confessing God's superiority over all others (v. 47).

The dream itself speaks of four world empires finally superseded by God's eternal kingdom. Coming here it foreshadows the revelations of chs. 7–12. (See further below, pp. 124f.)

Ch. 3: Nebuchadnezzar learns to fear the God of the Jews.

The story moves another step forward. The exiles suffered

persecution from time to time in Babylon, but this episode of the fiery furnace led to its cessation, for a time at least. Nebuchadnezzar is amazed by what he sees (v. 24) and decrees that all his subjects must now acknowledge the power of the Jewish God.

The thing that particularly impressed him about Daniel's friends was their absolute trust in God (v. 28), and indeed their faith is most impressive: 'the God we serve is able to save us ... But even if he does not ... we will not serve your gods' (v. 18).

Ch. 4: Nebuchadnezzar acknowledges God's sovereignty.
This chapter takes the form of the king's personal testimony about the wondrous working of God in his own life. He was shown in vision God's purpose to teach him 'that the Most High is sovereign' (v. 17). Daniel warned him that God would not release him until he acknowledged it to be true (v. 25), which in the end, after much unnecessary suffering, was precisely what he had to do (v. 37). It was not enough for Nebuchadnezzar to acknowledge God's power in a detached way. He had to be brought to a point of personally recognising God's hand in his own life. Once he did and repented, his healing and restoration followed automatically.

Ch. 5: Belshazzar discovers the cost of opposing God.
We now move to the end of the Babylonian period, indeed to its very last night. Belshazzar, far from learning respect for God's sovereign power through his forefather's experience, mocks God openly and so the writing is on the wall (vv. 18-24), both for him and for the Babylonian Kingdom!

The words MENE, TEKEL and PARSIN designate units of weight or coinage: the mina, shekel and half shekel, but they also have the root meanings: to number, weigh and divide. Daniel's interpretation depends on these root meanings. As in ch. 2, he is again rewarded by promotion, this time to become 'the third highest ruler in the kingdom', that is after Nabonidus and Belshazzar (v. 29). Though he only retained that honour for a few hours, the next king was to appoint him to a similarly high position (6.1-3). Note how Daniel sought no reward for himself (5.17); he knew that his wisdom was not his own, but from God—and some of the more spiritually perceptive at court knew it too (v. 11).

Ch. 6: Darius decrees national toleration for the Jewish faith.

The post-Babylonian age dawns on a different note. Darius the Mede is exceedingly well-disposed towards Daniel. After all, he represents the Persian regime the prophets foretold would deal favourably with the Jews (see above, pp. 30f).

This chapter tells of the testing of Daniel's faith. Hitherto he has known only success and honour, but now in his old age, his trial also comes. Like his friends before him, he remains faithful, with the result that, after the miracle at the lion's den, Darius, who already has an open heart towards Daniel's God, publicly acknowledges his sovereignty in words reminiscent of Nebuchadnezzar's confession in 4.3 (vv. 26f).

The lesson is clear: the God of Israel is the Most High, sovereign over the kingdoms of men. Whether world-emperors learn that truth the hard way, or refuse to acknowledge it, or accept it readily, they will all find that neither he nor his people are to be trifled with. They may persecute the Jews, whether willingly or not, but they will never destroy God's kingdom, and in the end will have to do what Darius did, namely desist from their persecution and recognise the validity of the true faith. The kings of Babylon and Persia had to learn that lesson; in the chapters that follow God reveals to Daniel that other kings yet unborn will have to learn it too.

3. THE UNFOLDING OF THE AGES (CHS. 7–12)

Daniel received his first two visions early in Belshazzar's reign and his second two soon after the beginning of the Persian era, when he must have been roughly 65 and 80 years old respectively. Along with Nebuchadnezzar's vision in ch. 2, they lead us down the centuries to times of intense

THE VISIONS OF DANIEL				
EMPIRES as symbolised in vision	CH. 2 Statue	CH. 7 Beasts	CH. 8 Ram & Goat	CH. 9 70×7	CHS. 10-12 King of North and King of South
Babylon	Gold	Lion	—	—	—
Persia	Silver	Bear	Ram		11.2-4
Greece	Bronze	Leopard	Goat*	7×7 + 62×7	Kings of South & North*
Rome	Iron	Monster	—		—
Kingdom of God	Rock	Man	—	Last 7	—
The End	—	—	8.17,19	9.26f	11.35–12.4
* Culminate in the persecution of Antiochus Epiphanes in 168 BC					

persecution, at which point God himself intervenes and ushers in his kingdom that is to last for ever.

Different theories exist about the historical identification of the kingdoms foreshadowed in the visions (which we cannot discuss here), but it is of the very essence of apocalyptic symbolism that it should be fluid, the happy result of which is that its message continues to have relevance for us as we face the future today.

Ch. 2: The enormous statue and the rock.

The image in four parts represents four successive empires, and since the first is identified as the Babylonian (gold), the others must be the Medo-Persian (silver), the Greek (bronze), and the Roman (iron, but with clay in the feet). Then in Roman times God himself and no human hand will carve out a kingdom that will supersede all earth's empires and last for ever (the rock). The reference is to the coming of Christ and the Church.

Another popular view regards the Medes and Persians as two separate empires, takes the fourth to be the Greek, not the Roman, and sees in the brutality of the iron a reference to the persecution of Antiochus Epiphanes in 168 BC. The main problem with this view is that there never was a Median empire. Those who hold it identify the time of persecution in all Daniel's visions that follow in the same way.

Ch. 7: The beasts from the sea and the man from heaven.
This vision covers the same outline as in ch. 2, but in greater detail, portraying earth's empires as four beasts of increasing ferocity emerging from the sea and God's kingdom as 'one like a son of man, coming with the clouds of heaven'. If we apply the same sequence as in ch. 2, then the winged lion is Babylon, the bear with the ribs is Persia, the four-headed leopard is Greece (divided among Alexander's four generals), the monstrous persecuting beast is Rome, and the human empire is God's kingdom. (The same alternative application as in ch. 2, to Antiochus's persecution, is again popular.)

For Christians the human figure signifies several interrelated things, as well as the last kingdom. 'Son of man' was Jesus' favourite title for himself and he did come bringing God's kingdom in Roman times. However, Daniel's vision also looks forward to the end-time judgment when he will come again, on the clouds of heaven, finally to establish his kingdom for ever (cp. Matt. 24.30f).

Ch. 8: The ram and the goat.
Daniel is now granted a closer look at the history of the next two empires, the Persian (the ram) and the Greek (the goat; see vv. 20f). In the earlier visions he was only shown in a fairly general way that times of oppression were in store for his people, but now he sees something of what it will mean for them: cessation of sacrificial worship, desecration of the sanctuary, devastation and destruction among men. The persecution is to happen during the reign of one of the later Greek kings (who must this time be Antiochus Epiphanes), and though he is reassured that it will pass and the sanctuary will be reconsecrated, the horror of what he sees leaves him exhausted and appalled.

PROPHECY OF THE END AND HISTORY

Why does Daniel jump from the persecution of 168 BC directly to the end of history? Why does Jesus do the same in Matt. 24 with his prophecy of the fall of Jerusalem in 70 AD?

Each persecution is like a seismic tremor heralding others of similar pattern but of greater or less violence, all of them precursors of a final great cosmic shaking.

Prophets usually bring a message to their own generation about what is to happen soon and about God's eternal purposes, but not often about distant intermediate history. Hence they describe the first tremor in detail, and possibly a second, but discerning the eternal pattern beyond it, skip over other intermediate tremors to the final upheaval of which they are the forerunners.

Since the pattern repeats itself and foreshadows the end, persecution continues to bear the same stamp and those living through it can still take encouragement by applying the prophecies about 168 BC, or 70 AD, or the end, to their own times.

For the first time we are told the vision concerns 'the time of the end' (v. 17) and teaching about it intensifies as the book proceeds. As we have already noted, it relates to God's judgment in history.

Ch. 9: The seventy 'sevens'.
The date is 538 BC and Daniel is praying for the exile to end soon. Jeremiah had said it would last seventy years, and if Daniel was counting from the time of his own captivity in 605 BC, then sixty-seven of those years had already passed. Perhaps he was hoping for assurance that the return would indeed begin in the next three years, but instead is granted revelation about dating the end.

If we take the figures literally and not symbolically, as some do, then the seven 'sevens' are 49 years of rebuilding the city in troubled times and the sixty-two 'sevens' are the next 434 years 'until the Anointed One comes'. Assuming that the time of rebuilding referred to is that of Ezra and Nehemiah, and we date it from Ezra's return in 458 BC, then the total of sixty-nine 'sevens' takes us to 25 or 26 AD, very near the start of Jesus' ministry. The final 'seven' then covers the period when 'the Anointed One will be cut off' by the crucifixion, which is indeed 'to put an end to sin, to atone for wickedness, to bring in everlasting righteousness', and so forth (vv. 26,24). If this interpretation is correct, the final 'seven' must symbolise the whole period of the end-time kingdom of God from Christ onwards, covering the destruction of Jerusalem by the Romans in 70 AD as well. Then also an 'abomination that causes desolation' stood in the temple in the form of Roman standards stamped with the emperor's head (cp. Matt. 24.15-31). Once more the vision culminates in the final end of all history. (Others again relate this prophecy to Antiochus Epiphanes' persecutions in 168 BC.)

Chs. 10–12: The Last Battle.
Though ch. 10 is written as an introduction to the revelation in the next, it is interesting in its own right. It reminds us that there is a spiritual dimension to the events of earthly history. The heavenly messenger, whose description (vv. 5f) reminds us of John's vision of Christ in Rev. 1.12-16, tells Daniel that he has had to interrupt his battle with 'the prince of Persia', that after him comes 'the prince of Greece', and that only Michael, the guardian prince of the Jews, helps him in his fight (vv. 13,21).

Man may imagine he is in sole control of the affairs of earth, but he is not. Heaven is very much involved too and, as we shall soon see, in the end the two spheres will interact in a cataclysmic way. That is why it is so important to remember the lesson of chs. 1–6, that God is sovereign over the kingdoms of men.

In 11.2-35 the angelic figure forecasts the development of history through the Greek period in great detail (see above, pp. 113–116), prophesying the wars and the increasing build-up of tension that climax in the persecution of the Jews under Antiochus Epiphanes.

Then, in vv. 36-45 the vista quite suddenly changes and we move out beyond the reaches of history as we know it into sweeping images of 'the time of the end' (v. 35). Antiochus is no longer just the king of Syria, but begins to assume the proportions of an evil cosmic ruler who successfully vaunts himself against gods and men, and under whose rule persecution, corruption and oppression intensify (vv. 36-39).

When the King of the South tries to stop him he sweeps through his and other lands with apparently irresistible force, as though he would conquer the whole world. But then alarming reports from the east and north reach him and he turns back and pitches his royal tents in Judea, in preparation for what will be his and this world's last battle (vv. 40-45).

We are told nothing of the course of this last battle, only that the archangel Michael will be involved in it and there will be great distress on earth, though through it deliverance will come to the people of God. Clearly we are here being granted a glimpse into time beyond time. We have now left the historical Antiochus far behind. The vision speaks of the end of all things, the winding up of history, the resurrection of the dead and the final judgment. Very few details are given (12.1-5).

When Daniel asks his visitors about the date and timing of these things, he is again told they will be associated with times of persecution, but the figures he is given are apparently as mysterious to him as they are to us today. Even Jesus, when his disciples asked the same question, clearly said that such dates and times are known only to the Father and are not revealed to us (Matt. 24.3,36; Acts 1.6f).

The Purpose of the Book of Daniel.

As well as covering the latest period of Jewish history, Daniel may have been one of the latest Old Testament books to be published. The stories about Daniel and his friends in chs. 1–6 must certainly have been written down after his time. The style of his visions in chs. 7–12 imply that he wrote them down himself soon after he got them, but he was told that they were not to be published in his own time (12.4). The book as we now have it, with visions and biography combined, may even be as late as the second century, about the time of Antiochus' persecution, which would indeed have been the sort of occasion on which Daniel himself must have expected it to be published (12.9), as an encouragement to the persecuted in those days.

The message is clear: Every emperor has had to acknowledge God's power in the end. The Babylonians were slow to do so; the Persians did so from the start (chs. 1–6). God is Lord of all and his kingdom will never be destroyed—the Greeks will discover that truth too. God will not allow persecution to succeed in its aim, but will intervene at his appointed time to establish his kingdom. Imperial power has mere feet of clay in comparison with God's rock-like power (ch. 2), is merely bestial, rising out of the depths, in contrast with the human face of God's power, coming down from heaven (ch. 7). Man's oppression may succeed for a while, but God knows the course history must take (chs. 8–9). He is sovereign over the kingdoms of men and they have only two alternatives: either to bow before him, as Nebuchadnezzar had to, or meet him face to face, as Belshazzar had to and as Antiochus must.

Nevertheless, these historical confrontations are but foreshadowings of God's final showdown with earth's oppressing powers. Daniel saw in his visions that God's kingdom would be inaugurated in Roman times with the coming of an Anointed One, one like 'a son of man', and that it will culminate in a cosmic judgment at the time of the end, after which the faithful who have died will rise and join the righteous still living to 'shine like the brightness of the heavens, like the stars for ever and ever' (12.2f).

What better prophetic preparation could there have been for the birth of Christ and the dawning of the New Testament age?

10

The Glory of the Son of God

THE GOSPEL ACCORDING TO JOHN

One of the less welcome legacies of the post-exilic era, particularly of the Greek phase of it, was that Palestinian Judaism became split by sectarian divisions. As well as militant Zealots, we find Pharisees, Sadducees, Essenes and Samaritans. John, however, only mentions two of them and they alone need concern us here.

The Pharisees were exclusivists (the name means 'separated'). Ardent believers in holiness and righteousness, their approach to the law was strict, sometimes too strict and legalistic, judging by Jesus' repeated criticisms of them. They were also thoroughly spiritual in their beliefs, in contrast with the Sadducees who said 'that there is no resurrection, and that there are neither angels nor spirits' (Acts 23.8). Many therefore became Christians (including Paul), though some of the converts from among them found it difficult to abandon their exclusivist attitudes (Acts 15.5). Because they had a personal faith they survived 70 AD, unlike most of the other parties, and became the leaders of the Jews. It is probably because they were the main party left at the end of the first century when John was writing that in his Gospel Jesus' opponents are referred to either as 'Pharisees' or simply 'Jews' rather than by other sectarian titles that were becoming obsolete. By 200AD Judaism and Pharisaism had become synonymous.

The Samaritans were descendants of the peoples resettled by the Assyrians around Samaria after 722 BC, but they only properly emerge as a separate religious group in the fourth century, when they built their own temple on Mount Gerizim, opposite Shechem. It was destroyed about 128 by the Hasmonean king, John Hyrcanus, but Gerizim remained their holy mountain (John 4.20). The only Scripture they recognise as sacred is their own version of the Pentateuch. We know little about their beliefs in Jesus' time, but many of them seem to have responded to the gospel. A tiny community survives today.

Alongside the sects of Judaism a new movement began to make its presence felt both in Palestine and abroad. At first it was known as 'The Way' (Acts 9.2), but before long its followers became known as 'Christians' (Acts 11.26). It proclaimed that the long period of waiting since the prophets had foretold a New Covenant was over. The promised new age had dawned with the birth of Jesus, a carpenter from Nazareth, whom they recognised as the expected Messiah (Greek: *Christos*). He had been executed as a blasphemer, but God had raised him to new life. They believed his death had sacrificial power for the forgiveness of all sin and that those who put faith in him would receive God's Holy Spirit.

Their preaching proved most effective in making converts, particularly since it was accompanied by a startling display of miraculous signs and wonders, so much so that persecution soon broke out against them. That, however, only resulted in further growth, as Christians in flight took their gospel to new towns and districts. Within thirty years they were to be found in almost every part of the Roman Empire.

About that time accounts of Jesus' life and ministry were beginning to appear in writing (the Gospels of Matthew, Mark and Luke). Letters by Paul, an apostle and evangelist of the faith, were also being read widely in the churches and cherished for their teaching, as were various letters written by other church leaders.

What Jews and many others found hardest to accept about this new movement was its teaching that Jesus was more than a great prophet or leader, but that he was also Son of God. Christians actually acclaimed this crucified 'criminal' as King and worshipped him as Lord. To Jews that was tantamount to blasphemy (or as Paul says, 'a stumbling-block'), to more rationalistic Gentiles it was simply foolishness, but to those enlightened by the Spirit, it was God's own wisdom and power (1 Cor. 1.23-25). It was mainly to help enquirers see this truth about Jesus that John's Gospel was written (cp. John 20.31).

John, the beloved disciple.

The Gospel refers to its author anonymously as 'the disciple whom Jesus loved' (21.20,24). He is mentioned as present at the Last Supper (13.23), the crucifixion (19.26f) and the resurrection appearance by the Sea of Galilee (21.7), and is probably the same as the equally anonymous 'other disciple' who, along with Andrew, followed Jesus from the start (1.35f), was known to the high priest and gained admission for Peter to his house at the time of Jesus' trial (18.15f) and went with Peter to the tomb on the resurrection morning (20.3). Since the second century it has been taught that this was in fact the apostle John, son of Zebedee, one of the inner circle of Jesus' disciples, along with Peter, Andrew and his own brother, James, and that he wrote his Gospel at the end of the first century by which time he was an old man living in Ephesus.

John's Gospel and the Synoptics.

Even the briefest glance at his Gospel shows how different it is from the Synoptics (the other three).

1. *It contains stories not told by the others*, such as:
   * Jesus' miracle at the wedding in Cana (2.1-11),
   * his conversations with Nicodemus (3.1-21),
   * and with the woman at the well of Samaria (4.1-29),
   * the healing of the paralytic at the pool of Bethesda (5.1-15),
   * the raising of Lazarus (11.1-44),
   * the washing of the disciples' feet (13.1-17),
   * the appearance to Mary Magdalene in the garden (20.10-18),
   * to doubting Thomas in the upper room (20.24-9)
   * and to seven disciples by the Sea of Galilee (ch. 21).

2. *It omits some of the most significant events of the other gospels*, such as the stories of:
   * Jesus' birth • his baptism • his temptation • the transfiguration • his agony in Gethsemane and • the institution of the Lord's Supper.

3. *It gives a different presentation of Jesus' teaching.*
   * There are no parables and very few short sayings, but

several long discussions and discourses, mostly of a deeper theological nature than we find in the Synoptics.

- Jesus makes no attempt to conceal his Messianic calling, but rather speaks openly about his eternal character as Son of God from the very start.
- Jesus gives almost no teaching on the kingdom and none on repentance, both so central to his message in the other gospels (cp. Matt. 4.17), but instead much about light, love, truth, rebirth, abiding, believing and other similar concepts which are not so central in them.

There are other differences that can be listed, but they should not be thought of as a challenge to our faith in the accuracy and truth of John's Gospel. If we adopt that approach to them we shall miss the whole point of what John is trying to teach us in his Gospel. It is best to read it as an independent, additional witness to Jesus' life and ministry and in so doing to recognise that what John wants us to learn about Jesus is different from what the others do.

Thus there are some details that John seems to put in a different place. But rather than regarding these as contradicting the Synoptics' accounts, they can be viewed as shedding additional light on some of the events of Jesus' and the disciples' lives.

- The call of some of the apostles is associated with John the Baptist some months before they left their fishing businesses, but that only shows they had already been introduced to Jesus and helps to explain why they so readily left all to follow him when he eventually called them to do so (1.35-42; Mark 1.16-20).
- The cleansing of the temple is set at the beginning of Jesus' ministry instead of at the end, but then if there were actually two purgings rather than one, we can understand all the better why his last one generated the murderous anger it did (2.12-25; Mark 11.18).
- According to John, Jesus' ministry in Jerusalem did not all happen in the last week of his life, but also during three earlier visits, but that would explain several things, for example, why Jesus once said, 'O Jerusalem, Jerusalem … how often I have longed to gather your children together, as a hen gathers her chicks under her

wings, but you were not willing!' (Luke 13.34)
- John places the story of Peter's miraculous catch of fish after the resurrection instead of at the time of his call, but that may show us only that his reinstatement involved a total reliving of his original call experience (21.1-14; Luke 5.1-11).

Such differences apart, John does in fact tell the same general story as the others and reproduces many of the same main features of it:
- the record of John the Baptist • the healing of an official's son • accounts of controversy between Jesus and his enemies • the feeding of the five thousand • the walking on the water • the anointing • the triumphal entry to Jerusalem • the last supper • the arrest • the trial • the crucifixion • the resurrection.

The accounts are in essence the same and many attempts have been made to produce harmonisations of them, but though it is an interesting enough exercise trying to do so, it is not one that will occupy our time here. Our concern for the moment must be to focus on the differences rather than the similarities, particularly with respect to John's portrait of Jesus. In so doing it is worth remembering that Matthew, Mark and Luke also differ from each other to some degree in their presentations of his life and ministry.

John's portrait of Jesus.
Mark portrays Jesus as a man of faith, authority and action, Matthew presents him as the Messianic King ushering in the kingdom of God, Luke emphasises the charismatic and prophetic aspects of his ministry. All of these, whilst recognising his divinity, tend in the first instance to highlight and focus attention on the activities of Jesus as a man. They are essentially records of the life and ministry of the carpenter's son from Galilee, written to show why we should believe in him as Messiah, Saviour and Son of God. The revelation of that deeper truth unfolds itself to the disciples and the crowds only gradually.

John's perspective is entirely different. He invites us from the beginning to view the divine light that shines in and through this man, to behold 'his glory, the glory of the one and only Son who came from the Father, full of grace and truth' (1.14). Hence his starting-point is not with Jesus' birth, but before creation itself.

1. INTRODUCTION (CH. 1)

John's desire is that we should perceive Jesus' glory, and so believe and find life in him. To highlight that glory he emphasises a number of important key words and concepts that we need to look at briefly in the course of our study, all of which he introduces in his prologue in 1.1-18. To avoid interrupting the flow of our reading too much, his use of these words is outlined in separate boxes scattered throughout this chapter. It would be worth casting a glance over them now before reading beyond 1.18.

1.1-18: The incarnation of the Son of God.

'In the beginning', when God created the heavens and the earth, all was darkness, but then God uttered his word, 'Let there be light,' and there was light. This light was not that of sun, moon or stars, for they were not yet created. No, rather it was the primordial, uncreated light of God himself that will still be shining in the end-time when sun and moon are no more (Rev. 21.23; 22.5). When it shone forth into pre-creation darkness it was as if the Master Craftsman had turned on a light in his cosmic workshop to enable him to perform his handiwork. And in the brilliance of that light creation sprang to life as God continued to utter his word (Gen. 1).

That remains God's creative way of dealing with darkness. We see it today in the process of conversion, for then, when God is about to create new life in us, he first speaks his word to us, perhaps through a sermon or a testimony, and that causes his light to shine in our personal darkness, which in turn leads to us finding our new life in him. God, after all, is light (1 John 1.5), and so it is only by his light entering the chaotic mess of our lives that he will ever sort us out (cp. 2 Cor. 4.6). Such also was his way of working when he sent Christ to recreate our world held by the darkness of sin.

SON OF GOD

John's Gospel discusses more fully than the others what it means for Jesus to be 'Son of God'.

Firstly, it means that he shares his Father's divine nature and that his life on earth is a continuation of a Sonship that has existed from eternity: *He was with God in the beginning* and is *the one and only Son who came from the Father* (1.2,14). Indeed his union with the Father is so close that he can say: *I and the Father are one* (10.30).

He is therefore the complete revelation of the Father: *No-one has ever seen God, but God the only Son, who is at the Father's side, has made him known* (1.18). *If you really knew me,* he said to Thomas, *you would know my Father as well* (14.7).

Such Sonship requires his complete obedience to the Father's will: *the Son can do nothing by himself; he can do only what he sees his Father doing* (5.19).

We too can experience the Fatherhood of God, but only through union with him: *to all who received him, to those who believed in his name, he gave the right to become children of God* (1.12).

And for those who do believe Jesus prays that they may know the same personal intimacy with the Father as he does: *that all of them may be one, Father, just as you are in me and I am in you. May they also be in us* (17.21).

It is only John that calls Jesus 'the Word', here, in 1 John 1.1 and in Rev. 19.13, but the same identification underlies Heb. 1.1-3, where it is said that while in the past God spoke through prophets and in other ways, 'in these last days he has spoken to us by his Son'. The word of God continues to be active in these 'other ways' today, but it has also now taken a more tangible and personal form, by coming to live among us and communicate with us in the 'flesh' of Jesus.

A word is a thought that has been given expression. God's Word is therefore his thought given expression and so is closely associated with his Wisdom that was also active in creation (Prov. 8) and finally in Christ (Col. 1.15-20; 2.3). His Wisdom is the content of his mind, his Word is the utterance of his Wisdom. With the coming of Jesus, his Wisdom which had hitherto contemplated men and creation from afar and his Word which had reached out to us from eternity through the moving of his Spirit in prophetic men, now comes among us in bodily form. In Christ there lodged the whole content of God's mind concerning men and all that he purposed to communicate with us. In other words, as we read and think about Jesus, we shall learn all we will ever need to know about what God wants to say to us.

As at creation, God's Word still causes 'life' to spring forth. John's Gospel speaks much of this life (esp. in chs. 3–6). It is found in Jesus, it is what he offers to all who believe in him, and it gives them 'light'. Consider what happens when a man is converted or baptised in the Spirit: a new life springs up within him, a new light shines in his face. That is what Jesus is speaking about when he says those who receive him will themselves have light (8.12) and become 'sons of light' (12.36)—naturally so, for they will be 'born of God'—and this is the very light of God himself (1.4-13).

It is this light of life in Jesus that is the 'glory' God wants to reveal to us through his Son, full of grace and truth. John himself saw it and he wants us to see it too (vv. 14-18). It is as though he bids us look at Jesus in much the same way as we would look at a stained glass window, not just to see the crafted glass, but to see also the sun that shines through it giving it its coloured splendour. Look at Jesus, yes, but look also at the light of God that shines through him making him what he is. Once you see that, then you lay hold of his grace and truth for yourself, of his light and life, of the very life of God, and at that point you believe and become a new man, born of God.

Note that this being born of God, or becoming his children, is not the natural right of every man, but is offered only to those who believe in Jesus. All men are God's creatures, but not all men are his sons. Only Jesus has the right to call God 'Father', but he confers the same privilege on those who come to believe in Jesus. To the Jews such talk was blasphemy (5.18).

In ch. 3 our being born of God is said to be the work of the Spirit, which is what Paul says too in Rom. 8.14-16 and Gal. 4.4-7, where he points out that it is by the Spirit's working we recognise our sonship and cry '*Abba*, Father'. This association of the Spirit and sonship is also seen clearly in the story of Jesus' own baptism in the other gospels,

---

LIGHT

Jesus brings 'light' into a world of darkness. *In him was life, and that life was the light of men. The light shines in the darkness, but the darkness has not understood it* (1.4f).

Before him another light shone for a while in John, but only to prepare for his coming. Jesus said of him, *John was a lamp that burned and gave light, and you chose for a time to enjoy his light* (5.35). But John *himself was not the light; he came only as a witness to the light. The true light that gives light to every man was coming into the world* (1.8f).

But the light is not just *in* Jesus; he *is* the light. And those who receive him find light and life for themselves. *I am the light of the world. Whoever follows me will never walk in darkness, but will have the light of life* (8.12; cp. 9.5). *I have come into the world as a light, so that no-one who believes in me should stay in darkness* (12.46).

Many, however, reject his light, because it shows up their own evil ways and brings them under judgment. *The light has come into the world, but men loved darkness instead of light because their deeds were evil. Everyone who does evil hates the light, and will not come into the light for fear that his deeds will be exposed* (3.19-21).

Those that do receive his light get lit up themselves, like little candles from a big one, and become *sons of light*, and so continue his work of being light in the world after he is gone from among them. *You are going to have the light just a little while longer. Walk while you have the light, before darkness overtakes you. Put your trust in the light while you have it, so that you may become sons of light* (12.35f; cp. Matt. 5.14-16).

---

where it is at the point of the Spirit's descent he hears his Father say the words 'my beloved son'. Again this teaching is not just doctrinal, but relates to our experience of God, as many have discovered after conversion and baptism in the Holy Spirit.

Indeed the whole of John's prologue speaks about our experience of God. The life in Jesus was not just 'the light', but 'the light *of men*' (v. 4). The whole point of Jesus' coming was, not simply to help us understand God's ways a bit better, but that we might ourselves have the light and the life. And, as we have already seen, that only happens through *believing*. John uses the word more than ninety times. Believing in Jesus is the only way to receiving God's life, perceiving the truth, being born of God, seeing his glory. In reading through the rest of the Gospel it is important to remember that. John has written precisely 'that you may believe that Jesus is the Christ, the Son of God, and that by believing you may have life in his name.' (20.31) Read it that way yourself now—so that you look for the glory in Jesus, believe in him, know you are born of God, and that you do have life in his name.

1.19-51: The unveiling of the Son of God.

John's Gospel, like the others, begins with the ministry of John the Baptist. Though we are told that he baptised, he is never actually called 'the Baptist' in this Gospel. Indeed he refuses to recognise any of the titles men want to give him. We know that Jesus recognised him as Elijah, the forerunner of his coming prophesied by Malachi (Matt. 11.14; Mal. 3.1; 4.5), but John thinks of himself as no more than 'the voice of one calling', preparing the way for the Lord. He is simply a witness (vv. 6f) come to 'testify that this is the Son of God' (v. 34). Jesus says he 'was a lamp that burned and gave light' for a time (5.35), but John knew that once Jesus' ministry was launched, his own function was completed, and so we later hear him say, 'He must become greater; I must become less' (3.30). His calling was simply to prepare for and point to Jesus in the beginning.

In keeping with this picture of John as witness, we are given his testimony about Jesus' baptism, rather than an account of the baptism itself. The purpose of this testimony is to point to Jesus as 'the Son of God', but in it he makes two statements that amount to a complete description of the purpose of Jesus' ministry, indeed of God's total purpose in his dealings with men since the fall of Adam: firstly that Jesus is 'the Lamb of God, who takes away the sin of the world', and secondly that it is 'he who will baptise with the Holy Spirit' (vv. 29-34).

In the Garden of Eden there were two special trees: the tree of the knowledge of good and evil and the tree of life. For partaking of the one man needs forgiveness, driven from the garden he has lost access to the other. The Bible's story tells how God has been putting all that right, through his promises to the patriarchs, through the preaching of the prophets, and so forth, but much more fully through Jesus. In the New Heaven at the end of time the matter will have been finally dealt with and man will again have free access to the tree of life (Rev. 22.1-3). In the meantime, Jesus has come that we 'may have life' (John 10.10), and that is granted, first by putting us right by the taking away of sin through the sacrifice of the cross and secondly by the infusion of God's life through baptism in the Holy Spirit.

Calling Jesus 'the Lamb of God' links him immediately with Passover. Just as the blood of a lamb on the sides and tops of their door-frames secured protection for the Israelites when the angel of death passed over and resulted in their salvation from the bondage of the Egyptians (Exod. 12.7), so now the blood of Jesus, the new Passover Lamb, secures our protection from the wrath of God and results in our salvation from bondage to sin (cp. 1 Cor. 5.7). The difference is that in Moses' time that salvation was only for Israel, whereas now it is to 'take away the sin of the world'. As we read on we shall see just how important Passover is in the drama of Christ's life as presented in John's Gospel.

John the Baptist's testimony speaks about Jesus being 'revealed to Israel' (v. 31). The other Gospels give more the impression that Jesus' baptism was an occasion of empowering for ministry, not unlike our own frequent experience of baptism in the Spirit today. John's intention, however, is that we should see unveiled the full glory of his God-ness that was there already from the beginning. It is, of course, possible to think similarly about our experience of baptism in the Spirit, that it is a drawing out or releasing of what is already there from the moment of conversion and first confession of faith. Paul also speaks of an experience of unveiling of glory in relation to receiving the Spirit in 2 Cor. 3.12-18 (cp. Rom. 8.18f). Anyhow, as Jesus' baptism in the Synoptics leads to a ministry of miracles that demonstrate the power of the Spirit at work in him, so in John it leads to a ministry of miracles that are signs of and that reveal his glory (cp. 2.11).

In the other gospels the disciples only gradually realise who Jesus is (cp. Mark 8.27-30). Here recognition is immediate, triggered off by John's testimony. Andrew sees he is Messiah, Nathanael even acclaims him 'Son of God'. But as the story progresses it becomes clear that the rate of revelation was not uniform among the disciples. Peter's confession comes at the end of ch. 6, Philip still has problems about believing at the Last Supper (14.8-11) and Thomas only believes after the resurrection (20.24-9).

In both the earlier cases the recognition follows an invitation to 'come and see' (1.39,46). That, of course, is the invitation extended by the whole Gospel, for it is only by seeing that we shall 'believe' and in doing so behold Christ's glory (1.14; see also 6.40; 12.44f).

On the relationship between the call stories here and in the Synoptics, see above, p. 133.

2. JESUS' PUBLIC MINISTRY (CHS. 2–12)

In these chapters we see Jesus make three round trips from Galilee to Jerusalem, apparently corresponding to three seasons of ministry. The other Gospels tell about his ministry in Galilee in one continuous block of narrative and end with an account of his last week in Jerusalem. In John's presentation as much of the action happens in and around Jerusalem as in Galilee.

First season (chs. 2–3)
- 1.43 – 2.12: in Galilee, at Cana (2.1) and Capernaum (2.12),
- 2.13 – 4.2: in Jerusalem (2.13) and the Judean countryside (3.22).

Second season (chs. 4–5)
- 4.3-54: in Samaria, at Sychar (4.4f), and Galilee, at Cana (4.46),
- 5.1-47: in Jerusalem, at first by the pool of Bethesda (5.2).

Third season (chs. 6–12)
- 6.1 – 7.1: by the Sea of Galilee, on the far shore (6.1) and in Capernaum (6.17),
- 7.2 – 12.50: in Jerusalem, particularly at the temple (7.14;

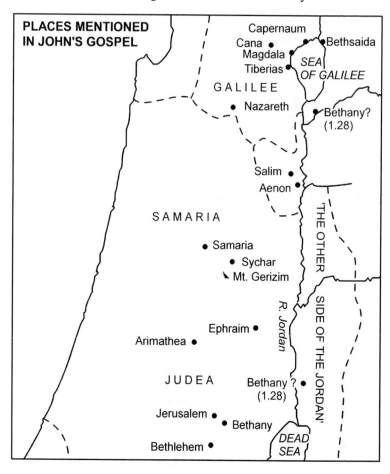

PLACES MENTIONED IN JOHN'S GOSPEL

Capernaum
Cana ●   ● Bethsaida
Magdala
Tiberias ●   *SEA OF GALILEE*
GALILEE
● Nazareth   ● Bethany? (1.28)
Salim ●
Aenon ●
SAMARIA
● Samaria
● Sychar
↖ Mt. Gerizim
R. Jordan
'THE OTHER SIDE OF THE JORDAN'
Ephraim ●
Arimathea ●
JUDEA   Bethany ? ● (1.28)
Jerusalem ●
● Bethany
Bethlehem ●   *DEAD SEA*

8.2; 10.22f), then away from the city in Transjordan (10.40),
then in Bethany (11.1), Ephraim (11.54), Bethany (12.1) and
finally back in Jerusalem for the last time (12.12).

Jesus' visits to Jerusalem are all associated with festivals.
He goes up the first time for Passover (2.13), the second for
'a feast of the Jews' (5.1) and the third for Tabernacles
(7.2). As Messiah his ministry must relate to every Jewish
festival, but since he is 'the Lamb of God', it is particularly
important to note what he did at Passover time. Three
Passovers are mentioned: at the first he cleared the temple

JESUS' SEVEN SIGNS
1. He changes water to wine (2.1-11).
2. He heals a royal official's son (4.46-54).
3. He heals an invalid by the pool of Bethesda (5.1-15).
4. He feeds the five thousand (6.1-15).
5. He walks on the water (6.16-21).
6. He heals a man born blind (9.1-41).
7. He raises Lazarus from the dead (11.1-44).

(2.13), at the second he fed the multitude in Galilee (6.4), at the third he was crucified (12.1 – 19.42). In clearing the temple he was preparing the place of the altar for his sacrifice; in feeding the five thousand he spoke about the bread of life, about eating his flesh and drinking his blood and about eternal life, thus preparing for the institution of his new Passover memorial meal, what we today call Communion; and, of course, in his crucifixion he offered the final Passover sacrifice for the taking away of the sin of the world. Jesus knew 'his time'. As the Lamb of God he had to die at Passover time, not before and not after.

While these various visits and themes run through this section and make up the skeleton that holds it together, the more immediate teaching is firstly about the 'life' that Jesus brings (especially in chs. 3–6), and secondly about his claims concerning himself (mainly in chs. 7–11), whilst overarching the whole is the theme of the revealing of his 'glory'.

Ch. 2: Jesus starts his ministry and begins to reveal his glory.

John records seven miracles, though in 20.30 he admits there were many more altogether. He calls them 'signs', because they are pointers for faith to the divinity that lies behind the flesh of Jesus: by them Jesus 'revealed his glory' so that men could 'put their faith in him' (2.11; cp. 2.23; 11.40). This self-revelation began hesitantly (2.4), but by the end of his public ministry Jesus looks forward with total assurance to the cross as the final unveiling of his glory (12.23-50).

It is important to note that, while his disciples saw his glory and believed, and many saw other signs and also believed (v. 23), there were plenty who saw nothing and even came demanding signs to prove his authority (v. 18). But Jesus was no wonder-worker using magical powers. A magician performs tricks to order; the work of Jesus is appreciated only through eyes of faith (cp. Mark 6.4-6).

Chs. 3–6: Jesus teaches about the life he brings.
The key to understanding these chapters is found in Jesus' words in 10.10: 'I have come that they may have life, and have it to the full.'

Ch. 3: First a man must be born again.
Jesus explains the starting point to Nicodemus, the point of entry into this life he offers, namely the birth of our spirit by the power of God's Spirit working within us (vv. 5-6).

Nicodemus has already come to some measure of belief, for he recognises the hand of God in Jesus' ministry (v. 2), and Jesus offers him the chance to enter into the livingness of what he has glimpsed. In doing that he introduces us to the need to be 'born again ... of the Spirit'. By natural birth we are born of flesh, but God is Spirit and so we cannot experience his life unless our spirit first comes alive. As nothing can give birth to flesh but flesh, so nothing can give birth to spirit except spirit, and that means God's Spirit. The experience is exactly the same as being 'born of God' (1.13). After the flesh we have a human father, after the spirit we can have God as our Father (1.12f). That, of course, is itself a result of believing, of openness to allowing God's Spirit to enter our lives and perform this work in us.

Nicodemus is puzzled, just as many still are today, for it is difficult to understand spiritual things without experiencing them for ourselves, but Jesus assures him he is speaking of what can be normal Christian experience, not something exceptional or unearthly (vv. 11f). If we grasp that fact, we will begin to appreciate what happened through and to Jesus himself, the Son of Man, that he was sent of God in his love to bring life through his death to all who believe, to give them light and truth (though many will not like that at all).

TWO WORLDS

In the Synoptic Gospels Jesus speaks much about 'the kingdom of God/heaven', but in John very little. Apart from telling Nicodemus how to see and enter the kingdom of God in 3.3,5, he only speaks of it again in 18.36, where he assures Pilate, *My kingdom is not of this world ... my kingdom is from another place.* However, the distinction between 'this world' and 'another place' runs through the rest of the Gospel, but is often spoke of in different language, which generally points to the fact that this world is at enmity with God (7.7; 15.18), ruled over by Satan (*the prince of this world*, 12.31; 14.30; 16.11) and in need of salvation. But God sent his Son for that purpose, because he loves the world (1.29; 3.16; 4.42; 6.33).

'Below and Above':
   Jesus says, *You are from below; I am from above. You are of this world; I am not of this world* (8.23).
   Jesus *comes down* from heaven and *ascends* to heaven (3.13; 6.33,41,50f,58,62; 20.17).

'Darkness and Light':
   John says, *The light shines in the darkness, but the darkness has not understood it* (1.5).
   Jesus says, *I am the light of the world. Whoever follows me will never walk in darkness, but will have the light of life* (8.12; cp. 9.5; 11.9; 12.35,46).

'Flesh and Spirit':
   Jesus says, *Unless a man is born of water and the Spirit, he cannot enter the kingdom of God. Flesh gives birth to flesh, but the Spirit gives birth to spirit ... You must be born again* (3.5-7).
   And again, *The Spirit gives life; the flesh counts for nothing* (6.63).

15.26f and 16.13f tell further how the Spirit helps us to appreciate Jesus more fully.

John the Baptist confirms that what Jesus is doing and saying is true. He therefore urges his own disciples to believe in him, if they would receive his gift of eternal life for themselves, and warns them that if they do not, then God's wrath must remain on them (vv.32-36). What Jesus brings is not just something it might be nice to have, but something essential and urgently important.

Ch. 4: The gift of God is living water welling up to eternal life.

In his conversation with the woman at the well Jesus says the life he offers will become in us 'a spring of water welling up to eternal life' (v. 14). He is, of course, alluding to the free flow of the Spirit in our lives (cp. 7.37-9), and that is why one of the first notable effects he mentions is a new relationship with God in worship, one that is 'in spirit and in truth' (v. 24). The phrase speaks of us knowing both the life-giving power of the Spirit working in us and also the truth of God's self-revelation in Jesus. The two are closely interrelated, because it is the Spirit that reveals Jesus (15.26; 16.14) and it is Jesus who gives the Spirit (7.36-9). Hence the Spirit is sometimes called 'the Spirit of truth' (14.17).

We now see Jesus rejoice at the response to his teaching and at the prospect of a plentiful harvest for eternal life in Samaria (vv. 32-8). The grounds for his hope are quite simply the measure of belief he has found there and his hope is fully vindicated as he watches more and more Samaritans believing (vv. 39-42).

Back in Galilee, his teaching finds confirmation in the healing of an official's son. Jesus tells him his son will 'live' and he takes him at his word. The resultant miracle then creates further belief in this man's household (vv. 43-54). The message is clear; it has been emphasised again and again throughout these last two chapters: that God's life in Jesus is obtained by believing.

Ch. 5: Whoever hears Jesus' words and believes has eternal life.

Back in Jerusalem, another healing leads to further conversations about Jesus' life-giving mission and again the theme is that the life he offers is obtained only by believing in him (vv. 24f,39f).

Interwoven with this general theme are two others, both of them highlighting particular aspects of it. Firstly, Jesus points out that he received his mission from his Father and that he can do nothing in it apart from what the Father commissions. Believing must therefore be more than just believing in Jesus himself, but also in the Father who sent

---

WITNESS

John identifies various 'witnesses' that 'testify' to Jesus' divine Sonship.

Firstly there is John (the Baptist). *He came as a witness to testify concerning that light, so that through him all men might believe. He himself was not the light; he came only as a witness to the light* (1,7f; cp. 1.15; 5.33,36).

Secondly there are Jesus' own disciples. To them he says, *You also must testify, for you have been with me from the beginning* (15.27).

And then the Scriptures witness to him: *You diligently study the Scriptures because you think that by them you possess eternal life. These are the Scriptures that testify about me* (5.39; cp. 5.46).

Jesus also speaks of his work and his miracles as witnesses. That is why John calls them 'signs', because they are pointers to who Jesus is. *The very work that the Father has given me to finish, and which I am doing, testifies that the Father has sent me* (5.36; cp. 10.25).

Jesus is, of course, his own witness: *Even if I testify on my own behalf, my testimony is valid, for I know where I came from and where I am going* (8.14; cp. 3.11).

But he also insists that his testimony is not just his own and that his Father witnesses with him: *I am one who testifies for myself; my other witness is the one who sent me—the Father* (8.18; cp. 5.31,37).

Then finally there is the witness of the Spirit. *When the Counsellor comes, whom I will send to you from the Father, the Spirit of truth who goes out from the Father, he will testify about me ... he will guide you into all truth ... He will bring glory to me* (15.26; 16.13f).

---

him (vv. 16-30).

The second theme concerns witnesses: John the Baptist, Jesus' own works, the Father and the Scriptures all testify to Jesus' life-giving power, but in the end of the day the only way we shall have that life is by coming to receive it from Jesus himself (vv. 31-40).

Ch. 6: Jesus is bread from heaven giving us life.
Two further miracles in Galilee, feeding the five thousand (vv. 1-15) and walking on the water (vv. 16-24), lead to Jesus teaching that he is 'the bread of life', or 'the bread of

God (that) comes down from heaven and gives life to the world', giving total satisfaction to man's hunger and thirst and assuring him of eternal life and resurrection at the last day (vv. 32-40).

Again belief is essential. That is stressed several times, but nowhere more forcefully than in vv. 28f, where Jesus, asked what works God requires us to do, answers, 'The work of God is this: to believe in the one he has sent.' Many say that cannot be all there is to it and quote passages like James 2.14-26 which speaks about faith without works being dead. But the works of which James speaks are those that arise out of faith, and is it not said in Heb. 11.6 that 'without faith it is impossible to please God'? Paul says the Jews miss the salvation that should be theirs by faith in Jesus because in their zeal for God they try to establish their own righteousness by their works (Rom. 10.1-3).

Some of the ways Jesus expresses himself in this chapter may seem offensive to unbelievers, particularly when he says it is essential to eat his flesh and drink his blood, but he does explain that the message is spiritual: 'The Spirit gives life; the flesh counts for nothing. The words I have spoken to you are spirit and they are life' (vv. 53-63).

One delightful little scene highlights the dynamic power of Jesus' life-giving ministry. In vv. 22-24 we read about the length the crowd went to to be with him. We see people today go to similar lengths when they know there is revival to be found at the end of their journey. But then, revival is about life, about bringing life back into the dead. The repeated message of John's Gospel is that that revival life is found in Jesus and nowhere else.

Peter's acknowledgment of Jesus and 'the Holy One of God' at the end of the chapter echoes his confession at Caesarea Philippi in the other Gospels (cp. Matt. 16.13-20), after which Jesus set out on his last journey to Jerusalem. Here also he goes up for the last time and the rest of the Gospel is set in and around Jerusalem.

Chs. 7–11: Recognising Jesus as the Christ.
The life-giving work of Jesus remains a prominent theme, but the overall emphasis shifts as people now question and debate his identity with increasing heatedness, as some

LIFE

Life is not just a quickening of the natural life in man, but is a gift from God, and so Jesus speaks of *the bread of God ... who comes down from heaven and gives life to the world* (6.33).

Hence it is called *eternal life* (6.27,40,47,54,68).

It resides in Jesus, who therefore says of himself, *I am the bread of life* (6.35), and even, *I am the life* (14.6).

But he acknowledges that he derives this life from his Father: *For as the Father has life in himself, so he has granted the Son to have life in himself* (5.26).

Jesus' mission is therefore to impart this divine life to men: *I have come that they may have life, and have it to the full* (10.10).

That, indeed, is why John wrote his gospel in the first place: *that you may believe that Jesus is the Christ, the Son of God, and that by believing you may have life in his name* (20.31).

(John's use of the word 'life' is discussed more fully in the commentary on chs. 3–6.)

recognise and others reject him.

Ch. 7: Can this be the Christ?

At Caesarea Philippi, when Jesus asked his disciples who people said he was, their answer indicated a variety of opinions (Matt. 16.13f). In this chapter John shows us something of the debates that lay behind that variety. But it was also at that time that Jesus first showed his own awareness of another more sinister opinion, that he should be put to death (v. 1; cp. Matt. 16.21). These debates lead us to the cross.

He therefore goes secretly to Jerusalem, but people are already discussing him everywhere (vv. 1-13). When he does show up they express amazement at his learning, though he says it is all from God, and that it is not appreciated by everyone, for there are those who want to kill him. One miracle performed on the Sabbath in particular has aroused considerable anger against him (vv. 14-24). The nonsense of it all is that they really know where he is from (vv. 25-9).

The temple guard is sent to arrest him, but many put their faith in him, and so once more he offers them life. Some

JESUS' SEVEN I AM'S
1. I am the bread of life. (6.35,48) 2. I am the light of the world. (8.12; 9.5) 3. I am the gate for the sheep. (10.7) 4. I am the good shepherd. (10.11,14) 5. I am the resurrection and the life. (11.25) 6. I am the way and the truth and the life. (14.6) 7. I am the (true) vine. (15.1,5)
Also: ... believe that I am he ... know that I am he. (8.24,28) Before Abraham was born, I am! (8.58)

respond, but opinion is still deeply divided (vv. 30-44). Meanwhile the temple guards are so moved by his teaching that they find they cannot arrest him, but the Pharisees say Jesus has deceived them. Nicodemus pleads for him to be allowed a hearing, but they round on him too (vv. 45-53).

At the beginning of this new phase in Jesus' ministry he rejects the temptation to seek publicity by man's ways of self-promotion (vv. 3-9). He knows the Father will glorify him (8.54)—at the right time (7.6). The same principles should be governing Christian leaders and churches today, but sadly too many choose the way Jesus' brothers recommended, and their advice, we are told, rose out of unbelief!

Ch. 8: Jesus is the light of the world.
Jesus again teaches about life, now proclaiming he is 'the light of the world' (v. 12). In the debates that follow he says that with life he also offers knowledge of the Father (v. 19), forgiveness of sin (v. 24), knowledge of the truth (v. 32), freedom from sin (vv. 31-6), and release from death (v. 51).

Running through these discussions is the constant thread of Jesus' awareness of impending death, that among his hearers are those who will see him killed. Hence he repeatedly draws very sharp contrasts: light and darkness (v. 12), knowledge and ignorance (vv. 14,19), above and below (v. 23), not understanding and believing (vv. 17-31), sons of Abraham/God and sons of the devil (vv. 31-47), the bondage of slavery and freedom of sonship (vv. 34-6), falsehood and truth (vv. 44f), God and Satan (vv. 42-7), honouring God and speaking as one demon-possessed (vv. 48-51).

In Jesus' mission the contrasts are clear. There is God, the world, and no grey in-between. Similarly there is no camouflaging his own identity. He works in harmony with the Father and in obedience to his will (vv. 14-18,28f, 49,54), but even more than that, he is himself from eternity: 'Before Abraham was born, I am!' (v. 58). This stark 'I am' echoes God's own words to Moses at the burning bush (Exod. 3.14), and the 'I am he' of vv. 24,28 (see NIV footnote) echoes God's self-definition in Isa. 46.4; 48.12. For the time being his claim may seem to some exaggerated and even blasphemous, but its truth will be revealed at the cross (v. 28). Jesus has absolute faith about that, and so sees no need whatsoever to glorify himself (v. 54; cp. 7.2-9).

Ch. 9: Jesus gives sight to the blind.
As a sign of the truth of his claim to be the life-giving 'light of the world' (vv. 3-5) Jesus heals a man born blind. The debate about him now waxes even hotter, and judgment begins to operate, separating believers from unbelievers (v. 39).

Here again we see why John calls the miracles 'signs', for in this one 'the work of God (is) displayed' (v. 3). Judgment comes into the discussion because this 'work' is only recognised by believing and refusal to believe implies that Jesus, and therefore God, is a liar.

Ch. 10: Jesus is the good shepherd.
Perhaps because of growing opposition and threat of persecution, Jesus assures the believers of his protective care: he is 'the good shepherd'; he knows his sheep and will even lay down his life for them; he has come that they may have life (vv. 1-13).

His ministry thus far has been entirely among the Jews, but now he speaks of 'other sheep' that will listen to his voice. Already he is looking beyond the cross to the resurrection ministry among the rest of mankind (vv. 14-18).

While his teaching brings peace to believers, to unbelievers it seems madness, and so again we find a sharp division. The hostility becomes violent and Jesus withdraws into Transjordan (vv. 19-42).

Ch. 11: Jesus is the resurrection and the life. He is the Christ!

The debate about Jesus' identity reaches its climax as he performs the final sign that demonstrates his Messianic life-giving power: the raising of Lazarus. When he tells Martha he is 'the resurrection and the life' (v. 25), she has now no hesitation in acknowledging him as 'the Christ, the Son of God' (v. 27). Her faith is fully rewarded, and above all in that finally she sees 'the glory of God' (v. 40).

In his first miracle his disciples saw his glory and believed (2.11). This last sign is performed precisely 'for God's glory so that God's Son may be glorified through it' (v. 4). Of course, perceiving that is still entirely dependent on believing (vv. 15,40).

All this proves too much for the Jewish authorities, who now plot to have Jesus put to death (vv. 45-57). But then 'it was almost time for the Jewish Passover' when the Lamb of God must be slain. In their minds it seemed time they took action, but in God's plan it was his time, not theirs.

Ch. 12: The hour has come for the Son of Man to be glorified.

'We have seen his glory,' says John (1.14), but its unveiling, though immediate to some (1.29 – 2.11), was gradual to others. Jesus repeatedly insisted that there would be a proper time for its full revelation (2.4; 7.8; 8.20) and now he knows that time has arrived. He therefore allows himself to be anointed. There is a double significance in this act: firstly, the word 'Messiah' means 'Anointed One' and speaks of his status as King of the Jews; secondly, the anointing is for burial, but it is in his death that his kingship is finally and fully proclaimed. The cross is his throne; his anointing is preparatory for both. And so as Messiah he publicly rides into Jerusalem on a donkey to claim his throne. (vv. 1-19)

Jesus finally acknowledges 'the hour has come' when some Greeks ask to see him. His mission to the Jews is complete and soon the gospel will go to the Gentiles (vv. 20-23). But before that can happen he must first die, otherwise no expansion can take place at all (v. 24). The challenge troubles him, but his Father's voice reassures him about his glory. (Vv. 25-28 = John's Gethsemane ?) As Jesus

GLORY

'Glory' is one of the most key words in John's Gospel. It signifies the visible manifestation of God. It was his glory that came among the Israelites at the tabernacle in the wilderness (Exod. 40.34-8), and again at the temple in Jerusalem (1 Kings 8.10f; Ezek. 44.4). It signifies his goodness and mercy (Exod. 33.18f) and is all of God that man will ever see here on earth. It may be reflected in people, as it was in the radiance that shone from the face of Moses, for example (Exod. 34.29; 2 Cor. 3.7). But its most powerful appearance ever was in Christ (Heb. 1.3). In the Synoptic Gospels the disciples saw it in him at his transfiguration (Mark 9.2-8).

John proclaims that that glory was there in Jesus from the very start. It is what he saw in Jesus and is what he bids us see in him: *We have seen his glory, the glory of the one and only Son who came from the Father, full of grace and truth* (1.14).

Jesus' miracles reveal (are 'signs' of) his glory, but that glory is only seen by those who believe. Thus in his first miracle Jesus *revealed his glory, and his disciples put their faith in him* (2.11). And again of his last miracle, the raising of Lazarus, he says, *It is for God's glory so that God's son may be glorified through it ... Did I not tell you that if you believed, you would see the glory of God?* (11.4,40)

Many fail to see the glory in Jesus because it is not discerned by physical sight, but by faith. Hence Isaiah saw it long before Jesus was ever born (12.37-41; cp. 20.29).

The ultimate showing of his glory was on the cross (12.23-28), the truth of which could certainly only be seen by faith (20.24-29).

Jesus' life, however, was one of selfless love and so he seeks not his own glory, but that of the Father who sent him (8.50), and before the crucifixion has to ask the Father to do for him what he must not do for himself: *Father, glorify your Son ... glorify me in your presence with the glory I had with you before the world began* (17.1,5).

Similarly, he prays that his disciples may see and even share his glory: *I have given them the glory that you gave me ... Father, I want those you have given me to be with me where I am, and to see my glory, the glory you have given me because you loved me before the creation of the world* (17.22,24).

This glory is still to be seen in Jesus, but it is veiled to human eyes because of the flesh and so is seen only by faith. When we do see it, however, we behold the grace, goodness and mercy of God.

speaks on, it becomes clear that the full revelation of that glory is indeed going to be on the cross (vv. 29-34).

His departure will mean extinction of the light he has brought, but not if men believe in him and become themselves 'sons of light'. His light will then be carried by them and so will continue to shine into the darkness of this world (vv. 35f).

Some accept his offer and believe, but even at this last stage in his preaching many still reject him (vv. 37-50).

3. JESUS ALONE WITH HIS DISCIPLES (CHS. 13–17)

In John's account of the Last Supper we read nothing about the bread and wine, but we do find some intimate details not recorded in the other Gospels: the foot-washing, the teaching on love and the Holy Spirit, and Jesus' last prayer.

Ch. 13: Now is the Son of Man glorified.
Jesus' last act is to serve his disciples (vv. 1-17), to show and teach them how to love one another (vv. 1,34f). When Judas leaves, the drama is as good as completed and so Jesus cries out, 'Now is the Son of Man glorified' (vv. 18-31). He then begins to speak to them about his approaching departure (vv. 33-38).

Chs. 14–16: Jesus' last discourse—on the Holy Spirit.
In his public ministry, by preaching and challenging his hearers, Jesus offered life through the Spirit to all who believe. Now with his disciples, in a context of love and intimacy, he speaks of a deeper experience of the Spirit among faithful friends. The discussion is exceedingly rich, but quite straight-forward.

Ch. 14: Fear not. I will send another Counsellor to take my place.
I am about to leave you, but do not be anxious, for I am only going ahead to prepare the way for you. Through me you will come to the Father (and no other way), but then you have already seen the Father in me (vv. 1-11).

THE HOLY SPIRIT

He is of God, for *God is Spirit* (4.24);
To Jesus *God gives the Spirit without limit* ((3.34);
and so Jesus *is he who will baptise with the Holy Spirit* (1.33).

However, the Spirit was not given to men in Jesus' lifetime; *those who believed in him were later to receive* the Spirit, after Jesus had *been glorified* (7.39). Hence, after his resurrection Jesus breathed on his disciples and said *Receive the Holy Spirit* (20.22—this must have been as a foretaste of what was to happen to them at Pentecost).

The Spirit gives life (6.63), and since *the Spirit gives birth to spirit* (3.6), we can be *born of the Spirit* (3.5,8), thus entering into the experience of the life of God's kingdom.

The life the Spirit gives them will be like *the wind* (3.8) or like *streams of living water* (7.38) and then they will *worship the Father in spirit and truth* (4.23f).

Since he is God's gift for believers, *The world cannot accept him, because it neither sees him nor knows him* (14.17). To the world he comes to *convict of guilt in regard to sin and righteousness and judgment* (16.8).

But to the disciples he is *another Counsellor* (Greek: *parakletos*) who will take Jesus' place and will be with them *for ever*, but to be *in* them, not just *with* them (14.16f). The Spirit is again called 'the Paraklete' or 'Counsellor' (KJV 'Comforter') in 14.26; 15.26; 16.7 and Jesus is called *parakletos* in 1 John 2.1 (NIV: 'one who speaks in our defence'; KJV 'advocate').

In 14.17; 15.26; 16.13 he is called *the Spirit of truth*. Since Jesus himself is the truth, his function is to remind believers about Jesus' teaching, to show them who he really is and to glorify him. Jesus said: He will *remind you of everything I have said to you* (14.26), *testify about me* (15.26), and *bring glory to me by taking from what is mine and making it known to you* (16.14).

And finally, *he will guide you into all truth*, and that not only covers the truth about who Jesus is and what he has said, but also *he will tell you what is yet to come* (16.13).

The Holy Spirit is therefore to be to believers all that Jesus was to the disciples, and even more, for he is to be with them and in them for ever. Jesus is a Paraklete, he is another Paraklete; Jesus is the truth, he is the Spirit of truth. So Jesus says, 'I will not leave you as orphans; I will come to you.'—that is, in the person of the Holy Spirit (14.16-18).

Do not be anxious, for you will be able to do all that I have been doing (and much more besides), because when I go to the Father I will send you another Counsellor, the Holy Spirit. He will teach you everything and remind you of all I have taught you (vv. 12-25).

So it is peace, not anxiety, I leave with you. In fact you should be excited about me going away because of all that will happen to you as a result (vv. 26-31).

Ch. 15: Stay faithful. The Spirit will help you.

Think of yourselves as branches of a vine (= Jesus) tended by the Father. As you remain in the vine, its sap (= the Spirit) will flow in you producing fruit. I am speaking to you of joyful things that operate by love and faithfulness (vv. 1-17).

However, let me warn you in advance so that you are not taken by surprise when it happens: there will be persecution, just like I have suffered. But take heart, for the Spirit will testify about me as you maintain your testimony (15.18 – 16.4).

Ch. 16: The Spirit will continue my ministry in you with great joy.

I tell you, it is to your advantage that I go away, otherwise the Spirit will not come. But when he comes, that will be exciting, for he will convict people of sin and he will guide you into all truth, tell you of things to come, glorify me and remind you of all I have taught you (vv. 5-15).

So now, I go soon, but I will see you again. You will be sad for a time, but again you will rejoice, and then no-one will be able to take your joy from you (vv. 16-22).

Then at last the way will be open for you to approach the Father yourselves. You won't need me to ask on your behalf, for you will be able to ask for yourselves. So ask, and you will receive, and your joy will be full! (vv. 23-28).

Ch. 17: Jesus' final prayer.

Jesus' thoughts are now entirely on the future. He knows in himself the work is as good as done, but he still needs to be sustained to see it through that final stage which will bring the full revealing of his glory (vv. 1-5).

TRUTH

If God, men and things testify to Jesus, he himself testifies to 'the truth', as he said to Pilate: *For this reason I was born, and for this I came into the world, to testify to the truth. Everyone on the side of truth listens to me* (18.37).

This truth is of God himself. It is God's own *word* (17.17), what Jesus calls *the truth that I heard from God* (8.40).

It is therefore more than just something to which Jesus testifies. Since he is the Word incarnate, it resides in Jesus himself, who is thus by his incarnation *full of grace and truth* (1.14,17). Indeed he can even say *I am the way and the truth and the life* (14.6).

To know and live by this truth is to *come into the light* (3.21), to hold to Jesus' teaching so that *the truth will set you free* (8.31f), and to be sanctified *by the truth* (17.17).

It is the function of the Spirit to reveal the truth to believers, that is primarily the truth about who Jesus really is. Hence he is called *the Spirit of truth* and Jesus says of him, *When he, the Spirit of truth, comes, he will guide you into all truth. He will bring glory to me by taking from what is mine and making it known to you* (16.13f; cp. 15.26).

And since truth and the Spirit are both of God, *true worshippers will worship the Father in spirit and in truth* (4.23f).

Conscious also of his disciples, that he will no longer be able to watch over them personally (v. 12), he commends them to the Father's protection, praying for their continued growth (vv. 6-19).

Finally he prays for future converts, that they may be one with the disciples, with each other, with himself and with his Father, seeing and sharing his glory and love (vv. 20-26).

4. THAT YOU ALSO MAY BELIEVE (CHS. 18–20)

In John's account of the arrest, trial and crucifixion, Jesus is manifestly the King of Glory, fully in control of events, and several people in the story are well aware of that.

Chs. 18–19: The King of Glory is crowned and lifted up.

Majestically Jesus presents himself to his captors, who fall to the ground before him (18.1-9). Refusing any help (18.10f), he is taken before Annas, where, while Peter denies him outside, he conducts himself with regal assurance and dignity. (18.12-27)

He is brought to Caiaphas, and then to Pilate, who finds himself discussing Jesus' kingship and ends up calling him 'the king of the Jews'. (18.29-40)

Rejected finally by the Jews, Pilate has Jesus flogged, but even so the soldiers clothe him and address him as a king: a crown of thorns, a purple robe and the acclamation, 'Hail, O king of the Jews!' Then follows Pilate's moving presentation of Jesus: 'Here is the man!' We see his fear on discovering Jesus' claim to be Son of God. We watch him hand Jesus over with the words 'Here is your king.' And finally he affixes the notice: JESUS OF NAZARETH, THE KING OF THE JEWS, refusing to alter it when requested. (19.1-22)

Throughout the story there is little doubt about who is really in control. Jesus tells Pilate, 'You would have no power over me if it were not given to you from above.' (19.11) He carries his own cross (19.17); he makes arrangements for the care of his mother (19.25-27); and at the end it is he who declares, 'It is finished' (19.30). Jesus knew throughout what had to be done, and he was the one who saw that everything was fully accomplished.

Truly he was King. The man 'who saw it has given testimony and his testimony is true. He knows that he tells the truth, and he testifies *so that you also may believe*.' (v. 35)

Ch. 20: My Lord and my God!

The resurrection is not Christ's glorification—that took place on the cross. Rather it is its rubber-stamping, the final proof or manifestation of his glory.

As John tells the story, he now highlights the challenge to the reader. The 'other disciple', though he still did not understand, 'saw and believed' (v. 8). Mary Magdalene recognised the truth and declared, 'I have seen the Lord!' (v. 18). Thomas said, 'Unless I see, I will not believe it' (v. 25),

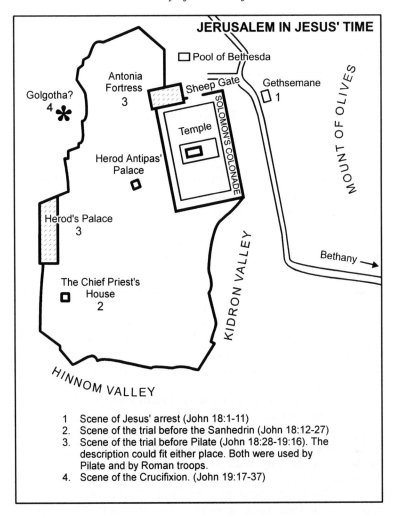

JERUSALEM IN JESUS' TIME

Pool of Bethesda

Antonia Fortress
3

Sheep Gate

Gethsemane
1

Golgotha?
4

Temple

SOLOMON'S COLONADE

MOUNT OF OLIVES

Herod Antipas'
Palace

Herod's Palace
3

Bethany →

The Chief Priest's
House
2

KIDRON VALLEY

HINNOM VALLEY

1   Scene of Jesus' arrest (John 18:1-11)
2. Scene of the trial before the Sanhedrin (John 18:12-27)
3. Scene of the trial before Pilate (John 18:28-19:16). The
    description could fit either place. Both were used by
    Pilate and by Roman troops.
4. Scene of the Crucifixion. (John 19:17-37)

but was challenged, 'Stop doubting and believe,' whereupon he cried, 'My Lord and my God!' (vv. 27f) Jesus' last
words are, 'Because you have seen me, you have believed;
blessed are those who have not seen me and yet have
believed.' (v. 29)

The purpose of John's Gospel should now be clear (20.31):

... written that you may believe that Jesus is the Christ, the Son of God, and that by believing you may have life in his name.

5. EPILOGUE: THE INFANT CHURCH

Ch. 21: Peter and the infant Church.

Jesus takes Peter through his original call all over again (vv. 1-14; cp. Luke 5.1-11 and see above, p. 134). He then reverses his threefold denial by taking him through a three-fold confession of love. Three times he gives him his new commission: 'Feed my lambs/sheep' (vv. 15-17), and twice he reminds him of the words with which he was first called: 'Follow me' (vv. 19, 22).

Jesus' last act before his final departure is to reinstate Peter and establish him as pastor of the infant Church which is to carry on his work on earth. The Gospel closes with this chapter, not as a tagged on extra, but as a reminder that Christ's work on earth had just begun, to be continued by those that believed in his name, led at first by Peter, and then by ...

But John hoped his Lord would return before that kind of sentence needed too much expansion (v. 23)!

Jesus gives the Holy Spirit to the infant Church.

At his first meeting with his disciples after his resurrection Jesus breathed on them and said, 'Receive the Holy Spirit' (20.22). Many puzzle over the relationship between that and the story of Pentecost in Acts 2, but the answer lies in the Gospel itself. Jesus offered the woman at the well 'living water' (4.10,14) and some time later in the temple made a similar offer to all who thirst and believe (7.38). In 7.39 John explains that this 'living water' is the Spirit and that it was given when Jesus was glorified. As we have seen, his glorification took place on the cross, and that is why John records that when his side was pierced there flowed out blood and water—the blood of his Passover sacrifice to save us from death and the water of his Spirit to give us life.

The flow of the Spirit of Christ for us began neither at Pentecost, nor in the upper room, but on the cross. The events that followed were simply stages in the developing history of the fulfilment of the promise of the Father to give us the Holy Spirit released at Calvary, a story still far from ended. The cross cannot be separated from Pentecost. As one beautiful old hymn, popular at the time of the Welsh revival of 1904, puts it:

> *On the mount of crucifixion*
> *Fountains opened deep and wide;*
> *Through the floodgates of God's mercy*
> *Flowed a vast and gracious tide.*
> *Grace and love, like mighty rivers,*
> *Poured incessant from above,*
> *And heaven's peace and perfect justice*
> *Kissed a guilty world in love.*

PART FIVE

STANDING FIRM AND GROWING IN CHRIST

In our Old Testament study we examined the great truths of God's sovereignty or Lordship and his wisdom. We then saw how these truths 'became flesh' and were revealed with sharper, more tangible clarity in the life of Christ and how we ourselves obtain the benefits of them when we come to believe in him, how by believing we enter into a new life of faith in the revelation of them. The crystallisation of that revelation comes for us when we acknowledge Jesus' divine Lordship and along with Thomas cry, 'My Lord and my God!'

Throughout Old Testament times these truths were revealed from heaven to and through men, but once the Jews grasped the revelation, they could only wait for God to act, trusting that what they had seen and heard would come to fulfilment when their Messiah came.

In New Testament times men encountered these truths incarnate in the person of Jesus and found that the encounter, if coupled with faith, resulted in them discovering new life in him. It was as if they were being grafted into a new vine, not just receiving understanding, for a new life began to flow in them as a result. Coming to faith in Jesus was being born again.

The challenge facing the infant Church was to enable the new-born children of faith to grow up in it and to remain firmly rooted and grounded in the richness of its revelation and blessing. John, as well as showing us God's wisdom and Lordship in Christ in his Gospel, addresses himself to this continuing challenge in his epistles, as also, of course, do the others whose writings we shall now be studying.

11

Remaining in Christ

1, 2 & 3 JOHN

John probably wrote his letters for believers who were feeling the first impact of an early form of Christian heresy known as Gnosticism. It taught a complete distinction between the spiritual world as good and the material as evil, holding that Jesus therefore could not have been both divine and properly human at the same time. John is clearly opposing some such false teaching in parts of his first two epistles when he asserts the full humanity of Jesus, but most of what he writes can also apply in any setting and so remains entirely relevant today.

1. THAT WE MAY HAVE FELLOWSHIP WITH GOD AND ONE ANOTHER (1 JOHN)

John wrote his Gospel 'that you may believe'; he wrote his first letter to instruct those who have believed how to live the Christian life and remain strong in it. His teaching is neatly summarised in the key words he uses, such as darkness, the world, light, life, truth, love, the Spirit, born of God. This is the same complex of terminology as in the Gospel and so we need not discuss it here again. There is, however, one set of words and phrases that we should particularly notice, since it seems to sum up John's main purpose in writing.

Several times he reminds us that we are called to *live in* God (2.6), *continue in* him (2.28) and *live in* the light (2.10).

The Greek verb he uses literally means 'remain' or 'abide' (so KJV) and in it is encapsulated almost everything he wants to teach us about the work of Christ through the Spirit. In the Gospel Jesus uses it in the passage about the vine (15.4-10): as branches must remain in a vine for the life of the vine to flow through them and produce fruit, so also must believers remain in Christ for his life (Spirit) to flow through them. They must remain in his love and allow his words to remain in them; otherwise they become dead and barren.

Similarly in his epistle John preaches the importance of letting Jesus' teaching and his Spirit remain in us: 'the word of God lives in you' (2.14); 'See that what you have heard from the beginning remains in you' (2.24); 'the anointing you received from him remains in you ... just as it has taught you, remain in him' (2.27); 'And this is how we know that he lives in us: We know it by the Spirit he gave us' (3.24).

John's plea is therefore quite simple: remain in God and let his word and his Spirit remain in you. Doing that will, of course, result in you living a properly Christian life: 'No-one who lives in him keeps on sinning' (3.6). John also speaks of Christian living as a way of 'walking' or 'doing': we must *walk in the light* and *live by the truth* (literally 'do the truth'; 1.6f)—indeed we 'must walk as Jesus did' (2.6). The reasoning is straightforward: 'God is light; in him there is no darkness at all. If we claim to have fellowship with him yet walk in the darkness, we lie and do not live by the truth.' (1.5f)

John's promise is that if we do walk this way, we shall have victorious confidence through our faith, we shall have rich fellowship with one another, we shall know how to deal with sin, the evil one and those that would lead us astray into false teaching, and above all we shall know the fullness of God's love in our lives and our relationships. This is an epistle that speaks love and assurance to believers.

In some ways it seems strange to call 1 John a letter at all, for it is addressed to no-one in particular. Its readers are simply called 'dear children' and 'dear friends'. That, however, only helps to make it seem more personal, as if addressed directly to us today.

1.1-4: Introduction.

The language of these opening verses echoes that of the Gospel's prologue, but now John writes, not simply to introduce us to Jesus, 'the Word of life', but that we may 'have fellowship' together and have 'joy complete' (1.3f); in other words, that we may live a full Christian life. The teaching that follows is therefore essentially very practical, though interspersed with such words of exhortation and assurance as we have already noted.

1.5 – 2.17: How to deal with sin and temptation.

Firstly, be truthful about your walk with God and each other, then confess your sin and set yourself to 'walk as Jesus did', by loving one another and knowing God has forgiven. You can do that with confidence, because just as Christ's sacrifice cancels sin at conversion, so his blood continues to purify us from all sin, that is every time we come back to him in repentance. (1.5 – 2.6)

Secondly, you know the call is to love, but you also know the light shines to dispel your darkness. So take courage, whatever age you are, for his word lives in you to strengthen you and give you victory in your battle against sin and evil. (2.7-14)

Thirdly, recognise that temptations of the flesh do not come from God. They are transient, whereas you, as a man of God, will live for ever. So love and obey God above everything in this world. (2.15-17)

2.18-27: Beware of false teachers.

You should not need anyone to tell you someone is a false teacher. You should easily recognise the truth yourself, for you know it perfectly well, since you have 'an anointing from the Holy One' (= the witness of the Spirit). Pay attention to what that anointing tells you and be led by it, because it is real, and you know it!

'Antichrists' are simply people who may at one time have seemed to be Christians, but whose teaching about Jesus has become distorted.

2.28 – 3.24: Living as God's children in his family.

God has invited us into a marvellous family with a wonderful Father and has given us beautiful things to look forward to (2.28 – 3.3). So no-one in his family can continue in sin—Jesus came to do away with all that! (3.4-6) In fact, if anyone does continue in sin, he is not really a child of God, but rather of the devil. (3.7-10)

There is only one way to live in God's family, and that is in love with one another, just as Jesus loved us. (3.11-18)

We have peace about our place in his family if 'our hearts do not condemn us'. Then we walk free and with confidence, knowing we have open access to the Father—and the key to such confidence and knowledge is the presence of his Spirit within us. (3.19-24)

Note there is a vast difference between having sinned (1.10) and keeping on sinning or continuing in sin (3.6). As Christians we have broken with, or, as Paul would say, 'died to' lives dominated and controlled by sin. If we have not, then we are not really Christians. However, we do still commit sins, and we deceive ourselves if we deny it, but God's will is not that we should go in condemnation for that, but that we should repent again and live (2.1f).

4.1-6: Beware of false prophets.
How do we 'recognise the Spirit of God', or 'recognise the Spirit of truth and the spirit of falsehood'?

Answer: You will know if the spirit of a prophet is from God by his teaching about Jesus (vv. 1-3) and by the inner acknowledgment of 'the one who is in you' (vv. 4-6). Cp. the similar advice in 1.18-27.

4.7-21: Love one another with God's love.
Christian living demands a special sort of love, God's own love. We see what that means when we consider how God demonstrated his love for us in sending his Son as the sacrifice for our sins. It is that kind of love he wants us to show toward each other. (vv. 7-12)

However, it is only possible to love one another in that way if his love is in us, but he himself makes that possible by coming to live in us, for 'he has given us of his Spirit'. 'God is love' and we receive his love as we acknowledge Jesus to be his Son. (vv. 13-16)

The teaching of these verses reminds us of what Paul says

in Rom. 5.5,8: 'God has poured out his love into our hearts by the Holy Spirit, whom he has given us' and 'God demonstrates his own love for us in this: While we were still sinners, Christ died for us.' It is only the power of the cross and of the Spirit that will ever enable us to love with God's love.

God's love in us is perfect love and so it drives out all fear and fills us with confidence. But love is only truly love if it issues in action! (vv. 17-21)

5.1-12: Our faith overcomes the world.

It is our faith that tells us Jesus is God's Son, and because of it we are born of God. These truths are confirmed to our hearts by our love for God and our obedience to his commands. (vv. 1-5)

Throughout his Gospel John emphasised the saving, life-giving power of believing. But faith is not just to bring us into salvation. It is also to sustain us in it and give us victory in life—in every aspect of life. As Paul would put it, Christianity operates 'by faith from first to last' (Rom. 1.17). The great men of God in ancient times all knew the truth of that; they approached everything in their lives by faith and 'were still living by faith when they died' (Heb. 11.13).

In conclusion John reminds us again of the very basis of our faith: that Jesus Christ (who 'has come in the flesh', 4.2) is the Son of God. There are various testimonies to that truth, but the most powerful are three in which we see or hear God's own witness: Jesus' baptism in water, the shedding of his blood on the cross, and his ministry in the power of the Spirit (all gathered into one at the moment of his death and glorification, see above, p. 160f). These constitute the testimony of God himself, and he cannot lie. Those who receive it carry it in their heart and to them it imparts eternal life. (vv. 6-11)

5.12-21: Final assurances and reminders.

Note the number of times John uses the words 'we know' in these few verses. His closing words, many of which re-echo things he has already said in the letter, are written to reaffirm faith and strengthen assurance:
- that we do have eternal life (v. 13),

- that God does hear our prayers (vv. 14f),
- that it is worth praying for others (vv. 16f),
- that we are free from sin (v. 18),
- that we are safe from the evil one (vv. 18f),
- that the revelation of truth is given to us in Jesus (v. 20).

And finally, 'Dear children, keep yourselves from idols.' A striking ending, but a strange afterthought? This is no mere afterthought, but a warning about man's greatest danger. Idolatry is a turning from God to worship other things, which will destroy all our assurance and is itself the root of all perversion (cp. Rom. 1.18-32).

2. ON OFFERING HOSPITALITY TO ITINERANT PREACHERS (2 JOHN)

Here we have a brief personal letter warning against offering hospitality to false teachers. Its vocabulary and expression echo 1 John in almost every line and so it may be regarded as a personal application of his teaching to the particular circumstances of some local church.

'The chosen lady and her children' to which it is addressed may be some local church and its members, in which case 'the children of your chosen sister' (v. 13) would be the members of a sister-congregation, though, of course, the references may equally well be to individuals, personal friends of John, for he also veils his own identity by calling himself simply 'the elder'.

What prompts him to write is the threat posed by heretical travelling preachers. Just like Paul on his journeys, early Christian evangelists depended on local believers for hospitality, and it was important that the churches should offer it so that the work of spreading the gospel might continue unhindered. Indeed hospitality was always associated with the ministry and gifts of the Holy Spirit and Christians were urged to give it (cp. Rom. 12.13; 1 Pet. 4.9), but now, with the growth of heresy at the end of the first century, it was becoming increasingly important to test the spirits of the preachers who came among them. John's test is that they should acknowledge the full truth of the incarnation (v. 7; cp. 1 John 4.2).

Of course, the danger associated with testing and discernment is that love can give way to suspicion and a critical spirit. John therefore urges his readers to continue to 'walk in love' as well as 'in the truth' (vv. 4-6). His words still have urgent relevance today, particularly in charismatic circles where every latest new inspirational teaching seems to generate a great deal of instant, unthinking enthusiasm.

3. ON JEALOUSY OF ANOTHER MAN'S ANOINTING (3 JOHN)

Here is another brief personal letter, this time clearly addressed to a particular individual, a friend of John's called Gaius. Again the topic is hospitality offered to visiting Christian brethren, though this time the problem is not heretical teaching, but bullying opposition to the work from one called Diotrephes, who was apparently one of the congregation's leaders, indeed liked to consider himself its chief leader. He was also opposed to John's letters being read in church. In him we see the pettiness and jealousy that still besets church leaders today.

The problem is a very ancient one among the Lord's people, and strangely, it seems to be where the Spirit is most active that it becomes most exaggerated. It was just such jealousy that roused Aaron to challenge Moses' leadership, that stirred Saul to murdering anger against David, that caused prophet to stand against prophet, and that set Jerusalem's religious leaders against Jesus. It seems that the man God blesses with spiritual anointing will inevitably have to live with jealousy. And the challenge has always been the same: to reassert the centrality of Christ and restore love and unity in the body. To that end John commends Gaius for his faithfulness to the truth and for the strength of his love, and encourages him to continue in them.

12

Jesus Lord of All

PAUL'S CAPTIVITY EPISTLES

If our appreciation of Jesus' glory results from the Spirit's working in us, so also does our appreciation of his Lordship. Before experiencing fullness of the Spirit, many Christians have difficulty in appreciating either. They may acknowledge both because they have been taught to do so, but it generally remains a serious puzzle how Jesus can be both human and divine and what it means for him to be Lord over our lives. After conversion and baptism in the Spirit it remains just as difficult to explain these things, but believing them ceases to be a problem. Instead the recognition that Jesus is Lord and God becomes a source of tremendous joy and a primary cause of the exuberant praise that has always been the hallmark of the charismatic Christian's life and worship. That same sense of joy and worship runs through all Paul's captivity epistles.

Turning to them, we step back in time some thirty years. When John was writing his Gospel and Epistles toward the end of the first century, Paul had already long finished his work. The four letters we shall be studying here were written from prison, some time during the period covered in Acts 23–28, probably towards the end of it, when he was in Rome in 62–64 AD. It is impossible to date them with any certainty, but Colossians, Philemon and Ephesians were apparently all written about the same time, and Philippians perhaps before them.

Paul's earlier letters were written in the heat of evangelistic work and reflect a mind largely preoccupied with the problems of new churches and young, enthusiastic Christians. Thus Galatians was born out of a fiery debate about whether Gentile converts should be circumcised and required to observe the Jewish law. 1 & 2 Thessalonians were written to encourage new converts and restrain over-enthusiastic views about the near return of Christ in a church that was only a few months old. 1 & 2 Corinthians were sent to correct a multitude of problems that had surfaced in one of Paul's mission churches. The mood of each is that of debate, dispute and discipline, with Paul writing now to plead, now to reprove, now in warmth, now in anger.

His captivity letters reflect a quieter atmosphere. Paul has been out of the hurly-burly of active evangelism for several years and has had time to reflect on the deep truths of his faith. It is the fruits of such contemplation that we shall be examining here.

It must be remembered, however, that these are not simply abstract theological essays. They are *letters*, written to living churches with real-life problems. Reading between the lines, it seems that heretical teachings were already beginning to appear, and so part of Paul's purpose in writing is to bring the churches back to the truth. In doing so, he has to reassert the absolute centrality of Christ, and that is the point at which these letters become particularly interesting for us here, namely in their teaching about the person and work of Christ. We shall see them asserting his Lordship— over life's circumstances (Philippians), over personal relationships (Philemon), over every power and all creation (Colossians), over history and the Church (Ephesians)—that he is the embodiment of God's wisdom, indeed that the fullness of the Godhead dwells in him. Their message is essentially the same as John's, and in it we shall also find most of the central strands of teaching about God in the Old Testament books we studied being gathered up together and applied to Christ.

The Lord's promise for his people in the New Covenant age contains three major, interrelated elements—that they will:
1. know God personally in a much more intimate way,
2. experience a break with their past lives of sin,
3. find a new potential for obeying God within themselves.

These things will happen as a result of God's own initiative and will be personalised in our lives by the action of his Spirit in us. Two well known prophecies in particular sum the matter up beautifully:

> *'This is the covenant I will make ...*
> *I will put my law in their minds*
> *   and write it on their hearts.*
> *I will be their God,*
> *   and they will be my people.*
> *No longer will a man teach his neighbour,*
> *   or a man his brother, saying 'Know the* LORD,'
> *because they will all know me,*
> *   from the least of them to the greatest,'*
> declares the LORD.
> *'For I will forgive their wickedness*
> *   and will remember their sins no more.'*
> (Jer. 31.33f)

> *I will cleanse you from all your impurities and from all your idols. I will give you a new heart and put a new spirit in you; I will remove from you your heart of stone and give you a heart of flesh. And I will put my Spirit in you and move you to follow my decrees and be careful to keep my laws. ... you will be my people, and I will be your God.*
> (Ezek. 36.25-8)

Paul's presentation of life in the New Covenant incorporates all three elements—that by the Spirit:

1. we know God as Father and Jesus as Lord (Rom. 8.15; 1 Cor. 12.3),
2. we are set free from the law of sin and death (Rom. 8.2),
3. we can live our lives by the Spirit, not the flesh (Gal. 5.13-26).

His teaching on Christian discipleship is similarly a balanced mixture relating to: knowing God in Christ, standing firm in our new freedom and faith, and growing as Christians. At some point in each letter we find a 'therefore': Because of what you now are in Christ, therefore press on to know him better, keep yourself free from sin, and continue to walk in God's ways. However, it is important to remember that the key to appreciating and applying this teaching fully lies, not just in understanding its theology, but in our own acknowledgment of Jesus as Lord and of the Spirit as our life-giver and guide.

1. JESUS CHRIST IS LORD (PHILIPPIANS)

Philippi is in Macedonia, north-east of Greece. We read about how Paul established a church there in Acts 16. He went there about 48/49 AD, early in his second missionary journey, in response to a vision of a man of Macedonia begging him to 'Come over and help us.' Immediately he arrived the Lord opened a door for him and on his first Sabbath the household of Lydia, a local business-woman, came to faith. His ministry apparently continued with the same happy momentum and soon he had established what would turn out to be one of his finest mission-churches, one of which he was always very proud and with which he maintained a most happy relationship.

His time in Philippi ended abruptly when an astounding miracle of deliverance led to him and his travelling companion, Silas, being arrested, beaten, imprisoned and finally expelled from the city, though only after their jailer was converted! The picture we are shown of Paul and Silas in jail that night, with their backs bleeding and yet praising God, is a powerful testimony to the work of the Spirit in their lives and to their faith in the Lordship of Christ.

Paul visited Philippi again about ten years later, towards the end of his third missionary journey, in 58 AD. On that occasion he came to collect offerings from his churches in Macedonia and Greece for the relief of poverty among the saints in Jerusalem (Acts 20.1-6). The Macedonians, who included the Philippians, had responded to Paul's appeal in this matter with overflowing generosity, and so he wrote to the Corinthians about them with warmest appreciation (2 Cor. 8.1-5).

When, probably about four or five years after that, he

came to write his letter to the Philippians, it was again to express appreciation for their warm generosity. Learning that he was in prison, they had taken up another collection, this time for Paul himself, and sent one of their members, called Epaphroditus, to him with it. Unfortunately Epaphroditus fell seriously ill and had to stay on in Rome, but now he had recovered, and so Paul sent him back home bearing this letter.

Its purpose was threefold: to thank the Philippians for their gift, to commend Epaphroditus for his help, and to encourage them all in faith and unity.

1.1-26: Personal greetings and news.
To all members and leaders of the Philippian church (1.2):

I thank God for you all and pray always for you (1.3-11).
I hope I may be spared to see you again soon (1.12-26).

The warmth of Paul's affection for this church is manifest. In some measure it must be a natural response to their recent expression of love for him, though that can hardly be the whole reason, for they had supported his ministry from earliest times (4.15f) and it is highly doubtful that his favour could have been simply won by gifts. It is for their partnership in the gospel he gives thanks. In 2 Cor. 8.5 he said that their giving to his earlier relief project reflected, not just personal generosity, but lives given to the Lord. To a man who has given his own life totally to God, it is that kind of heart dedication, not just gifts, that gives joy.

That same attitude of total dedication to the gospel is reflected in his rejoicing over the effect of his witness among the palace guard and over all the other preaching going on around him, some of which he did not like very much—even over the prospect of possible martyrdom.

This epistle is full of well known gems, one of which we find in 1. 21: 'For me, to live is Christ and to die is gain.' It is important to remember that this statement was not theoretical, but made by a man in prison expecting possible execution. The positive thankfulness, hope and joy of his letter is no mere response to a gift of money. It is an expression of faith in Christ's Lordship and of the hope of which he speaks in Rom. 8.5, a hope generated by the power of Spirit:

And hope does not disappoint us, because God has poured out his love into our hearts by the Holy Spirit, whom he has given us.

1.27 – 2.18: Stand firm in your faith and try to be like Christ.

The Macedonian churches had known the need to stand firm right from the start. At Philippi Paul was scourged and imprisoned, then Jewish agitation drove him from Thessalonica and Berea (Acts 16.22 – 17.15). Persecution continued after he left (1 Thes. 2.14), but through it the young Christians learned some precious lessons, one of which was how to rejoice in suffering.

The secret of such rejoicing lies to a considerable degree in appreciating and appropriating the mind (NIV 'attitude') of Christ—that he is himself both suffering servant and Lord of all.

In the little hymn in 2.5-11 we have one of the most profound statements of both the divinity and the humanity of Jesus: that 'being in very nature God', he 'made himself nothing' and became 'made in human likeness'. That is, he gave up all his 'equality with God' to become 'a servant', a man open to suffering and even death. Yet God has exalted him to reign as Lord over all creation.

We find similar teaching about Jesus' divinity and humanity in Hebrews, where we read that Jesus is 'the radiance of God's glory, the exact representation of his being' (1.3), and yet was 'made like his brothers in every way' (2.17), so that he could 'sympathise with our weaknesses' (4.15) and become our 'great high priest who has gone through the heavens' (4.14).

We have therefore every reason to rejoice whatever our circumstances. If Jesus, who himself suffered all we can ever suffer, now reigns over all things, good things await us in him. As Paul says elsewhere, 'our present sufferings are not worth comparing with the glory that will be revealed in us'(Rom. 8.18). In the meantime our calling is to have that same attitude of self-denying humility as he had, but equally to rejoice in the same hope. Peter puts it: 'Humble yourselves, therefore, under God's mighty hand, that he may lift you up in due time' (1 Pet. 5.6).

2.19-30: Honour men like this.

Timothy is well and I may be able to send him to visit you soon. Epaphroditus is also well, though he has been very ill. Give him a good welcome home; he deserves it.

It is not just for the things they have done that Paul particularly commends these men, but rather for their dedication of purpose in the Lord's service. He commends Timothy as one who 'has proved himself ... in the work of the gospel', unlike everyone else who 'looks out for his own interests, not those of Jesus Christ'. And he urges the Philippians to encourage Epaphroditus, not just because he almost died, but 'because he almost died for the work of Christ'. The Philippians would have understood such commendations, for they had a kindred spirit to these men themselves.

3.1-11: I want to know Christ.

'Watch out for those dogs!' Some believe Paul has interrupted the flow of his letter here to speak about a matter not directly related to the rest of what he was saying, to warn the Philippians about pressure from some Jewish Christians to have all converts circumcised and brought subject to the laws of Moses. But there is no interruption. Paul is urging the church to stand firm, to rejoice and to be like Jesus, and one thing that will undermine their faith and joy is falling back into religiosity, legalism and ritualism, which will turn their eyes off Christ. Paul knows that danger from his own experience, because he too was once a Jewish enthusiast, in fact more so than any of them, but he gave all that up for Christ. About such things they should be saying with him, 'I consider them rubbish, that I may gain Christ ... I want to know Christ'.

We sometimes call the Jewish Christians to whom he refers 'Judaisers'. They are called 'the party of the Pharisees' in Acts 15.5 and 'the circumcision group' in Gal. 2.12. They were highly critical of Paul's ministry in the Gentile world and caused him many problems. They had called him to account after his first missionary journey, but the apostles in Jerusalem had given Paul their approval (Acts 15 and Gal. 2). Clearly they were still active at the end of his ministry.

3.12 – 4.1: So I press on.

In his evangelism Paul had indeed pressed on, perhaps more than any other apostle, for he had preached 'from Jerusalem all the way around to Illyricum' (modern Albania) and was planning further missions to Rome and Spain when he was arrested (Rom. 15.19-24). That pressing on in ministry, however, issued from another pressing on—to get closer to Jesus. Too often we allow ourselves to be pulled back into condemnation and ineffectiveness by things in our past, while God's call is to go forward with hope and joy into his future, especially as 'our citizenship is in heaven. And we eagerly await a Saviour from there, the Lord Jesus Christ.' Such forward vision, says Paul, is the view of all 'who are mature'.

4.2-9: Be at peace with one another and rejoice in the Lord.

Other things besides Judaisers and their like can pull us back from pressing on to know Christ and thus spoil our confidence, growth and joy in the Lord, such as disagreements, anxiety and turning our minds off things that are pure. It is therefore important that our thoughts and life-styles are right. But in the meantime we can know God's peace if we rejoice now in faith that the Lord is near, that he does hear our prayers—indeed that he is Lord over every aspect of our lives, even though all that happens around us might seem to belie that fact.

Paul speaks about joy and rejoicing in this letter more than in any other. He himself rejoices in the privilege of suffering for Christ, even though uncertain of the outcome (1.18-29), and invites the Philippians to rejoice with him (2.12-18). He asks them to rejoice over men of God like Epaphroditus (2.29f). And now he bids them rejoice always, whatever their circumstances (4.4-7; cp. 1 Thes. 5.16-18), explaining that he has learned to do that himself (4.10-13).

It is worth recalling that he and Silas had already learned how to rejoice and praise God in that way when beaten and imprisoned at Philippi some fifteen years earlier. The lesson is one men of God have learned in every generation and are still learning today. One of the most vivid examples is Habakkuk, who proclaims that though everything in his world is going wrong, 'yet I will rejoice in the LORD, I will be joyful in God my Saviour.' (Hab. 3.18)

The teaching is not just Paul's and Habakkuk's, for Jesus also bids us 'Rejoice in that day and leap for joy' when persecution comes our way (Luke 6.23). But then he also tells us that that joy is his gift to us through the Spirit, and it is not something anyone will be able to take away from us (John 16.22-4; 17.13; cp. Gal. 5.22).

4.10-23: Thank you for your gift and for all your help.

Paul concludes on the same happy vein, speaking of his own personal contentment in all circumstances and thanking them for their generous gift. Oh that all men of Christ today displayed such grace!

Jesus Christ is Lord.

If this is a joy-centred letter, that is only because it is Christ-centred. And its Christ-centredness is most powerfully highlighted in the hymn proclaiming that 'at the name of Jesus every knee should bow ... and every tongue confess that Jesus Christ is Lord' (2.10f).

The title 'Lord' (Greek *kurios*) meant several things in Paul's day: head of a family or household, master of slaves, king or ruler, and even god. By the end of the first century it was applied with that last meaning to the Roman emperor, who was accorded the official title 'Lord and God'. In the Greek translation of the Old Testament, *kurios* was the word used to represent the Hebrew name of God, Yahweh. Hence the primitive Christian confession, 'Jesus is Lord', doubtless carried mixed overtones of all these different shades of meaning.

Paul, of course, had always acknowledged the Lordship of Jesus in his life as a Christian, but it is interesting that the strongest and one of the most joyful expressions of his acknowledgment of it comes in one of his later letters. Here we encounter a man who has indeed pressed on to know Christ and is now living very close to him. We shall find this strong sense of Christ's Lordship only grows stronger as we read his other captivity letters. The progression reminds us of that in John's Gospel, with Thomas's climactic acclamation: 'My Lord and my God!'

2. THE SOVEREIGN POWER OF CHRIST'S LOVE (PHILEMON)

At Colosse there lived a man called Philemon, a friend of Paul's and a 'home-group' leader in the local church. One of his slaves, Onesimus, had absconded with some of his money and made his way to Rome. There, after the money had run out, it seems, he had made contact with Paul in prison and the evangelist had led him to faith in Christ.

Paul loved him dearly, just like a son, and Onesimus became a strong support and helper to him in return. Paul would have liked him to stay, but legally he belonged to Philemon and had to be sent home. As a runaway terrible punishment awaited him, so Paul wrote this brief note commending him to Philemon, pleading that he be received home as no longer just a slave, but now a brother in Christ.

Paul does not argue about whether or not slavery is right in God's eyes. His purpose is more immediate, to tap the love that should exist between Christian brethren for Onesimus' sake. Though bound by the legal system of his age, he knew a power that transcended all laws. As he wrote elsewhere: 'The fruit of the Spirit is love, joy, peace ... Against such things there is no law' (Gal. 5.22f), for in Christ 'there is neither Jew nor Greek, slave nor free, male nor female' (Gal. 3.28). Both Philemon and Onesimus had the same Spirit of Jesus and the power of his love should transcend all legal rights and all human passions.

None the less, Paul is writing as a Christian leader and teacher, and so takes precautions to ensure that Philemon does allow himself to be governed by the love of Christ rather than his own indignation. Hence he writes lovingly but firmly about Christian duty as well as privilege, offers to make good Philemon's financial loss out of his own resources, proposes to come and visit him once released from prison, commends Onesimus in glowing terms in a separate letter to the church and sends another Colossian called Tychicus to accompany him on his journey home (cp. Col. 4.7-9). After all that Philemon must surely have had to let his Christian love prevail. Paul was a great realist! But then, don't we all need encouragement, sometimes in very practical ways, to walk true in Christ?

3. CHRIST, THE HEAD OVER EVERY POWER AND AUTHORITY (COLOSSIANS)

At the time Paul wrote his letter to Philemon, besides Onesimus he had the company of several others, including Mark, Luke and Timothy, but also two less well known Christians called Epaphras and Tychicus, both of them Colossians (1.1; 4.7-14).

It was Epaphras, not Paul, who first brought the gospel to Colosse (Col. 1.7). Though Paul was able to write to Philemon as a friend, it seems that most of the other Colossian Christians had never met him personally (2.1). The church may, however, have come into existence as an offshoot of his ministry at Ephesus during his third missionary journey, that is if Epaphras was one of those from the province of Asia who are said to have heard the word of the Lord through him at that time (Acts 19.10) and then took the gospel back home to Colosse.

Now Epaphras was a prisoner along with Paul (Philem. 23). He spent much time wrestling in prayer for his church (Col. 4.12), and no doubt told Paul all about it, both the blessings and the problems. As a result, Paul clearly felt some obligation to write pastorally to the church there, and also to its twin congregation in Laodicea (4.16).

Tychicus was the one who carried the letter to Colosse. Paul sent him to accompany Philemon's slave, Onesimus, on his journey home. In fact, he became something of a postman, for he also took the letter to the Ephesian churches (Ephes. 6.21f), and possibly another to Laodicea, one that we no longer possess (Col. 4.16).

It seems that the currently fashionable 'higher thought' of pagan philosophy was beginning to influence Christian understanding of the gospel in the province of Asia (Col. 2.8). By the second century that had led to the rise of Gnosticism there, the heretical teaching John may have been confronting in his letters (see above, p. 165). It was based on a belief that matter is evil, that God being good can have no contact with it, and that there must therefore be a hierarchy of intermediate spiritual beings or powers between him and the world, in which Christ holds a high-ranking, but not supreme, place. Perhaps it was some incipient form of this heresy Paul had to deal with among the Colossians, and hence his prayers for them to be granted wisdom and understanding by revelation from God himself, rather than through hollow philosophy, and his insistence that everything they will ever need is to be found in Christ.

Ch. 1: Paul prays for spiritual wisdom and reasserts the sufficiency of Christ.
Epaphras has told us all about your faith and your love and we are delighted. We pray for you all the time, 'asking God to fill you with the knowledge of his will through all spiritual wisdom and understanding', so that you may become strong (1.3-12).

Christ has given us everything: salvation, redemption, forgiveness (1.13f). Absolutely everything is in him—all God's fullness! There is no place for any watered down conception of Christ's divinity among us. We affirm that he is the image of God, that he was there before creation—indeed the whole created universe, visible and invisible, owes its origin and continued existence to him. But more than that, he is also the originator and head of our new order of things, what we refer to as 'the body, the church'. By virtue of the fullness of God dwelling in him he has broken the power of death by his own death and brought us reconciliation and peace. (1.15-20)

You know the truth of all that from your own experience in the faith. I certainly do, and that is why I serve him in the gospel, even at the cost of this suffering (1.21-29).

Ch. 2: And you have been given fullness in Christ.
That's the reason for my prayer for you, my prayer that you 'may have the full riches of complete understanding', because it is all in Christ 'in whom are hidden all the treasures of wisdom and knowledge'. (vv. 1-5)

So then, don't let anyone deceive you with empty, human philosophies. They cannot do what Christ has done for you. It is all in him! You know that yourselves, for when you were baptised, you died to your old life and God made you alive with Christ in a new way, free from sin and the bondage of every written regulation. (vv. 11-14)

But even more than that, he 'disarmed the (spiritual) powers and authorities ... triumphing over them by the cross' (v. 15). It was he who created them in the first place (1.16), but now he has rendered them powerless. Don't think you need to worship other spiritual beings (v. 18). Christ's Lordship is total. Your salvation is in him.

Again, don't let anyone deceive you with religious programmes either. They may have 'an appearance of wisdom', but they have no real value. Judging by the references to food laws, New Moons and Sabbaths, it may be that the same Jewish influences that had disturbed the church at Philippi were beginning to make some impact at Colosse too. (2.16-23)

Though the heresies and religiosities that would undermine faith in Christ are different today, the basic dangers are still the same. Our salvation lies entirely in him and nothing whatsoever can add to that. Many, however, are still led away into thinking that supplementary revelations, ascetic practices, ritual observances and such like can add to the benefits they have obtained in Christ. We therefore find Christians trying to top up their faith with beliefs and practices from other religions, or with the thought forms and ways of modern philosophies, such as secularism, humanism and atheism, as if faith in Christ were not good enough in itself. Insistence on supplementary revelations, regulations and doctrines as necessary for salvation is always a mark of heresy, for it implies deficiency in the work of Christ.

Col. 2 is a helpful chapter to keep in mind in discussions with Mormons, Jehovah's Witnesses, Moonies and the like—and sometimes with seemingly orthodox Christians as well.

Chs. 3–4: Set your minds on things above.
'Your life is now hidden with Christ in God', so:
- be rid of all your old ways (3.5-11),
- and clothe yourselves with the virtues of Christ, especially love (3.12-14),
- let his peace and his word rule in your hearts, and be filled with praise and thanksgiving (3.15-17).
- Apply all that to your family life (3.18-21),
- to your work (3.22 – 4.1),

- to your prayers and your conversation with each other (4.2-6).

Tychicus and Onesimus will give you our news. The others send you greetings (4.7-17).
  Signed: Paul. (4.18)

Christ and Wisdom.

As we have seen, Paul's main theme is that it is impossible to top up the work of Christ from any other source, be it philosophy, religion, further revelations, or whatever. All God's wisdom (2.3), indeed the fullness of God himself (2.9), resides in Christ, and it is that that is at the heart of 'the mystery of God' (2.2) that has been revealed with saving power to us in Christ.

Paul's teaching about Christ and wisdom goes back to his earlier missionary days and we find a full exposition of it in 1 Cor. 1–2. There, in discussing the contrast between what the world calls wisdom and what we see revealed in the cross, he firmly declares that 'to those whom God has called' Christ is 'the power of God and the wisdom of God' (1.24), that he 'has become for us wisdom from God' (1.30). That is why Paul says he is determined to preach nothing but 'Jesus Christ and him crucified', because it is only in him, not in any clever sermons, that God's saving wisdom and power will be revealed (2.1-5).

It is doubtless because he is again thinking of Christ as God's wisdom that Paul describes him in Colossians using the language he does. A comparison of Col. 1.15-20 with Prov. 8.22-31 helps to explain a lot of what Paul says about Christ's pre-existence and his role in creation (see above, p. 58). Another key passage is in the Apocryphal *Wisdom of Solomon*, 7.15 – 8.1, where Wisdom is called the 'artificer of all things' and 'an effulgence from everlasting light', who also has a saving role, for 'from generation to generation passing into holy souls she makes men friends of God and prophets'.

By New Testament times the Jews readily thought of Wisdom as the highest possible, pre-existent, divine reality under God himself, begotten before creation, a reflection of God's own light, active in creation, and active in revealing

God to men. Wisdom was God in action.

Paul's argument is therefore that in Christ God has revealed to us all of himself that he possibly could, so what more is needed? In Christ you have all God's wisdom you can possibly get, so why heed those that would tell you otherwise and would try to supplement the gospel with their various philosophies and practices? In Christ you have everything! 'He is the image of the invisible God ... God was pleased to have all his fullness dwell in him.'

Wisdom in Christian Experience.

In 1 Cor. 2.6-16 Paul says that it is only by the activity of the Spirit we receive understanding of the wisdom of God. 'God's secret wisdom' (v. 7), he explains, is something the world has never understood, but 'God has revealed it to us by his Spirit' (v. 10). To the unspiritual man it remains foolishness (v. 14), but to the spiritual man it is 'the mind of Christ' (v. 16).

The wisdom writers of the Old Testament already taught a connection between wisdom and the Spirit (see pp. 77f). The difference for us now is the embodiment of wisdom in Christ, but its unfolding is still given by the Spirit. Or, as John's Gospel puts it, the Spirit of truth leads us into all truth, bringing glory to Jesus (John 16.12-14). It is a common experience among Christians that baptism in the Spirit opens a vista of understanding about Christ and the purposes of God they were not able to attain otherwise. In 2 Cor. 3 Paul says such revelation is like the removal of a veil from our minds—and that, he adds, 'comes from the Lord, who is the Spirit' (v. 18).

Our clearest example of the operation of spiritual wisdom is, of course, in Jesus' own ministry. It was foretold that he would be endowed with 'the Spirit of wisdom and under-standing, the Spirit of counsel and power, the Spirit of knowledge and the fear of the Lord' (Isa. 11.2). As a child, he 'grew and became strong; he was filled with wisdom, and the grace of God was upon him,' and so he 'grew in wisdom and stature, and in favour with God and men' (Luke 2.40,52). In later life he had an answer for every necessity that amazed many: 'Where did this man get this wisdom?' they asked (Matt. 13.54).

We see this wisdom operating also among the early Christians. When Peter and John gave testimony before the Sanhedrin, realising 'that they were unschooled, ordinary men, they were astonished' (Acts 4.13). Similarly when Stephen argued, his opponents 'could not stand up against his wisdom or the Spirit by which he spoke' (Acts 6.10). And that was exactly what Jesus himself promised that his followers would find: 'I will give you words and wisdom that none of your adversaries will be able to resist or contradict' (Luke 21.15).

When Paul mentions 'the word of wisdom' at the head of his list of spiritual gifts in 1 Cor. 12.8 (KJV), it must be to such specific applications of wisdom that he is referring. We can therefore think of some such pattern of relationship and development as in the following chart:

WISDOM IN CHRISTIAN EXPERIENCE	
1 GOD'S WISDOM	*(active in creation)*
is	
2 revealed in Jesus,	*(active in incarnation)*
is	
3 given to us by the Spirit,	*(active in regeneration)*
and is	
4 expressed in a 'word of wisdom'.	*(active in ministry)*

The same Spirit of wisdom as Jesus and the apostles knew is still available for us, because Jesus, says Paul, 'has become for us wisdom from God' (1 Cor. 1.30). He therefore prays that God will 'give you the Spirit of wisdom and revelation, so that you may know him (Christ) better' (Eph. 1.17), and that he will 'fill you with the knowledge of his will through all spiritual wisdom and understanding' (Col. 1.9).

This wisdom clearly includes a deep understanding of God's word and his ways, of the Scriptures and the truth about God and his world. It is not gained by much study, but by revelation through the working of the Spirit. Hence it unlocks mysteries hidden to others, giving discernment and judgment beyond their reach (1 Cor. 2.10-16).

We receive wisdom through the Spirit by faith (Jas. 1.5-8). We can grow in wisdom through meditating on God's word (Ps. 119.97-104) and through being filled anew (Col. 1.9). We use wisdom in testifying (Luke 21.15), teaching (Col. 3.16), life's decisions (Jas. 3.13), and presumably also in exercising the twin gift of the 'word of knowledge' (1 Cor. 12.8, KJV), since knowledge is revealed information and we usually need wisdom to show us how to use that information.

Such is the gift of God to us in Christ through his Spirit!

4. CHRIST, THE HEAD OF THE CHURCH (EPHESIANS)

Ephesians was written about the same time as Colossians and carried by the same messenger, Tychicus (6.21f; cp. Col. 4.7f). Paul may have sent it, not just to Ephesus, but as a circular letter to other churches in Asia, among which Ephesus was the most important. The main reasons for believing something like that was the case are that Paul, though he addressed the letter to a church in which he had ministered for three years, included no personal greetings and wrote as if he had never met his readers (1.15; 3.2; 4.21), and also that some early manuscripts do not have 'in Ephesus' in 1.1. It may even be that this was the letter Paul expected to be passed on to the Colossians from Laodicea, though it is usually thought that that one is now lost to history (Col. 4.16).

Ephesians is one of Paul's richest and best loved letters. In Philippians he asserts Christ's Lordship over life's circumstances, in Philemon over personal relationships, and in Colossians over every power in creation. Now he asserts that same Lordship over all mankind and history through the Church. We have seen how he believes there is a divine purpose in history and how he speaks of it as a 'mystery' or 'secret' that is only revealed to men in Christ through the working of the Spirit. Of course, the whole of Scripture attests to the same truth, but now Paul summarises it beautifully in Ephesians.

God is a loving Father who desires men to live in harmony with himself and each other. However, the present state of the world is one of alienation: God and man, man and man at enmity with each other, and spiritual powers aggravating the rift. But God has always had a plan to restore harmony. That has remained a secret until recent times, but now it has been unveiled in Christ. In him all history finds new meaning, through the victory he won by his death, resurrection and ascension, by which he has opened the way for reconciliation to take place.

Today it is in the Church, which is Christ's body and over which he rules as the head, that this reconciliation is being worked out. There men find a new fellowship that transcends social and racial divisions, but since that fellowship is precious and has a continuing purpose of bringing reconciliation to the rest of mankind, Paul urges that it be cherished by its members, sustained by living godly lives and defended against the continuing assault of spiritual foes.

Ch. 1: We have every spiritual blessing in Christ.
Praise God for how he has blessed us in Christ! He has chosen us, adopted us as his sons, given us his grace, redemption and forgiveness, and has lavished his abundance on us. He has also given us revelation of his plan ('the mystery of his will'), which finds its focus in Christ who makes it all cohere. We were chosen for a purpose and sealed in it by the Holy Spirit, given us as a guarantee of our ultimate inheritance. (vv. 3-14)

I keep on praying God will give you understanding of all that ('the Spirit of wisdom and revelation'), that you may know him better, and that you may know the hope and the wealth of what you have been called into, as well as the power of it all, namely the power of Christ whom God has now raised and set above all other powers. God has appointed him head of the church, which is his body, in which everything is to be drawn into one. (vv. 15-23)

Ch. 2: We are given new life and made one in Christ.
Just think of it. You were once dead in your sins, held captive by the ways of this world, but God in his mercy has saved us and made us alive in Christ, raising us up with him into heavenly places. All that operates by his grace alone,

not our works. And it is only by faith we enjoy the benefits, for the only works he has called us to do are those he himself prepared in advance for us to walk in. (vv. 1-10)

Once Gentiles were excluded from God's people, but now they have been brought in through Christ's sacrifice. He has broken down all the barriers, making peace, breaking the curse of alienation, creating one new humanity. The church is like a great building rising on the foundation of apostles and prophets, with Christ as the chief cornerstone, to become a holy temple, a dwelling in which God lives by his Spirit. (vv. 11-22)

Throughout chs. 1–2 Paul repeatedly emphasises the richness of what is made available to us 'in Christ'. Note the expressions he uses: 'chose us ... to be adopted as his sons ... grace, which he has freely given ... redemption through his blood, the forgiveness of sins ... all wisdom and under-standing ... made known to us the mystery of his will ... chosen for the praise of his glory ... marked in him with a seal, the promised Holy Spirit (1.3-13) ... made us alive with Christ ... raised us up with Christ and seated us with him in the heavenly realms in Christ Jesus ... created in Christ to do good works (2.1-10) ... he himself is our peace ... to create in himself one new man out of the two (Jews and Gentiles) ... through him we both have access to the Father by one Spirit ... members of God's household ... in him you too are being built together to become a dwelling in which God lives by his Spirit' (2.11-22). Every one of these phrases, and many of the others as well, merits some comment. Unfortunately space does not permit that here, but it is well worth reading these chapters through slowly, pausing over each rich phrase, and thinking for a moment what it should mean for you.

Ch. 3: Paul speaks of his purpose in preaching.
My calling is to preach this good news, the full revelation of which has only recently been made available to us through Christ. It is my job as a preacher to unfold 'this mystery', this 'wisdom of God', which came through Christ and is now at work in the church.

I therefore pray that God will 'strengthen you with power through his Spirit' so that you will fully appreciate the comprehensiveness of the love of Christ I preach and thus be filled with 'all the fullness of God'.

Paul describes the gospel he preaches as 'the mystery made known to me by revelation' (v. 2). He speaks of it in much the same way in Gal. 1.11f: 'I did not receive it from any man, nor was I taught it; rather I received it by revelation from Jesus Christ.' This experience of revelation is what he alludes to in 2 Cor. 3.14-18, where he likens it to the lifting of a veil uncovering the meaning of Scripture ('the old covenant'), which, he says, comes from the Spirit. It is the same experience that Christians enjoy today when they are baptised in the Spirit. Through it the 'mystery' of the gospel is unveiled, Jesus is glorified to them and a new power to witness is imparted, such that it becomes almost impossible to restrain themselves from telling others about it all. It is such revelation through the Spirit that above all turns men into preachers and evangelists.

4.1-16: Maintaining and maturing in the unity of the body.

The church is Christ's own body and therefore very precious. Treat it as such and strive to maintain unity of the Spirit in it. Recognise its different leadership anointings, for they are Christ's own gifts and function to build up the body and make it strong. And remember that Christ is the head of the body, that it is he who holds it all together. (On the ministries, see below, pp. 193f.)

4.17 – 6.24: Therefore …

… live every aspect of your life 'in Christ'—your conduct, speech and thought, your family and workaday life, and your spiritual life. 'Be strong in the Lord.'

Don't live in your old pre-Christian ways. You have already been taught about putting off your old self and being made new in Christ. Don't give the devil a foothold and don't grieve the Holy Spirit. (4.17-32)

Be imitators of God. Live as children of light, not darkness. Find out what pleases God and do it. Be filled with the Spirit and praise God always and for everything. (5.1-21)

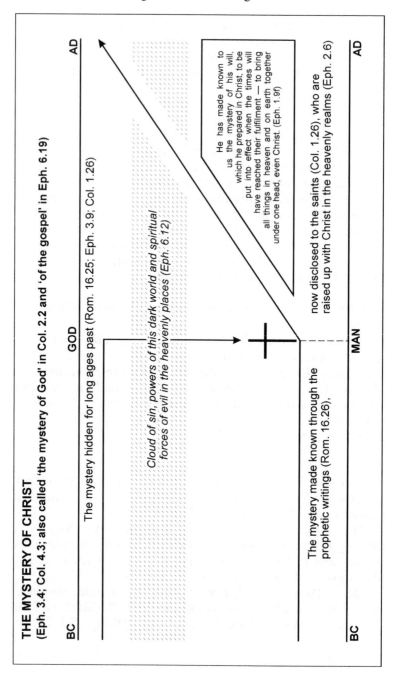

THE MYSTERY OF CHRIST
(Eph. 3.4; Col. 4.3; also called 'the mystery of God' in Col. 2.2 and 'of the gospel' in Eph. 6.19)

BC   GOD   AD

The mystery hidden for long ages past (Rom. 16.25; Eph. 3.9; Col. 1.26)

*Cloud of sin, powers of this dark world and spiritual
forces of evil in the heavenly places (Eph. 6.12)*

He has made known to
us the mystery of his will,
which he prepared in Christ, to be
put into effect when the times will
have reached their fulfilment — to bring
all things in heaven and on earth together
under one head, even Christ. (Eph. 1.9f)

now disclosed to the saints (Col. 1.26), who are
raised up with Christ in the heavenly realms (Eph. 2.6)

The mystery made known through the
prophetic writings (Rom. 16.26),

BC   MAN   AD

Let the principles of Christ's body govern your family life too, in all its aspects, and also your relationships at work, whether you are worker or boss. (5.22 – 6.9)

Protect the good you have in Christ. Be prepared like a soldier for action and stand firm in your faith. Keep alert, for our struggle is not just against men, but 'against the spiritual forces of evil in the heavenly realms'. (6.10-18)

And pray for me that I may continue to preach this gospel boldly. Tychicus will give you all my news. May God's peace and grace be with you all. (6.19-24)

Ephesians is a happy, praise-filled letter of encouragement. Its positive exhortation is perhaps best summed up in 5.18-20:

> *Be filled with the Spirit. Speak to one another with psalms, hymns and spiritual songs. Sing and make music in your heart to the Lord, always giving thanks to God the Father for everything, in the name of our Lord Jesus Christ.*

The Ministry Gifts of the Body of Christ (4.7-13)

In 4.11 Paul lists apostles, prophets, evangelists, pastors and teachers as the leading ministries of the church. A similar, but more extended, list is found in 1 Cor. 12.28, and that may be further supplemented with other, mainly subsidiary ministries listed in Rom. 12.6-8. Then in the pastoral letters we shall find Paul speaking of the offices of overseer (bishop), elder (presbyter) and deacon (servant). Perhaps the best way to understand the functions of all these ministries and their interrelationships is as follows:

- Pastors and teachers have to care for and teach their congregations;
- Apostles have a wider ministry to the churches at large;
- Evangelists are called to reach the unconverted;
- Overseers, elders and deacons have general responsibility for the welfare and running of their churches;
- Others have subsidiary ministries and support them in the work;
- Prophets are called to encourage those engaged in these ministries, for all need the encouragement of prophetic words that it is granted to some to give them.

Of course, the lines of demarcation are not always so clearly drawn. For example, the overseer, pastor, or evangelist may have a prophetic ministry as well as his own ministry of oversight, pastoral care, or evangelism, and so forth. It is never said that one man could only exercise one ministry, though as a general rule each individual will be seen to have his own particular, identifiable gift or ministry granted by the Spirit, each for the building up of the church.

These ministries will be found locally in individual congregations, but also regionally and globally throughout the whole body of Christ, for though Christ's body is universal, each congregation is called to be an expression of it. It is significant that the ministries of apostle, prophet and evangelist, as well as all the others, are being rediscovered and revived with renewed vitality in Pentecostal and Charismatic churches today. They are, after all, said to be God's gifts to the body, not just jobs and appointments in the church, and therefore rank alongside the other gifts of the Spirit in 1 Cor. 12 and Rom. 12.

It is, however, worth bearing in mind when we turn to the pastoral letters and read about the offices of overseer, elder and deacon, that in the body of Christ everything should operate by the enabling of the Spirit anyhow, and no less so among those ministries that at first sight may seem less supernatural than others.

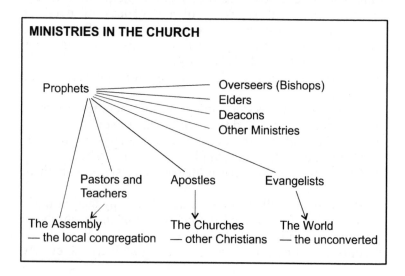

MINISTRIES IN THE CHURCH

Prophets

Overseers (Bishops)
Elders
Deacons
Other Ministries

Pastors and Teachers   Apostles   Evangelists

The Assembly
— the local congregation

The Churches
— other Christians

The World
— the unconverted

13

Guard the Good Deposit

PAUL'S PASTORAL EPISTLES

1 & 2 Timothy and Titus are called the 'Pastoral Letters' because they speak of pastoral affairs, mainly to do with church administration, sound teaching and consecrated living. Because their interest is so practical, they seem to be the least spiritual of Paul's letters, so much so that some scholars have questioned whether he actually wrote them himself. That question need not detain us here, for our interest lies elsewhere, mainly in what the Holy Spirit teaches us through these letters.

1. PAUL, TIMOTHY AND TITUS

Part of the problem about authorship is that it is impossible to fit the personal information given in these letters into any part of Paul's life as we know it from Acts. However, Acts ends with Paul in prison in Rome awaiting trial and gives no account of the outcome. Clement, bishop of Rome at the end of the first century, tells us in a letter he wrote to the Corinthian church (*First Epistle to the Corinthians, 5.7*), that before Paul died his missionary journeyings took him to 'the limits of the West', which in Roman times referred to Spain. Paul himself tells us in Rom. 15.24 that he intended to go there after visiting Rome, so perhaps he was released early in 64 AD, before the burning of Rome in July that sparked off Nero's persecutions, and was able to fulfil his ambition to preach the gospel in Spain. Later historians record that he was finally beheaded in Rome in 67 AD.

Now, his letters to the Philippians and Philemon, written while he was in prison in Rome before 64 AD, suggest he wanted to return east and revisit some of his friends there if released to do so (Phil. 1.25-27; Philem. 22). Assuming the letters to Timothy and Titus belong to these last years of Paul's life after 64, then it seems he fulfilled this ambition too. From them we can piece together the following history of his last years, though it must be admitted from the outset that there can be no certainty about the sequence we are about to outline. It is just one possible solution to an otherwise enigmatic problem.

64 AD   Paul is released from prison in the spring.
- He sails to Crete with Titus, whom he leaves there to organise the churches (Tit. 1.5)
- He sails to Ephesus where he leaves Timothy to do the same thing (1 Tim. 1.3f). If he did visit Philemon, it must have been at this time (Philem. 22).
- From Ephesus he goes to Macedonia, perhaps to Philippi, and from there writes to Timothy (first letter) and Titus about the ministries he has left them to do (1 Tim. 1.3).
- He spends the winter in Nicopolis where Titus rejoins him after being relieved by Artemas or Tychicus (Tit. 3.12).

65–67   Paul goes to Spain, possibly taking Titus with him.
67   Paul returns east.
- He visits Miletus where he leaves Trophimus because he is sick (2 Tim. 4.20).
- He goes north to Troas, where he leaves a cloak and some scrolls with one called Carpus (2 Tim. 4.13).
- From Troas he goes to Corinth where Erastus stays behind (2 Tim. 4.20).
- Then finally he is in Rome, a prisoner.

We have no idea whether he was arrested in Rome itself, or earlier in Troas or Corinth, but his imprisonment was probably brief and certainly he was harshly treated (2 Tim. 1.15f; 2.9). He is very much alone. Most of his companions have left him. Only Luke is with him and so he writes to Timothy (second letter) pleading with him to come quickly and bring Mark as well (2 Tim. 4.6-11).

We have no idea whether they arrived before he was executed. The second letter to Timothy may well have been Paul's last communication with one of his dearest and most faithful friends.

Timothy and Titus were to Paul what Peter and John were to Jesus, close and faithful disciples. The impression we get of them is that they were very different personalities.

Timothy was the son of a Greek father and a Jewess called Eunice (Acts 16.1; 2 Tim. 1.5). He lived at Lystra and was probably converted by Paul there on his first missionary journey, in 46 or 47 AD. He joined Paul and Silas at the beginning of his second evangelistic expedition, highly commended by his fellow Christians at Lystra and Antioch, but also by prophetic utterances that confirmed his call to this ministry (1 Tim. 1.18; 4.14). It was not long before he found himself entrusted with his first ministry, when he had to stay behind in Thessalonica with Silas and encourage the young church there, while Paul went south to Athens (Acts 17.14f).

On Paul's third journey, in 56 AD, during his long stay in Ephesus (Acts 19), Timothy was sent to Corinth to deal with the situation there, but he was, it seems, quite a timid young man and not able to handle the strong personalities involved (1 Cor. 4.17f; 16.10f), so Paul sent Titus later in the year.

In 59 AD Timothy accompanied Paul to Jerusalem where his master was arrested (Acts 20.4f) and he may have stayed with him throughout his imprisonment. He was certainly with Paul when he wrote to the Colossians and the Philippians, for Paul spoke exceedingly highly of his dedication to the Lord's service at that time (Phil. 2.19-24).

Then we come to the period of the Pastorals, when Paul left Timothy in Ephesus, still a fairly timid person in much need of encouragement (2 Tim. 1.7f). His physical frame apparently matched his personality, for we read that he suffered from frequent illnesses (1 Tim. 5.23). Nevertheless, no other companion of Paul's is so warmly commended for his loyalty, and so it is fitting that the last letter he wrote should have been addressed to him.

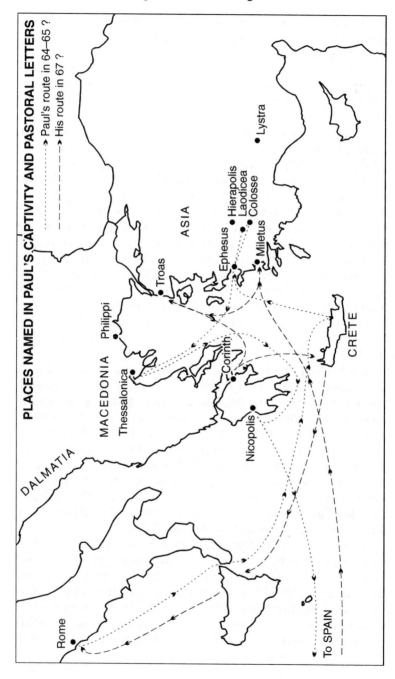

PLACES NAMED IN PAUL'S CAPTIVITY AND PASTORAL LETTERS

······▶ Paul's route in 64–65 ?
– – –▶ His route in 67 ?

DALMATIA

MACEDONIA
Thessalonica
Philippi

Nicopolis

Corinth

Rome

To SPAIN

ASIA

Troas

Ephesus
Hierapolis
Laodicea
Colosse
Miletus

Lystra

CRETE

Titus was a much stronger person. He is not named in Acts. We first meet him when Paul took him to Jerusalem in 48 AD to present him to the council there as an example of a Gentile convert (Gal. 2.1-3). We next hear of him at the time of the Corinthian crisis in 56 AD. Paul sent him to Corinth to organise a collection for the poor in Jerusalem (2 Cor. 8.6) and to iron out the problems that Timothy had not been able to handle. This was a time of great anguish in Paul's relationship with the church in Corinth (2 Cor. 2), but it seems that Titus had some measure of success in dealing with the situation, for when he rejoined Paul he came with good news (2 Cor. 7), and so Paul sent him back, carrying 2 Corinthians, to see to the completion of the collection and make final preparations for his own arrival (2 Cor. 8.16-24).

After his release from prison in 64 AD, Paul left Titus in Crete to deal with another difficult situation in churches again dominated by strong personalities. Later that year he summoned him to Nicopolis and may have taken him from there to Spain. The last we hear of him he is on mission in Dalmatia in 67 AD (2 Tim. 4.10).

Having spent so much time in Paul's company and having themselves gained so much first-hand experience, these two men had no need for Paul to instruct them about Christian ministry as if they knew nothing of it already. The Pastorals are written for a different purpose. Paul wrote to encourage his disciples in their work and to remind them of the importance and urgency of some very basic essentials. When we read them, in the midst of all the practical advice Paul gives, we need to take care that we do not miss his exhortation to hold on to and rekindle faith in the basic beliefs about Christ and the Spirit. There is even a danger of wanting to skip over the passages that discuss such things almost as if they were intrusions diverting our interest off the more 'important' instructions about ministry matters. Beware of letting that happen as you read. Paul's exhortation is basically to keep Christ central, to keep the fire of the Spirit alive, to hold fast to true Christian teaching and to pursue holiness of life.

2. HOW TO ADMINISTER THE AFFAIRS OF THE CHURCH
(1 TIMOTHY)

Paul has left Timothy in Ephesus to put right the affairs of the church there, but now he suspects his absence may be rather prolonged (3.14f). He therefore writes to encourage Timothy in the meantime not to neglect the 'gift' he received through prophecy at the time of his ordination (4.14), but to stand firm in his own 'good confession' of faith (6.16) and guard 'what has been entrusted' to him (6.20). The problem in Ephesus, which could crush this rather diffident young man, was mainly heretical teaching being propounded by some members of the church, some of them doubtless fairly strong personalities again. The heresy was probably some version of the mixed Gnostic and Jewish tendency we already encountered at Colosse. The antidote recommended here is basically strong, orthodox leadership and plenty of good, sound teaching.

Ch. 1: Hold on to faith and a good conscience.
I left you in Ephesus to oppose the false teachers there, those that lead people into discussions about myths and endless genealogies—relating to the intermediate spiritual beings of the Gnostic systems (? see above pp. 182f)—and also those that make an imbalanced use of the law. If you want to see what they are doing in right perspective, then contrast it with what you know about Christ's basic call to love (v. 5), about the glorious gospel that was entrusted to me (v. 11), about the effect it has had on my life (vv. 12-17). Timothy, you know what is good—hold fast to that!

Ch. 2: Teach your people to pray.
God wants everyone to be saved. That is the gospel and it is to that end that I preach. So teach your people to pray to God for all men, but without ostentation that will only draw attention to self. Men should pray without anger or disputing and women in quietness and submission, as befits both sexes.

Ch. 3: Choose good leaders.

Choose overseers and deacons carefully, because their lives will be an example to the church. And that is utterly important, because we are dealing with 'the mystery of godliness', not just administrative systems.

Ch. 4: Do not hesitate to confront heresy.

Don't be surprised that there is false teaching around. That's what we were told would happen. You must oppose it and warn your people against it. But the best antidote is that you live in the full confidence of your gospel and of your own spiritual gift. Preach it, teach it, guard it and live up to it.

Chs. 5–6: Some further pieces of advice.

Paul now gives Timothy some mixed instructions about:
- his conduct towards people (5.1f),
- support for and the role of widows in the church (5.3-16),
- support for and disciplining of elders (5.17-22),
- treating his illnesses (5.23),
- discerning sin: Don't worry about how to do that, for it will not be able to be kept hidden, nor will goodness (5.24f),
- conduct of slaves towards their masters (6.1f),
- the danger of wrong attitudes to money in ministry (6.3-10).

Timothy, shun all thought of financial gain and pursue righteousness, faith, love and the like. Aim for eternal life and hold on to your good confession, just as Jesus did (6.11-16). Teach the rich to have the same attitude too (6.17-19). And again I say, don't be influenced by false teaching, but guard the deposit entrusted to you (6.20f).

3. ENCOURAGE GODLY LIVING (TITUS)

The problems confronting Titus in Crete were somewhat different from those Timothy had to deal with in Ephesus. Cretans were a naturally unruly people and their lack of moral and social grace was undermining church life. Paul's exhortation is therefore to upright, disciplined living. His repeated use of such words as blameless, holy, good, self-controlled, upright and disciplined tells all. The answer to the Cretan problem, however, was not much different from the answer to the Ephesian one: appointment of trustworthy leaders, sound teaching, personal example and constant reminders of what God has done for us in Christ.

Ch. 1: On congregational life.
Choose elders who are men of integrity and sound faith. Good overseers are essential because there are too many religious charlatans around. They profess to know God, but their deeds deny him.

Ch. 2: On family life.
Older men, older women, younger men, younger women and slaves all need to be taught godly living, both by your example and through your preaching, 'so that in every way they will make the teaching about God our Saviour attractive' (v. 10) and will be ready for 'the glorious appearing of our great God and Saviour, Jesus Christ' (v. 13).

Ch. 3: On life in society.
The call is again to temperate, godly living. And the reason why is because it was from unruly, sinful living that God saved us in the first instance, 'through the washing of rebirth and renewal by the Holy Spirit whom he poured out on us generously through Jesus Christ' (vv. 5f). Paul writes, 'I want you to stress these things', because it is the power of the gospel, not just moral preaching or administrative organisation that makes men godly. Despite all his practical and seemingly churchy advice, Paul's teaching is thoroughly focused on the power of Christ through the working of the Holy Spirit.

**4. BE STRONG IN THE GRACE THAT IS IN CHRIST
(2 TIMOTHY)**

Turning to this epistle we find that the atmosphere has changed radically. Paul is no longer a free man, but a prisoner facing almost certain death. He is lonely and far from comfortable in his chains. Winter is approaching, and so he will need the cloak he left at Troas (4.13,21). But more than that, he longs for the company of Timothy himself.

Timothy may still be in Ephesus, but it is no longer the problems of the church there that concern Paul. This is a very personal letter to his dear disciple, encouraging him in his own life and ministry: to keep clinging to sound doctrine, to defend it against all error and to stand firm in his faith like a good soldier of the Lord.

Ch. 1: Be faithful.
Remember how you began your life as a Christian and 'fan into flame the gift of God, which is in you through the laying on of my hands' (v. 6). Do not be ashamed to testify, nor to suffer for the gospel, for God has blessed us richly in Christ. 'Guard the good deposit that was entrusted to you— guard it with the help of the Holy Spirit who lives in us' (v. 14).

Ch. 2: Teach others.
Teach the things you have heard from me to reliable men, and stand firm like a good soldier. Keep Jesus central to your teaching, and 'Keep reminding them of these things' (v. 14). Avoid all false teaching, wrong living and pointless argument. Teach to bring to repentance and knowledge of the truth.

Ch. 3: Stand firm.
All sorts of terrible and wrong ways of living will multiply, as will wrong teachings, leading many astray, but you know my teaching and how I lived for Christ, so continue in what you have learned. You know how it makes you wise for salvation.

Ch. 4: Preach the word.
The times are urgent and there are plenty of people who will teach other things, so 'I give you this charge: Preach the word … correct, rebuke and encourage … Do the work of an evangelist', for my own ministry is now all but finished. Timothy, it's over to you now. 'Do your best to come to me quickly … before winter … The Lord be with your spirit. Grace be with you.'

This is a precious letter. Besides providing us with a portrait of the great apostle in his last days, it should encourage us to complete our own work for the Lord with all diligence, so that we too can be counted faithful like Paul and Timothy, and also to seek out others whom we can make disciples and to whom we can hand over our charge, so that they can continue it in Christ's name, in the same way as Paul handed his charge over to Timothy.

I have fought the good fight, I have finished the race, I have kept the faith. Now there is in store for me the crown of righteousness, which the Lord, the righteous Judge, will award to me on that day--and not only to me, but also to all who have longed for his appearing.
(4.7-8)

14

Constant in Wisdom, Faithfulness and Truth

JAMES, 1 & 2 PETER, JUDE

The letters of James, Peter, John and Jude are often referred to as the Catholic or General Epistles, because they are addressed to a wider audience than a local church or an individual (that is, apart from 2 and 3 John). Hence, unlike Paul's letters that are all known by the name of the congregation or person to whom they are addressed, these letters are known by the names of their authors.

The fact that they are placed at the end of the New Testament tells us nothing about the date when they were written: John's letters seem to come from the end of the first century, but James may have been written in the fifties. Nor does it tell us anything about their value in relation to the other letters. Nevertheless, because they are short and tucked away at the end of the Bible, they do tend to get forgotten, though they all contain some excellent spiritual gems that we neglect to our own great loss.

1. IF ANY OF YOU LACKS WISDOM (JAMES)

James addresses his letter to 'the twelve tribes scattered among the nations'. Since it is not an evangelistic letter, it is unlikely he is thinking of the Jewish people, but rather the Christian Church regarded as the new Israel of God, the inheritor through Jesus the Messiah of the covenants made

with God's ancient people Israel. We may therefore take his
address to refer to 'Christians everywhere'.

The author simply calls himself 'James, a servant of God
and of the Lord Jesus Christ', and gives us no other hint of
his identity. James was a common enough name in New
Testament times. Two of Jesus' twelve apostles bore it:
James son of Zebedee and James son of Alphaeus (Matt.
10.2f), but most people believe our author was another
James, the brother of Jesus, sometimes called 'James the
Just', who became leader of the church at Jerusalem.

He and his brothers had difficulty in believing during
Jesus' lifetime (Mark 3.21; John 7.5), but Jesus appeared to
him after the resurrection (1 Cor. 15.7) and they joined their
mother, the apostles and others in Jerusalem to pray and
wait for the Spirit at Pentecost (Acts 1.12-14). By the time
Paul's first missionary journey was over James had become
one of the leading elders in Jerusalem, perhaps *the* leading
elder, since it was he who gave the final ruling at the
conference in 48 AD (Acts 15.12-21; Gal. 2.9,12). He was
certainly established as chief elder by 58, for when Paul
returned to Jerusalem that year it was to 'James and all the
elders' that he reported (Acts 21.18). The Jewish historian
Josephus (*Jewish Antiquities* 20.9) tells us that he was
stoned to death in 62 AD by decree of the Jewish high priest
and the Sanhedrin.

If this James was the author of the epistle, then clearly it
must have been written before 62, that is before Paul arrived
in Rome. It would then predate all the letters of Paul we
have studied in this volume, though not necessarily his
earlier missionary letters. At the time of writing some of
these, Paul was having an extremely difficult time with
opposition from the Judaising 'circumcision party' (see
above, p. 178) who were objecting to his teaching that
permitted Gentiles to become Christians without having to
submit to all the demands of the law of Moses. Paul's
answer, which we have preserved in some detail in Galatians and Romans and which we touched on in Philippians,
was that the law was given by God as a tutor to prepare us
for Christ, but now that Christ has come we do not need to
get stuck in its slavish, preparatory teaching any more, but
can graduate to the fuller and freer maturity that is found in

him. That, however, is only made possible by faith in the effectiveness of Christ's death for releasing us from sin's bondage and faith in the new life and power available to us through the gift of his Spirit (Gal. 3.23 – 4.7). Our gospel is therefore about faith from first to last; that is the sum and substance of the matter (Rom. 1.16f). And now through faith:

> *we have been released from the law so that we serve in the new way of the Spirit, and not in the old way of the written code.*
>
> (Rom. 7.6)

Now James, being head of a thoroughly Jewish church, must have found himself under considerable pressure to enter this debate, particularly from the strong Pharisaic party in his congregation who were doing their utmost to correct, as they thought, Paul's incomplete gospel (Gal. 2.12f). Reading 2.14-26, where he speaks of faith without deeds being dead, it seems he did express an opinion, and one which on the surface looks as if it contradicts Paul's teaching. That, however, can hardly be the case, for James, we know, approved of Paul's gospel (Acts 15.12-21; Gal. 2.9f). In actual fact, what the two men say is totally in harmony. The works Paul opposes are those that would draw men back from saving faith in Christ into seeking salvation through legalistic religion; the works James advocates are not such legalistic substitutes for, or additions to faith, but deeds that grow out of and demonstrate the reality of our faith. Paul would have heartily approved of everything James wrote, just as James approved of Paul's teaching.

James' letter is no naive retort to Paul's gospel. Far from it. It is rather an expanded version of the kind of teaching we find at the end of Paul's letters, where he gives instruction about putting faith into practice in everyday Christian living. The whole theme of James is precisely that: practical religion. It perhaps helps to think of it as a Christian counterpart to the Old Testament book of Proverbs, a collection of short passages and sayings on a variety of different themes giving very practical advice about many aspects of Christian living and behaviour. Another near relation to it is

Jesus' own Sermon on the Mount in Matt. 5–7.

This is not an evangelistic letter that preaches the gospel. Indeed Jesus is only named in it twice. It does, however, demand that we live out the gospel to the full and that we maintain the highest standards in doing so. In our day, when Christianity far too often seems to be so much a matter of words and talk, it is good to have this strong reminder that words alone are not enough, that there must also be deeds to match them.

The letter's advice is so clear and practical that it scarcely needs comment here. The main topics covered are:

Ch. 1: on persevering in times of trial (vv. 2-4,12),
    obtaining wisdom (vv. 5-8),
    handling wealth and poverty (vv. 9-11),
    dealing with temptation (vv. 13-18),
    hearing and doing the word (vv. 19-27);
Ch. 2: on avoiding favouritism(vv. 1-7),
    loving your neighbour(vv. 8-13),
    faith and deeds (vv. 14-26);
Ch. 3: on the responsibility of a teacher (vv. 1f),
    controlling the tongue (vv. 3-12),
    recognising true wisdom (vv. 13-18);
Ch. 4: on not coveting (vv. 1-3),
    not compromising (vv. 4-10),
    not criticising (vv. 11f),
    not boasting (vv. 13-16);
Ch. 5: on the dangers of wealth (vv. 1-6),
    Christian patience, particularly in suffering (vv. 7-12),
    praying for the sick (vv. 13-16),
    praying with faith (vv. 17f),
    and reclaiming backsliders (vv. 19f).

Two contrasting things have happened in today's renewal movements. On the one hand they have developed ministries to the sick and to the poor and needy and have become actively involved in social care programmes and political action. On the other they have been criticised for being too much about praise, prophecy, preaching, prayer meetings and the like and not enough about caring for orphans, widows and the poor. Either way, it is good to have this letter from a time when the church was thoroughly charismatic. Note, however, that James, though utterly practical, never ceases to be spiritual as well. His opening words are about persevering in faith and seeking spiritual wisdom (1.2-8) and his closing exhortation is to pray in faith for healing and miracles (5.13-18), whilst in between he gives teaching about resisting temptation (1.12-15), spiritual warfare (4.7) and discerning spiritual gifts (1.16-18; 3.13-18). The spiritual dynamic of the gospel is certainly not lost in this most practical of letters. We could well sum up his teaching by rephrasing an old maxim: God does not want Christians to be so spiritually minded that they are of no earthly use, and yet he does very much want them to be spiritually minded, otherwise they will indeed be of no earthly use.

2. A FAITH AS PRECIOUS AS OURS (1 AND 2 PETER)

We know more about Peter than any other early Christian leader, apart from Paul, and if anyone's life-story bears testimony to the transforming power of the Holy Spirit, it is his. Unlike Paul, he was not dramatically converted from a position of antipathy, but was well disposed to Jesus from the start, just like many in our churches today. And yet he discovered, as fully as any fresh convert, the power of God to make him a new man in Christ.

He came from Bethsaida, was married and worked with his brother, Andrew, as a fisherman on the Sea of Galilee. Andrew introduced him to Jesus (John 1.35-42, 44) and some time later he abandoned his work to follow Jesus and join his band of twelve apostles (Mark 1.16-18; Luke 5.1-11). Along with James and John he had the privilege of being close to Jesus at some of the most memorable moments in his ministry, such as the raising of Jairus' daughter (Mark 5.35-43), the Transfiguration (9.2-8) and the agony in Gethsemane (14.33). Occasionally we see him taking the lead or acting as the group's spokesman, as when he stepped out on the water with Jesus (Matt. 14.28-32), when he acknowledged Jesus as the Christ (16.16), or when he spoke up at the Transfiguration (17.4). Sometimes his speech and action demonstrated courage, sometimes mere impetuosity, but Jesus recognised him as 'the Rock' (Cephas from Aramaic, Peter from Greek) and future leader of the Church (John 1.42; Matt. 16.18), even though he knew he would deny him when the time of testing came (Matt. 26.31-35 and esp. Luke 22.31f). After his resurrection Jesus acknowledged his remorse and singled him out for special favour (Mark 16.7; Luke 24.34), then finally re-established him in pastoral oversight of the infant church by renewing his call on the shores of Galilee (John 21).

After Jesus' departure, supported by John, he became the chief leader and spokesman of the church in Jerusalem (Acts 1-5). He and John seem to have enjoyed special friendship during Jesus' lifetime, for apart from being members of the inner circle of disciples, we find them acting together from time to time, as at the preparation of the last Passover (Luke 22.8) and the first inspection of the empty tomb (John 20.1-9). Both were known to be 'unschooled, ordinary men' and so it has often been questioned whether Peter, a mere Galilean fisherman, could have written the two quite fluent Greek letters bearing his name. However, a radical change had taken place in his life. He was no longer a mere fisherman. He was now a man filled with God's Holy Spirit and even the Jewish authorities were astonished by the assurance with which he and John spoke (Acts 4.8,13).

Experience of leadership, preaching and travelling in the service of the gospel in subsequent years would only have added maturity to that initial boldness. The accounts of his defence of Cornelius' conversion (Acts 10.1 – 11.18) and later of the incorporation of the Gentiles through Paul's ministry (Acts 15) certainly demonstrate how much his wisdom was respected by the church.

However, his ministry is not remembered only for its wise leadership, but also for its dynamic power and its moments of Pentecostal anointing. Apart from performing some outstanding miracles (Acts 3, 5, 9), he became the church's leading preacher in the early days. It was also he who first explained the meaning of Pentecost (Acts 2), who ensured that Philip's converts at Samaria received the Spirit (Acts 8), and whose preaching led to Cornelius being baptised with the Holy Spirit (Acts 10–11). There can surely be little doubt where the source of Peter's strength as a Christian leader lay: in the love, acceptance and encouragement shown him by Jesus during his earthly life, in the knowledge of his forgiveness and salvation, and in the rich empowering of the Holy Spirit he knew after Pentecost. It is his high valuation of these rich blessings that shines through above all else in the letters he has left us.

After the conference in Jerusalem in 48 AD (Acts 15) we lose track of Peter. Paul tells us he visited Antioch where the two of them had something of a disagreement (Gal. 2.11-14). The reference to a group of his followers in Corinth suggests he may have preached there (1 Cor. 1.12). The fact that his first letter is addressed to churches scattered throughout much of the region of modern Turkey suggests he may have travelled extensively there too. Tradition has it that he eventually settled in Rome where he was martyred during Nero's persecution, in or soon after 64 AD.

It is often thought we have his own account of Jesus life in Mark's Gospel, since Mark, according to a second century bishop called Papias, joined him in Rome (cp. 1 Pet. 5.13), became his 'interpreter' and edited the stories of Jesus' life as he learned them from him (Eusebius, *Ecclesiastical History* III.39). Be that as it may, it is good to have at least these two letters and to hear the apostle speak personally through them of his appreciation of the richness of the blessing he knows in Christ.

The two letters are very different from each other, both in style and expression, but that is probably because Silas, Paul's missionary companion, who was also with Peter at the time, apparently helped him with the writing of the first one, and so perhaps its style is as much his as Peter's (5.12). Though no indication is given of the date of writing, both letters seem to come from Peter's last years in Rome.

1 PETER

'She who is in Babylon' in 1 Pet. 5.13 is probably a cryptic reference to the (Peter's) church in Rome. Babylon, because of its fury against the Jews at the time of the exile, became a

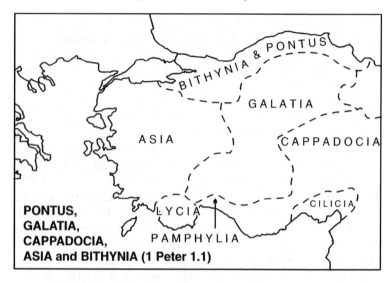

PONTUS,
GALATIA,
CAPPADOCIA,
ASIA and BITHYNIA (1 Peter 1.1)

symbol of oppressive imperial power persecuting the people
of God, which in later New Testament times meant Rome,
of course (cp. Rev. 17.5). In Peter's day persecution of
Christians was not yet policy throughout the whole empire,
but Peter, aware that the suffering must spread, wrote to
some of the churches he knew to encourage them and
prepare them for the ordeal that must one day come their
way. In doing so he has left us one of the most hope-filled
and encouraging letters in the Bible. His theme is basically
that we have been given something wonderful from God and
have a marvellous hope to look forward to, so prepare to
stand firm, cherish all the Lord has done and live your
Christian life out to the full.

1.3-12: Praise God for our hope and salvation.
You have been born anew into a living hope of an eternal
inheritance through Christ. You may suffer a little now, but
that will only serve to test and refine your faith. You love
Jesus, you believe in him and you are filled with inexpressi-
ble joy, all because you are receiving the salvation of your
souls. The prophets saw that coming and longed to know
when; now it has been told to you by men empowered by the
Holy Spirit sent from heaven.

1.13 – 2.3: Therefore, prepare your minds for action.
Live in readiness, holiness, reverent fear and appreciation of all God has done for you in Christ. Love one another. Be rid of all malice and pretence. Seek pure spiritual food—now that you have tasted that the Lord is good.

2.4-12: You are a people for God's praise.
You are being built like living stones into God's spiritual house, in which Jesus is the chief cornerstone (though some stumble over him). You are a chosen people, a royal priesthood, to declare God's praise. Live as such, that the world may see your good deeds and glorify God.

2.13 – 3.7: Advice for Christian daily living and relationships.
Governing authorities: Submit to them for the Lord's sake and show proper respect to all men. (Written at a time of persecution!)

Slaves: Submit to your masters, even if they ill-treat you. Consider how Jesus submitted to insult and how that had saving power.

Wives: Submit to your husbands and win them for Christ by true inner genuineness arising out of your new life in Christ.

Husbands: Treat your wives with the same genuineness.

3.8-22: Apply the same principles to all your relationships.
Live in love and harmony. Don't return evil for evil, but blessing, because that's what you are called to. Make Christ Lord in your heart and be always prepared to explain your faith. Give a good impression for Christ and so shame your persecutors. Don't be afraid to suffer unjustly, because that is how he died for your sins, the righteous for the unrighteous—he even went to preach to the spirits held bound since Noah's day. Your baptism is the pledge of all that.

Ch. 4: Live for God, whatever the cost.
Have done with the ways of the flesh and 'live according to God in regard to the spirit' (vv. 1-6; cp. Gal. 5.13-26).

Use your gifts in love, according to the strength God provides you (vv. 7-11; cp. Rom. 12.1-9)).

Rejoice in your suffering and don't be ashamed of Christ (vv. 12-19; cp. Matt. 5.10-12).

Ch. 5: A closing word to elders and young men.
Elders, shepherd the flock with willing hearts and the Chief Shepherd will reward you (vv. 1-4). Young men, stay humble, trust God and watch out for the devil. Be prepared to suffer for a while, but know that God will himself restore you (vv. 5-11).

2 PETER

Peter's second letter, like his first, was again written to uphold the faith, but this time in the face of different dangers. The problem was now heresy, not persecution. False teachers were abroad advocating free morality and scoffing at the hope of Christ's return, which is itself a good safeguard of Christian conduct. Peter's appeal is quite simply that our faith is far too precious to let it be adulterated by such rubbish.

This letter raises a number of questions we are not able to answer with any certainty. In 3.1 Peter says it is his second letter, but we cannot tell whether the first was 1 Peter, or another now lost, for he gives no hint about who he is addressing in this one. Most of ch. 2 is paralleled in Jude's letter and that amongst other things has led some to question whether Peter is even its author. (On the relationship between the two, see below on Jude.) Its own testimony is that it is from the Peter who was present at Christ's Transfiguration, and at a time when he believed his departure from this life was near (1.12-18), which suggests it was composed in Rome about the same time as 1 Peter and by the same author. The differences in style in his two letters must then be accounted for partly by the fact that Silas helped him write the first, and that the second was written either by himself or with the help of someone else who is not named this time.

Whatever the historical facts, the message is basically the same as in 1 Peter, that our faith is far too precious to lose.

Ch. 1: Be eager to make your calling and election sure.
Through Christ God's divine power has given us everything
we need for life and godliness, so keep building the best
Christian virtues on the foundation of the precious promises
he has given you. You will receive a rich welcome in his
kingdom.

My own life is almost over, but while I have time left I
must go on reminding you of these things, because they are
so important. They are not based on invented stories, but on
personal, eye-witness experience of Christ's glory. It was all
foretold by the prophets anyhow, and prophecy is not just
man's thoughts, for it originates in God.

Ch. 2: Beware of false teachers.
They will lead you into heresies that deny the Lord himself.
They will exploit you with made up stories for their own
financial gain. Beware, for their judgment will be terrible.
You will easily know them. They will not be afraid to
slander heavenly beings and blaspheme in matters they
don't understand. They are carousers, adulterous and
greedy. By appealing to the lustful desires of sinful nature
they will pull you back into the very depravities from which
Christ rescued you. Beware.

Ch. 3: Be ready for the Lord's coming.
Don't be put off by scoffing at your faith in the Lord's
return. It is as sure as creation itself. If it seems delayed to
you, know that God's patience is only to allow more time
for repentance. But the day will surely come, and suddenly.
In the meantime, therefore, do just as Paul advised: Prepare
for its coming by seeking to grow in godliness. And remember, beware of lawless men who would steal your assurance.

3. KEEP YOURSELVES IN GOD'S LOVE (JUDE)

Jesus had two disciples called Judas or Jude: Judas Iscariot
and Judas of James (Luke 6.16; John 14.22; Acts 1.13). The
first committed suicide and the second's name means 'son',
not 'brother' of James. The author of the epistle is therefore

usually identified as a third Jude, one of Jesus' brothers and so also brother of James who was chief elder in the church in Jerusalem and author of the letter bearing his name (Matt. 13.55; Mark 6.3). Unfortunately we know nothing more about him, though the fact that he identified himself by naming James rather than Jesus as his brother suggests he may have been writing officially as a member of the Jerusalem church, for Paul calls its members 'men from James' in Gal. 2.12. The letter must then be dated before the city was sacked in 70 AD, perhaps even before James' martyrdom in 62 (see above, p. 206).

The Christians to whom he wrote were clearly confronted with the same kind of heretical teaching as Peter had to oppose. Indeed most of this epistle is so like 2 Pet. 2 there can be little doubt that either one is dependent on the other or both made use of some earlier tract against false teaching. Jude's style is more crisp and colourful than Peter's. His allusions to two extra-Biblical, Jewish traditions not in 2 Pet. 2, about Michael's dispute with the devil over Moses' body (v. 9) and Enoch's prophecy of judgment (vv. 14f), suggest he was probably writing to Jewish readers. Peter, living in the Gentile world, would have considered these traditions too obscure for some of his readers.

The nature of the heretical teaching is the same as in 2 Peter, as is the terrible judgment forecast for its propagators. Jude identifies the root of their perversion not so much in their doctrine as in their motivation: they are men 'who follow mere natural instincts and do not have the Spirit' (v. 19). Hence his exhortation to his readers: 'But you, dear friends, build yourselves up in your most holy faith and pray in the Holy Spirit' (v. 20). This gulf between the understanding of those with and without the Spirit is one Paul speaks about in 1 Cor. 2 and 2 Cor. 3 (see above, pp. 185f) and is one many Christians find tiresome today. It is not always so grotesquely highlighted as Jude's readers were finding, but the pressure to abandon the things of the Spirit in favour of more rationalistic or natural ways is something all men of the Spirit have to contend with in some measure. It is therefore good to have Jude's concluding reminder that God is indeed 'able to keep you from falling and to present you before his glorious presence without fault and with great joy' (v. 24).

Though this is only a short letter and its author is virtually unknown to us, we would certainly be very much the poorer today without it. Its final admonitions and doxology provide a most fitting conclusion to the whole body of New Testament epistles, and to our study of the Lordship of God and Christ in this volume:

> *But you, dear friends ... Keep yourselves in God's love as you wait for the mercy of our Lord Jesus Christ to bring you to eternal life. ...*
>
> *To him who is able to keep you ... to the only God our Saviour be glory, majesty, power and authority, through Jesus Christ our Lord, before all ages, now and forevermore! Amen.*

PART SIX

CONCLUSION

15

God's People still a Waiting People

By New Testament times history had taught the Jews the absolute lordship of God and the seriousness of their calling to be his holy people. How they interpreted that calling varied a great deal among the sects that emerged, but most Jews were now total monotheists, dedicated to the pursuance of righteousness of life.

One lesson they learned was about God's absolute sovereignty and his power to fulfil his promises. They saw the sovereign ways in which he had upheld them during the times of the Babylonian and Persian empires (Ezra, Nehemiah, Esther, Daniel) and many of them became aware of the world-wide scope of his lordship (Ruth, Jonah). They therefore became a waiting people, encouraged from time to time by the last of their prophets (Haggai, Zechariah, Joel, Malachi) and by men who saw visions of their more remote future (Zechariah, Daniel).

As they waited they acknowledged God's Lordship in their worship, maintained at a level of faith and praise through continuing use of the old hymns and songs of the temple (Psalms, Lamentations). Also the sayings of the wise were studied to learn the deeper meaning of life and the purposes of God (Proverbs, Job, Ecclesiastes).

As we have seen, none of these aspects of their faith was simply a matter of the intellect, but rather of response to the moving of God's Spirit in their hearts and in history, most of it the sort of thing familiar to charismatics today.

The long age of waiting came to an end with the birth of Jesus, whom many recognised as the expected Messiah, Son of David and Son of God. He brought a new age for mankind, a new light into the world, a new zeal, a new hope, life in a new dimension—all of it made possible by the power of

the Holy Spirit released through him. It was like the dawn
dispelling the darkness and heralding a new day of sunshine.
But while it is full of hope, it remains dawn and we are still
a waiting people, waiting for the full sunrise when Christ
comes again. But sufficient has been given us through Jesus
to enable us to rejoice in this present time beyond anything
the world can understand. We have the 'firstfruits' of the
Spirit (Rom. 8.23) as a 'deposit guaranteeing our inheritance' (Eph. 1.14; cp. 2 Cor. 1.22; 5.5), and in his strength
we rest assured in hope as we expectantly wait.

In the meantime life has to be lived in the Church and the
world. The New Testament does not ignore that fact. Indeed,
most of Paul's letters end with instructions about applying
our faith in the daily business of life, and we have seen how
John, James and Peter also give guidance about the practical
details of Christian discipleship.

The waiting Church is well served with advice, instruction and encouragement, not only in these letters, but right
through the New Testament. And the teaching is always 'in
the Holy Spirit', even in the little letter from Jude, whose
antidote to heresy is to build yourself up in faith by praying
in the Holy Spirit (v. 20). The key to James's 'wisdom'
teaching lies in the wisdom from above, from God, that he
bids us seek (1.5-8; 3.13-18). Similarly, the instructions to
Timothy and Titus become little more than legalistic
directions about church order and discipline if we fail to
note that at the heart of it all lies a personal call to stand
firm in and teach the faith revealed, established and sustained by the anointing of the Spirit and his gifts (1 Tim.
4.11-14; 2 Tim. 1.13f; Tit. 3.3-8). The New Testament is
prophetic/charismatic all the way through. That, indeed, is
the whole point of its teaching: that Jesus came to take away
our sin and give us the Holy Spirit in whose strength we are
now to live our lives for God—and that means our lives in
every aspect and detail.

But while we wait, we are also encouraged by prophetic
teaching and vision about the future hope for the people of
God, the return of Christ and the resurrection to eternal life.
Jesus himself introduced it in Matt. 24-25, Mark 13 and
Luke 21; Paul expands on it in Rom. 9-11, 1 Thes. 4–5, 2
Thes. 1–2 and 1 Cor. 15; Peter adds his touch in 2 Pet. 3; but

its most extensive treatment is in Revelation. John's vision is fully discussed in Volume Three, but it inevitably forms the climax of any study of what the Spirit has said and is still saying to the churches through the Scriptures.

As we have reviewed the Writings of the Old Testament and their sequel in the New, we have listened to many voices singing the praises of God as Lord and King over private lives and over history. We have seen God's Wisdom expressed in his Word, and his Word become flesh in Jesus to dwell among us that we might behold his glory. We have heard the praises of Christ's glory in the writings of John and Paul in particular, and as we contemplate them, we cannot but cry with Thomas, 'My Lord and my God'. Then finally, we are carried in vision with John into heaven to see God's throne and the Lamb that was slain and

> *every creature in heaven and earth and under the earth*
> *and on the sea, and all that is in them, singing:*
> *'To him who sits on the throne and to the Lamb*
> *be praise and honour and glory and power,*
> *for ever and ever!'*

(Rev. 5.13)

That vision carries us through the drama of history and its last days to the end beyond all ends, when in God's New Jerusalem his servants stand before his throne and the Lamb, when they see him face to face, when they need no light of lamp or of the sun, since the Lord God gives them light, when they with him will reign for ever and ever (22.3-5). In the light of that vision, our hearts that have already cried 'My Lord and my God', must surely now cry with John and all the early saints, 'Amen. Come, Lord Jesus.' (22.20)

And all of that comes from the Spirit, who together with the bride (the Church), calls us to come, and to invite others to come, with the open offer:

> *Whoever is thirsty, let him come; and whoever wishes, let*
> *him take the free gift of the water of life.*

(22.17)

The offer still stands today.

Amen. Come, Lord Jesus.

The grace of the Lord Jesus be with God's people. Amen.
(22.21)

Chronology

The dates given to Biblical events are often approximations, some of them open to a great deal of debate.

In the Old Testament, for example, some prefer to date the exodus in the fifteenth century, or place Joel in pre-exilic times. Dates for the kings of Israel and Judah are notoriously difficult to pin down.

In the New Testament there are also many problems: There are several views about dating Jesus' birth, the crucifixion can be placed any time between 29 and 33 AD, dates for Paul's life are subject to a lot of discussion, and so forth, but the discrepancies seldom amount to more than two or three years.

The dates used here are widely accepted ones and, despite the uncertainties, they provide a convenient framework for tracing the Bible stories. Fortunately precise dating of Biblical events seldom affects our appreciation of spiritual truths much.

The dates given to extra-Biblical events are also generally open to discussion. Different scholars use different systems for the history of the second millennium BC, though the discrepancies are seldom much more than 10 or 20 years either way. Dating becomes more precise the nearer we approach Christian times, though plenty of uncertainties remain.

THE SECOND MILLENNIUM B.C.

	PALESTINE	EGYPT	MESOPOTAMIA
3000		26-25th c.: The Pyramids	Sumerian City States 2360-2180: Empire of Akkad
2000	The Patriarchs		Fall of Ur 1950 Rise of City States: Mari, Babylon, etc.
1720	Hebrews go down to Egypt.	Hyksos ('Foreign Kings') come to power.	Emergence of Assyria
1570		Hyksos expelled	Ascendancy of Assyria
1400	The Exodus ? The Conquest ?	1400-1350: Amarna Period	
1290	The Exodus ? The Conquest ?	1290-24: Rameses II	
1224	The Judges Philistines settle	1224-11 Merniptah - battles with Sea Peoples 1183-52 Rameses III – battles with Sea Peoples	[Fall of the Hittite Empire] Period
1100	Fall of Shiloh Samuel	End of Egyptian Empire	of weakness
1050	Saul		in
1010	David		Mesopotamia

THE DIVIDED KINGDOM

	JUDAH	ISRAEL	INTERNATIONAL
970	Solomon		
931	Rehoboam 931-14 Abijah 914-11 Asa 911-870	Jeroboam I 931-10	
		Nadab 910-09 Baasha 909-886	
		Elah 886-85 Omri 885-74 Ahab 874-53	Expansion of Assyria begins
	Jehoshaphat 870-48	*Elijah* Ahaziah 853-52	Assyrian advance halted at Qarqar 853
850	Jehoram 848-41 Ahaziah 841 (Athaliah 841-35) Joash 835-796	Jehoram 852-41 *Elisha* Jehu 841-14	Jehu pays tribute to Shalmaneser III 841
800		Jehoahaz 814-798 Jehoash 798-82	
	Amaziah 796-67	Jeroboam II 782-53	
	Uzziah 767-42	*Amos* Zechariah 753-52 Shallum 752	
750	*Isaiah* Jotham 742-35 *Micah*	Menahem 752-42 *Hosea* Pekahiah 742-40 Pekah 740-32	Tiglath-Pileser III takes Damascus 732
	Ahaz 735-15	Hoshea 732-22 ------------------722	Sargon II deports the people of Samaria 722
700	Hezekiah 715-687		Sennacherib besieges Jerusalem 701
650	Manasseh 687-42		
	Amon 642-40 Josiah 640-09 *Jeremiah* *Zephaniah* *Nahum* *Habakkuk* Jehoahaz 609 Jehoiakim 609-597		Rise of Babylon Fall of Nineveh 612
600			

	JUDAH	ISRAEL	INTERNATIONAL
	Jehoiachin 597 Zedekiah 597-87 *Ezekiel* ------------------587 *Obadiah*		Nebuchadnezzar takes Jerusalem 597
550	*Isaiah 40-55*		

THE POST-EXILIC PERIOD

	PALESTINE	INTERNATIONAL
	THE PERSIAN PERIOD	
539		Cyrus takes Babylon
538		Cyrus' Edict allows exiles to return
537	Exiles start to return and Sheshbazzar is made Governor	
535(?)	Zerubbabel is appointed Governor	
520-15	The Temple is rebuilt *Haggai & Zechariah*	
522-486		Darius I
486-465	*Joel ?*	Xerxes I
465-424	*Malachi*	Artaxerxes I
458	Ezra arrives with more exiles	
445	Nehemiah is made Governor	
423		Xerxes II
423-404		Darius II
404-358		Artaxerxes II
	THE GREEK PERIOD	
336-323		Alexander the Great conquers and establishes his Greek Empire
323		After his death, the Empire is divided between his generals
	Palestine is taken under the rule of the Egyptian Ptolemies	

	PALESTINE	INTERNATIONAL
200	The Seleucids take Palestine	
		Antiochus IV Epiphanes (175-63)
168	The Temple is profaned and the Maccabean Revolt begins	
164	The Temple is rededicated and Judas Maccabeus establishes the Hasmonean Dynasty	
THE ROMAN PERIOD		
63	Pompey takes Jerusalem	
39-4	Herod the Great rules Palestine	
27		Augustus Emperor (–14 AD)
5	Birth of Jesus Christ	
4	Palestine divided between Herod's sons: Archelaus (*Judea & Samaria*) Herod Antipas (*Galilee & Perea*) Philip (*Iturea & Traconitis*)	

THE EARLY CHURCH

	BIBLICAL		IMPERIAL
27	Jesus begins his ministry	14-37	Tiberius Emperor
30/31	The Crucifixion	26-36	Pilate Procurator of Judea
35	Paul's Conversion		
38	Paul visits Jerusalem	37-41	Gaius (Caligula) Emperor
38-45	Paul in Syria and Cilicia	41-54	Claudius Emperor
43	Herod's Persecution (Acts 12)	41-44	Herod Agrippa I, King of Judea
45	Paul & Barnabas in Antioch		

230 Chronology

	BIBLICAL		IMPERIAL
45-46	Famine relief taken to Jerusalem		
46-47	First Missionary Journey		
48	Jerusalem Conference *Galatians* ?		
48-51	Second Missionary Journey *1 & 2 Thessalonians*	49	Claudius expels Jews from Rome
51-53	Paul back in Antioch	51-52	Gallio Proconsul of Achaia
	Galatians ?	52-60	Felix Procurator of Judea
53-59	Third Missionary Journey *1 & 2 Corinthians* *Romans*	53-90	Agrippa II, King of Northern Palestine
		54-68	Nero Emperor
59	Paul arrested in Jerusalem		
59-61	Paul held at Caesarea		
61	Paul sails for Rome	60-62	Festus Procurator of Judea
62-64	Paul held in Rome *Philippians* *Colossians* *Philemon* *Ephesians*		
64-7	Paul freed & goes to Spain? *Mark's Gospel* Paul returns to Asia? *1 & 2 Timothy* and *Titus*	64	Neronian persecution
67	Paul & Peter martyred in Rome? Jerusalem Church moves to Pella *Matthew* and *Luke-Acts* ?		
70	Fall of Jerusalem	70-79	Vespasian Emperor
73	Fall of Masada		
		81-96	Domitian Emperor
85+	*John's Gospel* and *Epistles*		
95	*Revelation* Clement of Rome's letters *To the Corinthians*	95	Domitian's persecution

Glossary and Index

(REFERENCES TO MAPS ARE IN ITALICS)

People

Places

Theological & Historical
Titles & Themes

John 10.22, 116

Hasmonean, dynastic name of the Maccabean kings 116f, 131

Hebrew, language of the Jews 10, 12f, 22, 37, 53, 31, 80, 89, 109, 180

Hellenism, name given to the culture of the Greek empire (*Hellas* is the Greek name of Greece) 12, 115–7

Heresy, false teaching about Christ 165, 170f, 173, 182–4, 200f, 214–6, 222

Hospitality, a recognised ministry in the early Church 170f

Israelites, God's chosen people 3, 15, 17–21, 32, 39f, 55f, 60, 81, 140, 153

Jews, name given to descendants of Israel after the exile 6–14, 26–49, 64, 89, 101f, 108–31, 137, 142, 151f, 158, 164, 173, 177–90, 200, 205–7, 216, 212, 216

Joy/Rejoice, gift of God xix, 8, 40, 42, 66, 80, 83, 89–91, 95f, 98, 104, 156, 167, 172, 176–81, 212, 214, 217, 222

Judaisers, circumcision party or party of Pharisees in the early Church 178f, 206

Judaism, the faith and culture of Jews after the exile 7–9, 12f, 22, 26, 41, 43, 46, 117, 130

Judges, leaders in Israel in thirteenth-eleventh century BC 18, 46

Judgment, of God 5, 9f, 15, 19–21, 24, 88, 94f, 108, 120, 125–9, 138, 151, 155, 215f

King, of Israel or a foreign state 6, 9f, 16–19, 31, 59, 77, 86, 90, 93–5, 110, 113, 115, 123f, 128, 180

King, God or Christ as King xivf, 4, 85, 88–91, 94, 104, 131, 134, 152, 157f, 223

Kingdom of God, God's rule in this world xivf, 3f, 8, 16–18, 20f, 88, 108, 119–29, 133f, 145, 155, 215

Lamb of God, title of Jesus as the final Passover lamb 139f, 142f, 152, 223

Lament(ation), psalm of distress calling to God for help 9, 22–4

Last Battle, at end of history 120, 127f

Last Supper, the Lord's Supper, Holy Communion 89, 99, 132, 134, 141, 143, 154

Law, the law of Moses 5f, 9f, 18, 21, 26, 30, 39–44, 46, 55, 81, 88, 90, 93, 95, 98, 112, 121, 130, 173f, 178, 200, 206f

Levites, temple servants 11, 40–2, 82f

Life, of God given to men xvii–xix, 18, 62–4, 73–7, 135–40, 143–60, 164–6, 169f, 189f, 201, 207, 213, 217, 221–3

Light, of God, reflected in Christ and Christians 133–9, 144f, 147, 150f, 154, 157, 165–7, 185, 191, 221, 223

Lord, God or Jesus as xvif, 4, 49, 85, 129, 131, 158–60, 164, 172–80, 184, 188, 217, 221, 223

Love, of God, Christ or Christians xvii, 77–80, 83, 88, 91–3, 99, 101–6, 108, 132f, 144f,

153–7, 160f, 165–71, 176f, 181–4, 189, 191, 200f, 211–4, 217

Maccabees, leaders of the Jews against the Seleucids after 168 BC 14, 116f

Messiah, Hebrew for 'the Anointed One', 'Christ' in Greek xvi, 6–8, 10, 21, 86, 88, 92, 95, 97, 131, 133f, 141f, 152, 164, 205, 221

Ministries, early Christian 170, 191, 193f, 196f, 199, 203f, 210

Mishnah, authoritative collection of Jewish oral law 13

Mystery/Secret, of Christ, of God, of the gospel 91, 108, 185f, 188–92, 201

Nations, other than Israel, see also Gentiles 15, 25, 98, 205

New Heaven, New Jerusalem, at the end of time (92, 95), 140, 223

Obedience, response called for by the Law and by faith xvif, 3, 6, 17f, 26, 47, 86, 95, 136, 169

Orthodox, eastern branch of the Church 13

Paradise, the garden of God (Eden) to be restored to man one day 8

Passover, spring festival celebrating the exodus and salvation 33, 89, 97, 140, 142f, 152, 160, 210

Patriarchs, forefathers of Israel 21, 139

Pentateuch, the 'Five Books' of the Law, Genesis to Deuteronomy xvi, 3, 10, 131

Pentecost (= Fifty Days), festival seven weeks after Passover, commemorating God's coming on Sinai 91, 155, 160f, 206, 210f

Pentecostal(ism), present-day Pentecostal Movement 81, 194

Persecution, of Jews and of Christians 11, 47, 70, 87, 93, 108, 112, 115, 121–9, 131, 151, 156, 177, 180, 195, 211–14

Pharisees, largest party in Judaism in Jesus' day 7, 9f, 13, 64, 130, 149, 178, 207

Philistines, foreign peoples who settled in south-west Canaan 6

Prayer, 35f, 39f, 74, 79f, 85–7, 90–100, 112, 170, 182f, 185, 189, 200, 208f, 216, 222

Priests, whose function was to offer sacrifices and teach the law xvif, 4, 9, 11, 17, 31f, 36, 38–41, 55, 97, 132, 159, 177

Procurator, title of Roman provincial governors 117, 119

Promise, of God or Jesus (see also Covenant) 4–8, 10, 16–21, 23f, 26f, 86, 89, 97, 139, 161, 173, 215, 221

Prophecy, message given from God 55, 86, 88, 91, 109f, 126–9, 174, 192, 200, 208, 215, 222

Prophet(s), men moved by God's Spirit to speak his message xv–xviii, 3–6, 9–11, 17–26, 43, 46f, 55, 76, 81f,109, 112, 123, 131, 134, 136, 140, 168, 171, 185, 190, 193f, 212, 215, 221

Protestant, reformed tradition in the Church 12f

Summary Outline and Reading Guide

The following pages serve a double purpose:

1. They show at a glance the contents of the main Biblical books covered in this volume.
2. They divide these books up in such a way that reading them can be spread evenly over a period of about six months.

As you read your Bible, keep your mind open to hear what the Holy Spirit has to tell you. Allow him to speak to you personally through its pages.

Watch carefully for what God does and says, and for how the men of Old and New Testament times respond to him, because that is what the Way of the Spirit is all about.

And don't forget to keep asking yourself what lessons you should be learning from their experience, so that you can apply them to your own life as a Christian.

(The reading scheme outlined here forms the basis of the home study course advertised on p. 249.)

Week 1

Why the Exile?
Gen. 12: God's promise to Abraham.
Exod. 20: God's law given to Moses.
2 Sam. 7: God's covenant with David.
Deut. 30: Obedience, disobedience and repentance.
2 Kings 21: The state of the nation before the exile.
Ezek. 7: A prophet's last warning.
2 Chron. 36: God's hand of judgment falls.

Week 2

Jerusalem during and after the Exile (Lamentations and Ezra 1–6)
Lam. 1: Is any suffering like my suffering?
Lam. 2: The LORD has abandoned his sanctuary.
Lam. 3: Let us return to the LORD.
Lam. 4–5: It happened because of our sins. Restore us, O LORD.
Ezra 1–2: The first group of exiles returns home.
Ezra 3–4: The foundation of the temple is laid.
Ezra 5–6: The temple is rebuilt.

Week 3

Ezra's Reforms and Nehemiah's Walls (Ezra 7–10; Neh. 1–7)
Ezra 7–8: Ezra comes to Jerusalem.
Ezra 9–10: Ezra's Reforms.
Neh. 1.1 – 2.10: Nehemiah comes to Jerusalem.
Neh. 2.11 – 3.22: He starts work on the city-walls.
Neh. 4: Handling the opposition.
Neh. 5: Troubles within.
Neh. 6–7: Completing the wall.

Week 4

Jews and the Law, Jews and Gentiles (Neh. 8–13; Ruth)
Neh. 8: Ezra re-establishes the Law.
Neh. 9–10: Renewing the covenant.
Neh. 11.1 – 12.26: The population of Jerusalem.
Neh. 12.27-47: The dedication of the walls.
Neh. 13: Nehemiah's return visit.
Ruth 1–3: Ruth and Boaz.
Ruth 4: Ruth and David.

Week 5

A Reluctant Prophet and a Brave Queen (Jonah and Esther)
Jonah 1–2: Jonah runs away from God's call.
Jonah 3–4: A severe lesson about God's compassion.
Esther 1–2: Esther becomes queen.
Esther 3–4: She is asked to expose a plot against the Jews.
Esther 5–6: The king hears her plea.
Esther 7–8: The king executes justice.
Esther 9–10: The triumph of the Jews.

Week 6

Proverbs for Attaining Wisdom (Proverbs 1–15)
Chs. 1–2: The value of wisdom.
Chs. 3–4: Get wisdom, get understanding.
Chs. 5–7: Beware of folly.
Chs. 8–9: Wisdom's invitation.
Chs. 10–12: Various Proverbs of Solomon.
Chs. 13–15: More Proverbs of Solomon.

Week 7

Various Collections of Proverbs (Prov. 16 –31)
Chs. 16–19: Further Proverbs of Solomon.
20.1 – 22.16: The Proverbs of Solomon continue.
22.17 – 24.34: The sayings of the Wise
Chs. 25–26: More Proverbs of Solomon.
Chs. 27–29: Yet more Proverbs of Solomon.
Ch. 30: The sayings of Agur son of Jakeh.
Ch. 31: The sayings of King Lemuel and a portrait of a noble wife.

Week 8

The Meaning of Life (Ecclesiastes)
Chs. 1–2: So much in life is meaningless.
Chs. 3–4: Indeed everything in life is meaningless.
Chs. 5–6: Some advice on making the best of this meaningless life.
Chs. 7–8: The value of wisdom and justice.
Chs. 9–10: Wisdom and folly.
Chs. 11–12: The conclusion of the matter.

Week 9

Job's Suffering and his Complaint (Job 1–21)
Chs. 1–3: Prologue, then Job speaks.
Chs. 4–7: Eliphaz and Job.
Chs. 8–10: Bildad and Job.
Chs. 11–14: Zophar and Job.
Chs. 15–17: Eliphaz and Job.
Chs. 18–19: Bildad and Job.
Chs. 20–21: Zophar and Job.

Week 10

It is the Breath of the Almighty that gives Understanding (Job 22–42)
Chs. 22–24: Eliphaz and Job.
Chs. 25–27: Bildad and Job.
Chs. 28–31: Job, longing for wisdom and better times, calls on God.
Chs. 32–4: Elihu interrupts and speaks of God's justice.
Chs. 35–7: He lifts Job into the contemplation of God.
Chs. 38–9: God reminds Job about the mystery of the world around him.
Chs. 40–1: God reminds him of more wondrous mysteries of creation.
Ch. 42: Job's confession and restoration.

Week 11

Prayers for use in time of need (Psalms)
Pss. 55–7: For deliverance in persecution.
Pss. 13, 22: In time of suffering and dereliction.
Pss. 17, 26: Prayers for justice.
Pss. 51, 130: Prayers for forgiveness.
Pss. 42–3: Expressions of longing to be near to God.
Pss. 27, 31: Waiting on God in time of need.
Pss. 91, 121, 131: Assurance that God will protect.

Week 12

Songs of Praise (Psalms)
Pss. 8, 104: To God the Creator.
Pss. 65, 84: To God the bounteous provider.
Pss. 105, 114: To God the Lord of history.
Pss. 68, 149: To God the mighty, the victorious.
Pss. 46–8: Celebrating the coming victory of God.
Pss. 96–99: The LORD reigns.
Pss. 107, 145: To God my helper.

Week 13

Messianic and Communal Hymns (Psalms)
Pss. 2, 18: The LORD delivers and establishes his anointed king.
Pss. 21, 110: Christ as priest and king.
Pss. 35, 69: The suffering Messiah.
Pss. 45, 118: The joy of Christ and the Church.
Pss. 34, 37: The blessedness of a life committed to God.
Pss. 16, 61: The promise of life.
Pss. 23, 95: The LORD our creator and shepherd.

Week 14

His Banner over me is Love (Psalms and Song of Songs)
Ps. 139: Where can I flee from your presence?
Pss. 80, 85: Will you not revive us again?
Ps. 126: This is what revival was like.
Song 1–2: First meeting and the development of a loving relationship.
Song 3–4: An invitation to a deeper relationship.
Song 5–6: The testing of love.
Song 7–8: The triumph of love.

Week 15

The Most High is Sovereign over the Kingdoms of Men (Daniel)
Chs. 1–2: Nebuchadnezzar recognises the superiority of Daniel's God.
Chs. 3–4: Nebuchadnezzar comes to acknowledge God's sovereignty.
Chs. 5–6: Belshazzar opposes God, Darius honours the Jewish faith.
Ch. 7: The beasts from the sea and the man from heaven.
Ch. 8: The ram and the goat.
Ch. 9: The seventy 'sevens'.
Chs. 10–12: The Last Battle.

Week 16

Jesus begins his Public Ministry (John 1–7)
Ch. 1: The incarnation and unveiling of the Son of God.
Ch. 2: Jesus starts his ministry and begins to reveal his glory.
Ch. 3: First a man must be born again.
Ch. 4: The gift of God is living water welling up to eternal life.
Ch. 5: Whoever hears Jesus' words and believes has eternal life.
Ch. 6: Jesus is bread from heaven giving us life.
Ch. 7: Can this be the Christ?

Week 17
Jesus ends his Ministry and draws apart with his Disciples (John 8–14)
Ch. 8: Jesus is the light of the world.
Ch. 9: Jesus gives sight to the blind.
Ch. 10: Jesus is the good shepherd.
Ch. 11: Jesus is the resurrection and the life. He is the Christ!
Ch. 12: The hour has come for the Son of Man to be glorified.
Ch. 13: Now is the Son of Man glorified.
Ch. 14: Fear not. I will send another Counsellor to take my place.

Week 18

It is finished! (John 15–21)
Ch. 15: Stay faithful. The Spirit will help you.
Ch. 16: The Spirit will continue my ministry in you with great joy.
Ch. 17: Jesus' final prayer.
Ch. 18: His arrest and trial.
Ch. 19: The King of Glory is crowned and lifted up.
Ch. 20: My Lord and my God!
Ch. 21: Peter and the infant Church.

Week 19

Remaining in Christ (1, 2 & 3 John and Philippians)
1 John 1.1 – 2.27: Dealing with sin, temptation and false teachers.
1 John 2.28 – 4.6: Living in God's family and avoiding false prophets.
1 John 4.7 – 5.21: God's love in us and our faith overcome the world.
2 John: On offering hospitality to itinerant preachers.
3 John: On jealousy of another man's anointing.
Phil. 1–2: Stand firm in your faith and try to be like Christ.
Phil. 3–4: Press on to know Christ, and rejoice in the Lord.

Week 20

Christ, the Head (Philemon, Colossians, Ephesians)
Philemon: The sovereign power of Christ's love.
Col. 1–2: Paul asserts the full sufficiency of Christ.
Col. 3–4: Set your minds on things above.
Ephes. 1–2: We have every spiritual blessing in Christ.
Ephes. 3: Paul speaks of his purpose in preaching.
Ephes. 4.1 – 5.21: Life in the Spirit.
5.22 – 6.24: Daily living and spiritual warfare.

Week 21

How to Administer the Affairs of the Church (1 Timothy and Titus)
1 Tim. 1–2: Hold on to faith and teach your people to pray.
1 Tim. 3: Choose good leaders.
1 Tim. 4: Do not hesitate to confront heresy.
1 Tim. 5–6: Some further pieces of advice.
Tit. 1: On congregational life.
Tit. 2: On family life.
Tit. 3: On life in society.

Week 22

Constant in Wisdom, Faithfulness and Truth (2 Timothy and James)
2 Tim. 1–2: Be faithful and teach others.
2 Tim. 3–4: Stand firm and preach the word.
James 1:Perseverance, wisdom, wealth, temptation, doing the word.
James 2: Favouritism, loving your neighbour, faith and deeds.
James 3: A teacher's responsibility, the tongue, true wisdom.
James 4: Coveting, compromising, criticising, boasting.
James 5: Wealth, patience, healing, faith, backsliders.

Week 23

A Faith as Precious as Ours (1 & 2 Peter and Jude)
1 Pet. 1.1 – 2.12: A people for God's praise, prepared for action.
1 Pet. 2.13 – 3.22: Advice for Christian daily living and relationships.
1 Pet. 4–5: Live for God, whatever the cost and whatever your calling.
2 Pet. 1: Be eager to make your calling and election sure.
2 Pet. 2: Beware of false teachers.
2 Pet. 3: Be ready for the Lord's coming.
Jude: Keep yourselves in God's love.

Home and Further Study Courses

The present book can be used as the working manual for a six-month home study course suitable for use by groups or individuals. The additional materials available are: a book of weekly work sheets and a set of six tapes, each with four 20-minute talks relating to the week's reading. Assistance by correspondence can also be arranged if required.

Six levels of study and training are now available through
The Way of the Spirit:

1. SHORT BIBLE READING COURSES
• 4-6 weeks • on certain Biblical themes • for home or group study.

2. THE FULL BIBLE READING COURSE
• 4 six-month parts • giving complete coverage of the Bible • for home, correspondence, group, church, or college use.

3. BIBLICAL COMMENTARIES
• 8 weeks • more detailed studies of single books of the Bible • for home or group study.

4. BIBLICAL AND PROPHETIC FAITH (CERTIFICATE)
• 2 years • full Bible course plus discipleship and ministry training • local group, class and seminar teaching.

5. PROPHETIC BIBLE TEACHING (DIPLOMA)
• 1 year • part-time training for local church or group Bible teaching • three short residential schools and monitored home study.

6. PROPHETIC BIBLE TEACHING (FULL-TIME TRAINING)
• variable duration depending on qualifications and experience • a course for training Bible teachers for more long-term works • full-time residential training.

For details of any of these courses please write to:
The Way of the Spirit, Lamplugh House, Thwing,
Driffield, East Yorkshire YO25 3DY